"Rice gives us a splendid overview of ꜰ   nsightful
responses to major criticisms. He does so with a gentle spirit that identifies areas of
agreement between its critics and proponents. He carefully notes areas of difference
among open theists on several topics. Lastly, he explores open theism in relation to
topics such as the Trinity, the church, and eschatology. This is a clearly written guide
to contemporary open theism."

John Sanders, professor of religious studies, Hendrix College

"Richard Rice's book provides something lacking until now: a broad overview of the
open theist movement that places it in its historical perspective. A partisan himself, Rice
is consistently fair and accurate, both in setting out open theism and in discussing
objections to the position and replies to them. His theological reflections provide one
theologian's perspective on the broader implications of the position and constitute an
invitation to others to develop their own open theist theologies beyond the rather
narrow range of questions that have dominated most of the literature. This book is required reading for all who have been challenged by this dynamic theological movement."

William Hasker, professor emeritus of philosophy at Huntington University,
former editor of *Faith and Philosophy*

"Richard Rice offers a very accessible, evenhanded coming-of-age discussion of open
theism—past, present, and future. Starting with an engaging account of its origins and
fiery, unwelcomed entry into conservative Christian strongholds, Rice goes on to give
an instructive overview of the important theological debates open theism has sparked
in mainstream theological and philosophical circles. Finally, Rice points to interesting
ways in which the basic tenets of open theism can contribute to a fuller, richer understanding of key theological concepts such as the Trinity, Christology, the church, and
last things. A must-read for anyone who wants to understand why open theism
continues to have so much appeal to thoughtful Christian laypeople looking for ways
to reconcile their theological beliefs about God and the world with their lived experience."

David Basinger, vice president for academic affairs, Roberts Wesleyan College

"In this well-written, impressively comprehensive, and compellingly argued work,
Richard Rice outlines the past, present, and (what may be) the future of open theism.
Reflecting an admirably irenic spirit at every turn, Rice discusses not only the mul-
titude of theological and philosophical issues that separate open theists from their
critics, but also that distinguish different varieties of open theism from one another.
Whether you're an advocate, critic, or just an interested bystander, after reading *The
Future of Open Theism*, I suspect you'll be surprised by how much about open theism
you did *not* know! This is simply indispensable reading for anyone interested in this
important topic."

Greg Boyd, senior pastor of Woodland Hills Church in St. Paul, Minnesota,
author of *God at War* and *Is God to Blame?*

"Richard Rice offers us a fantastic book on a subject he knows intimately: open theology. The book explores precursors to this contemporary movement while addressing open theism's critics and explaining its varieties. Rice summarizes main ideas while breaking new ground to explain how the open view beautifully portrays doctrines central to Christianity. This book is now the ground floor for discussions of open theism in the present and future!"

Thomas Jay Oord, author of *The Uncontrolling Love of God* and *God Can't*

THE FUTURE OF OPEN THEISM

FROM ANTECEDENTS

RICHARD RICE

TO OPPORTUNITIES

ivp
Academic
An imprint of InterVarsity Press
Downers Grove, Illinois

InterVarsity Press
P.O. Box 1400, Downers Grove, IL 60515-1426
ivpress.com
email@ivpress.com

*InterVarsity Press® is the book-publishing division of InterVarsity Christian Fellowship/USA®, a movement of
students and faculty active on campus at hundreds of universities, colleges, and schools of nursing in the United
States of America, and a member movement of the International Fellowship of Evangelical Students. For
information about local and regional activities, visit intervarsity.org.*

*Scripture quotations, unless otherwise noted, are from the New Revised Standard Version of the Bible,
copyright 1989 by the Division of Christian Education of the National Council of the Churches of
Christ in the USA. Used by permission. All rights reserved.*

Cover design and graphic elements: Bradley Joiner
Interior design: Daniel van Loon

ISBN 978-0-8308-5286-4 (print)
ISBN 978-0-8308-3938-4 (digital)

Printed in the United States of America ∞

Library of Congress Cataloging-in-Publication Data
A catalog record for this book is available from the Library of Congress.

P	25	24	23	22	21	20	19	18	17	16	15	14	13	12	11	10	9	8	7	6	5	4	3	2	1
Y	38	37	36	35	34	33	32	31	30	29	28	27	26	25	24	23	22	21	20						

For Gail

The Companion of My Life

▸▸▸▸▸▸▸▸▸▸▸▸ CONTENTS ▸▸▸▸▸▸▸▸▸▸▸▸

:::::: ACKNOWLEDGMENTS ::::::

AFTER COMPLETING GRADUATE SCHOOL, I joined the faculty of Loma Linda University in the mid-1970s, so it could take a book nearly as long as this one to list all the people I am indebted to in one way or another—teachers, colleagues, students, and friends. The following is therefore a severely abbreviated list.

I enjoyed the academic life from college through graduate school and recall with appreciation my teachers along the way, including professors Roy Branson, Dan Cotton, James Cox, Raoul Dederen, Fritz Guy, Earle Hilgert, Gottfried Oosterwal, Royal Sage, Walter Specht, and Herold Weiss. At the University of Chicago Divinity School, I was enriched by the instruction of professors Brian Gerrish, Langdon Gilkey, James Gustafson, Bernard McGinn, Schubert M. Ogden, Norman Perrin, and David Tracy, my dissertation advisor.

I have appreciated the academic expertise and personal friendship of numerous colleagues on the religion faculties of both Loma Linda University Health and La Sierra University, as well as the leadership provided by deans John Jones, Gerald Winslow, and Jon Paulien.

To paraphrase Reinhold Niebuhr, nothing worth doing can be accomplished alone, and I feel a special connection to a number who have found the open view of God helpful and have given careful thought to the issues it raises. These include David Basinger, Gregory Boyd, William Hasker, Thomas Oord, Clark Pinnock, and John Sanders, as well as other theologians and philosophers whose works I have cited in the following pages.

I am grateful to the numerous people at IVP Academic who have undertaken the many tasks involved in the production of this book. I especially want to thank two editors, David Congdon, who encouraged the book's initial development, and David McNutt, who has provided valuable guidance in bringing it to publication. I would also like to thank John Sanders for his helpful suggestions for improving the manuscript and two anonymous readers for theirs. My editorial assistant, Gayle Foster, also contributed by carefully reading the manuscript and preparing the bibliography.

Finally, nothing would be possible without the love and support of family, the ones who ultimately make our lives worth living. Watching our daughter Alison and son Jonathan grow to adulthood, achieve professional success, and become loving parents themselves has been a constant source of joy. My wife, a faculty colleague who interrupted her own education years ago so I could complete mine, is the object of my lasting gratitude and ever growing affection. I dedicated my first book to her and I've done the same with this one.

HOW DID OPEN THEISM GET STARTED?

Open theism first attracted the attention of Christian theologians some twenty-five years ago when IVP published a symposium volume by five conservative scholars under the title, *The Openness of God: A Biblical Challenge to the Traditional Understanding of God*.[1] Their contributions explored the topic of God's relation to the world from a distinct vantage point with five specific concerns in mind—its biblical, historical, theological, philosophical and practical aspects.[2] Within a short time, the ideas presented in the book generated vigorous discussion.

According to the openness of God, God's essential nature is love, and out of love God chose to bring into existence a world containing creatures endowed with the capacity to love him in return. As a personal being, God seeks a personal relationship with the creatures, so God is intensely interested in, and genuinely affected by, their actions and decisions. God is open to the world, and the world is open to God. Both Creator and creatures contribute to the ongoing course of events, and God experiences these events as they happen. In giving those who bear his image the freedom to return his love, God ran the risk that they might pursue their own goals rather than God's. But despite the pain their rebellion brought him, God's commitment to their welfare remains unconditional, and he continues to pursue his goals for creation. The dramatic interchange, the give-and-take, between God and humans that we find in the Bible strongly suggests that God experiences events as they

---

[1]Clark Pinnock, Richard Rice, John Sanders, William Hasker, and David Basinger, *The Openness of God: A Biblical Challenge to the Traditional Understanding of God* (Downers Grove, IL: InterVarsity Press, 1994).

[2]At the time, the expression *free will theism* was sometimes used to refer to views later associated with openness.

happen. From God's perspective, therefore, past and future are not the same. In other words, time is real for God.

A lot has happened in the years since the publication of *The Openness of God*. My purpose in this discussion is to recount some of the notable steps in the development of open theism so far and then to explore some of the ways in which it may continue.

In chapters one and two we'll look at the arrival of open theism, beginning with the work of several thinkers who anticipated its concerns, largely from their individual study of the Bible. Then we'll review the contents of the 1994 publication, as well as additional expressions of open theism by some of its early proponents.

Whether it comes up in formal discussion or casual conversation, the topic of God easily gives rise to a host of philosophical and theological issues. So it is no surprise that proposals that deal with God from a novel perspective should generate questions and criticisms. After all, the concept of God is central to Christian theology—so important that it affects the entire range of Christian beliefs. To quote Paul Tillich, "The doctrine of God . . . is the beginning and end of all theological thought."[3]

Those of us who contributed to *The Openness of God,* along with others who supported its ideas, knew that we were describing a concept of God that differed from more widely accepted views. But we were taken aback at the intensity of the criticism and the price certain open theists were forced to pay. In chapter three we will review some of the back and forth between open theists and their critics that occurred within roughly the first decade after the 1994 publication.

Once the first waves of criticism subsided, and it appeared that the open view of God would survive the rather harsh responses that greeted its earlier expressions, a number of more extended and substantive engagements began. As the tone softened, the depth of discussion increased,

---

[3]*Biblical Religion and the Search for Ultimate Reality* (Chicago: University of Chicago Press, 1955), 82. Cf. Schubert M. Ogden: "Rightly understood, the problem of God is not one problem among several others; it is the only problem there is" (*The Reality of God and Other Essays* [New York: Harper & Row, 1966], 1).

and soon rather complex arguments arose concerning various features of open theism, along with their scientific and philosophical implications.

As the range of issues that captured their attention expanded, variations in the views of open theists themselves emerged. Chapter four considers a few examples of the exchanges open theism has generated concerning philosophical issues such as the nature of time, the nature of the future, and the fulfillment of divine purposes. In chapter five, we will bring the first phase of our discussion to a close by reviewing some of the different approaches open theists have taken to issues such as the origin of evil, the necessity of creation, and the nature of divine activity.

WHAT DOES OPEN THEISM REPRESENT?

One of the questions that hovers over the openness of God is just what this particular development represents. For a number of people who embrace the more familiar view of God, open theism not only varies from the traditional view, it denies God's most fundamental qualities. In an early review of *The Openness of God* in *Faith and Philosophy*, Edward Wierenga focused on the ways open theism differs from traditional theism and found all the arguments for doing so unpersuasive. This is how he described "the complex web of theological and philosophical claims" behind open theism: "First, the authors deny that God has the traditional attributes of simplicity, impassibility, immutability, and eternality. Second, they hold that God is omniscient, but only in an attenuated sense."[4] The use of words like "deny" and "attenuated" is typical of the way open theism was often characterized. People viewed it as detracting from, rather than affirming, certain divine qualities, suggesting that the primary task open theists faced was to overcome the objections their position raised.

Paradoxically, however, those who opposed open theism early on may have perceived its revolutionary potential more clearly than those of us who proposed it. What open theists themselves viewed as a modest revision in the traditional view of God—one more in keeping with the

---

[4]Edward Wierenga, review of *The Openness of God*, by Clark Pinnock et al., in *Faith and Philosophy* 14, no. 2 (April 1997): 248.

biblical portrayal of God's relation to the world—others perceived as a radical departure from orthodoxy. Admittedly, the subtitle of the 1994 work, *A Biblical Challenge to the Traditional Understanding of God*, may have been provocative. It underscores the fact that open theism varies from the traditional view of God and suggests that the latter is less than truly "biblical."

At any rate, there seems to be no smooth transition from the "traditional" view of God to the open view. The contrasts between them are too stark. In fact, their differences are reminiscent of the contrast between scientific paradigms that Thomas Kuhn describes in *The Structure of Scientific Revolutions*. On Kuhn's account, the most noteworthy advances in science occur when "normal science," the steady acquisition of data within a well-established, widely accepted perspective, accumulates enough "anomalies" to challenge its plausibility, and someone comes up with a significantly different approach. The result is a revolution, a radical large-scale transformation in the way people look at things. What is distinctive about such a transition is the incommensurability between the old and new paradigms. There is no clear path from one to the other. Within the new paradigm, everything looks different. In Kuhn's words, "After a revolution scientists work in a different world."[5] Not surprisingly, it takes time for a new paradigm to catch on. There may be considerable resistance from those who have operated within the old, and then it can take a while before the value of the new paradigm becomes evident.[6]

In many of the interactions between open theists and theologians who embrace the more traditional view of God, one has the sense that they are operating from different paradigms. What open theists see as essential to the Christian view of God, classical theists view as problems that can be effectively solved within the classical paradigm. For example, there are biblical texts that assert that God does not change and others that assert that God does. Which are considered central to a

---

[5] Thomas Kuhn, *The Structure of Scientific Revolutions*, 2nd ed. (Chicago: University of Chicago Press, 1970), 135.

[6] The total solar eclipse of May 19, 1919 provided scientists with a way to acquire experimental data that supported the general theory of relativity, which Albert Einstein had proposed in 1915.

biblically based concept of God, and which are considered peripheral and subject to qualification, will vary depending on one's theistic paradigm. For divine determinists, biblical descriptions of God changing his mind are figures of speech that are incidental to the basic portrait of God as the glorious all-determining sovereign who controls the world in all its detail. For open theists, such descriptions are powerful indications of God's responsiveness to human actions and decisions, and of the temporal, or successive, nature of divine experience.[7] Both groups look at the same landscape, but see it in a different light. A puzzling detail or an apparent paradox that is incidental from one perspective may represent a profound insight, indeed, an indispensable truth, from another.

When presented with a novel picture of God, many, like Wierenga, are inclined to note the things that it implicitly or explicitly denies. But for open theists, their position is noteworthy for the range of values it attributes to God, including the distinctive experiences of momentary sensitivity and responsiveness to others—seeking their cooperation, taking delight in their creativity, rejoicing when they return his love, and experiencing disappointment with their failures, suffering their sorrows. For open theists, it is the view of God as utterly impassible and immutable that denies important things to God, in particular, the elements of genuine personal interaction, such as momentary responsiveness and sensitivity to the experiences of others in all their complexity.

It is true that open theism was from the beginning envisioned as an alternative to views of God that had widespread acceptance in the Christian world, whether we call it *classical theism*, *traditional theism*, or use some other designation, and that its elements were often as not developed in contrast to corresponding themes in the rejected position. But here I would like to take a different path and articulate open theism "from the inside," as it were. For its proponents, open theism is not merely

---

[7]These are not the only alternatives, of course. For example, Reformed theologians often affirm the concurrence of divine ruling and human action through a version of compatibilism. Similarly, Arminians typically hold that human freedom is compatible with exhaustive divine foreknowledge, accounting for it in different ways, including Molinism and simple foreknowledge.

a corrective to a few well-known theological conundrums, but a sweeping vision that places everything we might say about God in a new light. If there is one thing that supporters and critics of open theism seem to agree on, it's that a great deal about God and God's relation to the world looks different from the openness perspective.

Kuhn, of course, invoked the notion of a paradigm shift to describe dramatic changes in scientific perspective, and there are significant differences between theology and science, both in the sort of evidence to which they appeal and in the communities to which they belong. The evidence to which Christian theologians appeal, at least conservative Christians, is not subject to new empirical discoveries or the invention of new instruments. And when the convictions of a theologian change, it raises questions of a personal sort that scientists typically do not face. As one of the characters in an Iain Pears novel asks, "How is that when a man of God shifts his opinion it proves the weakness of his views, and when a man of science does so it demonstrates the value of his method?"[8] So, while paradigm shifts in either are not always welcome, they are far less welcome in religion than in science. Since theology is concerned with the essentials of eternal salvation, theological investigation bears a burden from which scientific inquiry is exempt. For many, like Kuhn, science is better described as an account of "the community's state of knowledge at a given time," rather than "some one full, objective, true account of nature."[9] But the claims made for theology are never that modest.

The challenge to debate such matters has occupied a good deal of the energy of open theists. But the attractions of open theism are not likely to emerge if we wait until the various objections to it are overcome. What I suggest here is that we treat the openness of God as a paradigm in the sense that Kuhn describes it—as a new way of looking at things, one that changes many previously accepted explanations. So, once we have considered aspects of the development of open theism in chapters one through five, we'll inquire as to its transformative possibilities. Accordingly,

---

[8]Iain Pears, *An Instance at the Fingerpost* (New York: Riverhead Books, 1988), 551.
[9]Pears, *Instance at the Fingerpost*, 171.

our guiding question in chapters six through eleven is this: What do the elements of Christian faith look like from the perspective that open theism provides?

As an introduction to part two, I suggest in chapter six that we dispense with the popular description of open theism as proposing a "limited" view of God. The connotations of that way of describing open theism are inherently negative, even when used by its supporters. Those who embrace the open view of God do so because they believe that it enhances and enriches our concept of God rather than limiting it.

The discussions in chapters seven through eleven deal with a selection of specific questions that some of the ideas basic to open theism raise. For open theists, the future is open, or indefinite, and God's experience of the world is therefore temporal or sequential.

Does the concept of temporality apply to God's inner life as well as God's experience of the world? Chapter seven argues that it does and connects the idea of divine temporality with a trinitarian concept of God.

Another idea basic to open theism is the reality of human freedom, understood as libertarian freedom, or "freedom to do otherwise," as it is often defined. But the more we learn about the physical basis of our experience, the more people wonder about the extent or even the existence of human freedom. Chapter eight examines some of the current arguments related to human freedom and argues that there is important evidence that we are, indeed, significantly free.

The doctrine of incarnation is basic to the Christian understanding of salvation, and it raises questions about the nature of Jesus' earthly life, especially his moral experience. Chapter nine explores the central issues involved in Jesus' temptations and the question of whether or not his victory was inevitable.

The conviction that nothing is more important than a personal relationship with God, and that it depends on our individual decisions, raises questions in the minds of many people about the importance or even the value of Christian community. Chapter ten argues that participating in the community that Jesus established is not merely a consequence of the experience of salvation, it is essential to it.

Finally, there are divergent views among Christians about the nature of the life to come. Chapter eleven presents reasons to believe that everlasting life is an important aspect of the Christian view of human destiny and is best conceived as an everlasting series of experiences.

A final word. Since I was one of the contributors to the 1994 volume, my own commitment to the open view of God is obvious. So this discussion will inevitably reflect my own attraction to open theism. At the same time, I'll be speaking *as* an open theist, but not necessarily *for* open theists. As we shall see, there is considerable diversity in the views of those who accept the central ideas of open theism, but open theists have generally avoided attempts to define boundaries in ways that would generate unfruitful exchanges. I appreciate this reluctance, and I hope our openness to one another's views will continue.

PART I

THE ORIGINS

AND

DEVELOPMENT

OF OPEN

THEISM

CHAPTER ONE

ANTECEDENTS TO OPEN THEISM

PEOPLE SOMETIMES SAY NOTHING ever happens for the first time. And though *The Openness of God* attracted the attention of a new arrival when it appeared in 1994, people had been discussing many of its central ideas for a long time—for centuries as a matter of fact. In the "Open Theism Timeline" he prepared in 2013, Thomas Lukashow traces the antecedents for open theism back to the seventeenth century (and even beyond), citing numerous works on divine knowledge of the future, human freedom, and closely related topics. There are a number of more recent precedents for open theism as well.

In this chapter, we will review the work of several Christian thinkers who explored these themes, often at considerable length, not that long ago. Their efforts show that the central issues that concern open theists have occupied thoughtful people for quite some time, a number of whom, though lacking formal theological training, developed impressive arguments for their convictions.

JACOBUS ARMINIUS

For many people, Jacobus Arminius (1560–1609) was an essential figure, perhaps *the* essential figure in the history of "free will theism." In reaction to Calvin's doctrine of predestination, Arminius maintained that one's salvation requires a positive personal response to God's gracious invitation. Since we are free to accept or reject God's invitation, God's will is not all-determining. God allows the creatures to make decisions and contribute to the ongoing course of events.

Like many free will theists, Arminius accepted God's absolute foreknowledge, but he admitted that he did not have a good explanation for it. "The knowledge of God," he states, "is eternal, immutable and infinite, and . . . extends to all things, both necessary and contingent. . . . But I do not understand the mode in which He knows future contingencies and especially those which belong to the free-will of creatures."[1]

Arminius had his own suggestions for resolving this dilemma, and other free will theists have theirs as well, from middle knowledge to simple foreknowledge. Those who espouse "open theism" dissolve the dilemma by maintaining that future free decisions are logically unknowable, or "not there to be known." So the fact that God's (fore) knowledge does not include them does not, in any way, detract from divine omniscience. God still knows all there is to know. But this is getting ahead of our story. Our purpose in this chapter is to look at some of the figures whose ideas anticipated open theism and preceded its emergence as a distinct theological development.

ADAM CLARKE

There are precedents for open theism in the writings of several nineteenth-century figures. One was Adam Clarke (1760–1832), an English Methodist theologian, whose six-volume commentary on the New Testament exerted a significant influence on Bible students for two centuries.

Clarke appends some thoughts on "that awful subject, the *foreknowledge* of God" to his comments on Acts 2. To summarize Clarke's argument, God ordains that certain creatures have freedom, their free actions and decisions are therefore contingent, and God's knowledge of these contingencies is itself contingent. If creatures are not genuinely free, "then God is the only operator" and "all created beings are only instruments." "By contingent," Clarke asserts, "I mean such things as the infinite

---

[1]"A Discussion on the Subject of Predestination, Between James Arminius, D.D., Minister at Amsterdam, and Francis Junius, D.D., Professor of Divinity at Leyden," in *The Writings of James Arminius*, trans. James Nichols and W. R. Bagnall, 3 vols. (Grand Rapids: Baker, 1956), 3:66.

wisdom of God has thought proper to poise in the possibility of being or not being. . . . [They] are such possibilities, amid the succession of events, as the infinite wisdom of God has left to the creatures to determine."[2]

Without contingency, there would be no free agency, and that would leave God as the sole actor, making him "the author of all the evil and sin that are in the world." If God predetermines everything, and his determinations are all necessarily right, then nothing the creatures do is wrong. This would mean that "sin is no more sin" and distinctions such as "vice and virtue, praise and blame, merit and demerit, guilt and innocence, are at once confounded, and all distinctions of this kind confounded with them." The contingency that creaturely freedom involves provides a basis for moral responsibility. There is a distinction, then, within God's decisions regarding creation. God "has ordained some things as absolutely certain; these he knows as absolutely certain. He has ordained other things as contingent; these he knows as contingent."

The contingency that creaturely freedom and moral responsibility necessarily require has important implications for divine foreknowledge. God's knowledge of contingencies must itself be contingent. "It would be absurd to say that he foreknows a thing as only contingent which he has made absolutely certain. And it would be as absurd to say the he foreknows a thing to be absolutely certain which in his own eternal counsel he has made contingent."

Though Clarke insists that there is a difference between God's knowledge of necessities and his knowledge of contingencies, he seems to collapse the two with his view of divine eternity. Strictly speaking, he argues, God does not have foreknowledge, because nothing is either past or future to God. Since God exists in eternity, "he is equally everywhere," in both the past and the future. Indeed, he "exists in one infinite, indivisible, and eternal NOW." As a result, God sees the future as clearly as he sees the past. God may not decide everything that happens, but God knows everything that happens. So, from God's perspective, there is nothing indefinite about the future. As William M. King observed,

---

[2]Adam Clarke, *The New Testament of Our Lord and Savior Jesus Christ with a Commentary and Critical Notes*, vol. 1, *Matthew to the Acts* (New York: Abingdon-Cokesbury Press, n.d.), 702.

Clarke "flirted with a denial of absolute prescience in his Commentary on Acts," but ultimately shied away from it.[3]

LORENZO McCABE

Another nineteenth-century Methodist who addressed the topic of divine foreknowledge—and was not reluctant to deny it—was Lorenzo Dow McCabe (1817–1897), author of two books on the subject.[4] In *Divine Nescience of Future Contingencies a Necessity*, McCabe, for years a professor at Ohio Wesleyan University, discusses no fewer than fifteen reasons for this thesis, ranging from "the necessity of things," through "the divine perfection," "the utility of prayer," "a satisfactory theodicy," and "a universal atonement," among other things, to "the reality of time."

Not surprisingly, McCabe focused on the issue of divine foreknowledge, the topic that gives rise to the most persistent challenges to open theism. Like open theists a century later, he drew on the resources of philosophy, scriptural exegesis, and religious experience to support his concept of divine nescience.[5] As a Methodist, McCabe affirmed the reality of human freedom, and he insisted that free actions are of necessity contingent. But it is precisely on this point that freedom and the traditional view of divine foreknowledge come into conflict. How could contingent events be known before they occur? Absolute divine foreknowledge excludes all contingency. It "makes every event of the future just as absolutely certain as does the doctrine of unconditional predestination which declares there is a *causal* necessity."[6] Indeed, "if God proposes to deal with us on the principle of contingency, our future choices ought to be as truly contingent in his mind as they are contingent in ours."[7]

It was not just that absolute foreknowledge conflicts with human freedom that bothered McCabe. Even more upsetting was the picture of

---

[3]William McGuire King, "God's Nescience of Future Contingents: A Nineteenth-Century Theory," *Process Studies* 9, nos. 3-4 (Fall 1979): 114n1.

[4]Lorenzo McCabe, *Divine Nescience of Future Contingencies a Necessity* (New York: Phillips and Hunt, 1882), and *The Foreknowledge of God and Cognate Themes in Theology and Philosophy* (Cincinnati: Cranston and Stow, 1878).

[5]King, "God's Nescience," 105.

[6]McCabe, *Foreknowledge of God*, 341.

[7]McCabe, *Foreknowledge of God*, 306.

God as a timelessly omniscient being. Remove all notion of contingency from God, and we are left with a God who is "immovably fixed," locked in "the iceberg of indifference," in short, a God who is not, in any meaningful sense, a personal, or "personic," being.[8]

What makes the concept of absolute foreknowledge so objectionable, then, is what it takes away from God. It robs God of an entire range of positive experiences, including delight, enjoyment, curiosity, love, novelty, surprise and wonder, the thrill of "new thoughts, new desires, purposes and plans."[9] And it prevents God from sharing and suffering in the moral struggles of humanity.[10]

Unlike the immutable deity of Christian tradition, a truly personal being is one who can deliberate and make decisions, one whose actions are necessarily "successive and hence separable and distinguishable in duration."[11] In other words, a truly personal God is one whose experience involves temporality. God's relation to creation is a changing process, and since God's activity is a temporal one, God himself is "in time."[12] Unless God undergoes actual development in his relation to the contingent world, we cannot describe him as having free will and as a center of personal consciousness. So, the traditional defense of divine foreknowledge, resting as it does on notions of divine immutability and timelessness, is unacceptable.

Another problem with the traditional view is its failure to do justice to biblical accounts of God, in particular, descriptions of conditional prophecies, such as those of Jeremiah. It seems clear from such passages that God does not know what decisions human beings will make in the future and that God's experience registers those decisions only when they occur. Indeed, they show that "the conduct of men perpetually changes God's feelings and modifies his treatment of them."[13]

---

[8]McCabe, *Foreknowledge of God*, 210; McCabe, *Divine Nescience*, 289; and McCabe, *Divine Nescience*, 67; *Foreknowledge of God*, 211, respectively.

[9]McCabe, *Divine Nescience*, 20.

[10]McCabe, *Foreknowledge of God*, 245-46.

[11]McCabe, *Foreknowledge of God*, 276.

[12]McCabe, *Foreknowledge of God*, 387. Though a common way of expressing the notion of divine temporality, the expression "in time" has unfortunate connotations. We will discuss these in chapter 7, "Open Theism and the Trinity."

[13]McCabe, *Foreknowledge of God*, 64.

Finally, absolute foreknowledge and the attendant notion of divine timelessness conflict with the value of prayer. If God is timeless, how could prayer make sense? How could it have the slightest influence on God's "thoughts, feelings, purposes and volitions"?[14]

McCabe insisted that his revisionary ideas do not detract from God's essential qualities. For one thing, he found a parallel between omnipotence and omniscience. Just as omnipotence is "circumscribed by the possible," "omniscience must be limited to the knowable," and this excludes future contingencies.[15] For another, he described the interactive relationship between God and creation as a "voluntary self-limitation," a choice for God, not a necessity.[16] And perhaps most significantly, he distinguishes between God's "subjective" and "objective" lives. In God's objective life, that is, "his life, experience, interest, and enjoyment," is necessarily contingent, while his subjective life is eternal and "may not be a process of becoming and of passing away."[17]

When it comes to God's relation to the world, this view of God brings with it an open-ended view of history and an interactive view of divine providence. For McCabe, creation was a "pure venture" on God's part, a great and fair experiment. While God's purposes must ultimately prevail, just how this will happen is "unfixed, undetermined, and therefore uncertain."[18] Moreover, the fulfillment of these purposes requires human cooperation; it is not something God can determine unilaterally. What God ultimately wants is a kingdom of "co-creators, co-causes, co-originators, and co-eternal with himself in the realm of the contingent."[19]

In defending his view of God, McCabe exhibits the conviction of later open theists that it takes nothing away from God for us to reject absolute foreknowledge and embrace divine temporality. Instead, it significantly enriches and enlarges our picture of God. The view that God is actively

---

[14]McCabe, *Divine Nescience*, 99.

[15]McCabe, *Divine Nescience*, 24.

[16]McCabe, *Foreknowledge of God*, 205.

[17]McCabe, *Divine Nescience*, 283. McCabe's distinction between God's subjective and objective lives bears a striking similarity to Charles Hartshorne's dipolar theism.

[18]McCabe, *Divine Nescience*, 28.

[19]McCabe, *Divine Nescience*, 22.

engaged in the world, responding and reacting to the actions and decisions of humans, provides us a far more personal picture of God than the one that absolute foreknowledge requires.

Yet, however interesting McCabe's views are in light of our concerns today, they had little influence on his contemporaries and went largely unnoticed. But even so, his formulations provide an interesting precedent for later reflections on the nature of God. As William King concluded, "With the limited theological and exegetical resources at his disposal, [McCabe] was still able to articulate a doctrine of God that was somewhat ahead of its time."[20]

In another study, David Alstad Tiessen finds in McCabe's work a nineteenth-century Wesleyan precedent for open theism. The two views share a commitment to the primacy of scriptural revelation, an emphasis on God's concrete personality, a distinction between God's unchanging nature and his experience and action, along with similar concepts of creation, divine will, knowledge, and perfection.[21] There are differences, of course, such as the prominent role that the social Trinity plays in the openness model. But the similarities are strong enough to regard McCabe's views as a "proto-openness model" of God.[22] Tiessen draws another interesting conclusion from his study as well. The fact that McCabe operated in a "pre-process milieu," he argues, shows that open theism cannot be dismissed as "a twentieth-century capitulation to process theology. . . . [It] is a model with deeper roots than might appear at first glance."[23]

JULES LEQUYER

Another nineteenth-century figure whose ideas anticipated the concerns of open theism was Jules Lequyer (1814–1862), an obscure French genius,

---

[20]King, "God's Nescience of Future Contingents," 114.

[21]David Alstad Tiessen, "The Openness Model of God: An Evangelical Paradigm in Light of Its Nineteenth-Century Wesleyan Precedent," *Didaskalia* (Spring 2000): 94. See also Tiessen, "The Openness Model of God: An Examination of Its Current and Early Expression in Light of Hartshorne's Process Theism" (MDiv thesis, Providence Theological Seminary, 1998).

[22]Tiessen, "The Openness Model of God: An Evangelical Paradigm in Light of Its Nineteenth-Century Wesleyan Precedent," 100.

[23]Tiessen, "The Openness Model of God: An Evangelical Paradigm in Light of Its Nineteenth-Century Wesleyan Precedent," 101.

who published nothing during his lifetime, but whose writings attracted the attention of a wide range of thinkers, from French existentialists to the American pragmatist William James and the process philosopher Charles Hartshorne. According to an informative article by Donald Wayne Viney, Lequyer's philosophy of freedom develops in detail the idea of the openness of God.[24]

Lequyer affirmed a compatibilist idea of human freedom and he equated freedom with creativity. In creating beings who were free, God created beings who were themselves creative, so their decisions bring into existence something for which God is not responsible. Not only are these decisions independent of God, they have an effect on God. And this requires a revision in the classical notion of God as pure act with "no admixture of potency"—the view that God is wholly simple, eternal, immutable, and impassible, complete in himself, independent of and utterly unaffected by anything other than God. Since God's creatures have a genuine effect on God, there is a qualified sense in which the Creator himself is also created.

Another noteworthy element in Lequyer's thinking is a denial of absolute foreknowledge. If the creatures have creative freedom, God cannot know ahead of time what their decisions will be. As a result, God's experience of temporal reality must itself be temporal. Lequyer rejects the argument of Boethius that God experiences simultaneously events that occur successively. The fact that God knows future events as possibilities, not actualities, does not limit God's knowledge.[25]

Thinkers who affirm libertarian freedom and take Christian tradition seriously inevitably face questions about prophecy and providence, and Viney explores Lequyer's answers to both. Lequyer distinguishes between absolute and conditional prophecies. By acting, or not acting, in a certain way, God may guarantee the fulfillment of "absolute prophecy," like Peter's denial of Jesus. Knowing the state of Peter's heart, God anticipated that he would deny Jesus and decided not to interfere. When it comes to conditional prophecy, what eventually does or doesn't occur depends on

---

[24]Donald Wayne Viney, "Jules Lequyer and the Openness of God," in *Faith and Philosophy: Journal of the Society of Christian Philosophers*, 14, no. 2 (April 1997): 212-35.
[25]Viney, "Jules Lequyer and the Openness of God," 217.

how humans respond to God's commands, with Jonah's prediction of Nineveh's destruction being the classic example. Such prophecies pre-suppose human freedom.[26]

As for divine providence, the same factors at work in prophecy account for the achievement of God's purposes, namely, God's extensive knowledge of the consequences of free decisions, and God's active role in fulfilling absolute prophecies.[27]

Viney concludes with this assessment of Lequyer's legacy. He "anticipated and expanded upon the idea of the openness of God." With his solution to the ancient problem of divine foreknowledge and human freedom is born "not only a critique of traditional arguments but new ways of conceiving the divine life and its relation to the flux of time."[28]

GORDON C. OLSON

Though McCabe's views on divine foreknowledge did not attract a following during his lifetime, they were appreciated by others who wrote on the topic years later, such as Gordon C. Olson (1907–1989) and H. Roy Elseth. Olson, by trade a tractor design engineer and moral government teacher, wrote two noteworthy books on the nature of God, some thirty years apart, *The Foreknowledge of God*[29] and *The Omniscience of the Godhead*.[30] In one section of a later book that deals with a wider range of issues, *The Truth Shall Make You Free*, Olson summarizes his views on "the nature and character of God."[31]

There are aspects of Olson's account that will no doubt trouble theologically informed readers. His account of the trinity verges on tritheism,[32]

---

[26]Viney, "Jules Lequyer and the Openness of God," 226-27.

[27]Viney, "Jules Lequyer and the Openness of God," 227.

[28]Viney, "Jules Lequyer and the Openness of God," 227-28.

[29]Gordon C. Olson, *The Foreknowledge of God* (Arlington Heights, IL: The Bible Research Corporation, 1941). In the preface Olson acknowledges a debt to the work of Lorenzo McCabe.

[30]Gordon C. Olson, *The Omniscience of the Godhead* (Arlington Heights, IL: The Bible Research Corporation, 1972).

[31]Gordon C. Olson, *The Truth Shall Make You Free* (Franklin Park, IL: The Bible Research Corporation, 1980). This is the title of section three. The book comprises fifteen sections, each consisting of an extended paragraph outline and containing an abundance of biblical references.

[32]For example, Olson often uses the word *Godhead* as a plural ("the Godhead are") and speaks of a "plurality of divine persons." He also identifies the biblical view of God as both a "trinity of personal spiritual beings" and a "divine unity of personalities," "a compound oneness."

and his argument that we can infer what God is like from our analysis of human experience because we are created in God's image could lead to unwarranted anthropomorphism. But he offers impressive arguments that sequence, succession, duration—call it what you will—is intrinsic to the biblical portrayal of God, and the sheer number and variety of descriptions make it difficult to dismiss them as mere concessions to our finite minds. Since there is "a true chronology of divine succession in the Divine existence,"[33] we cannot bring our thinking about God into line with the Bible unless we think of God's experiences and actions as taking place over a duration of time.

As a result, the familiar idea that God is "above time," and sees all of human history in one indivisible perception, is incompatible with what the Bible says. Indeed, "the theological dogma that God is an 'eternal now,'" the belief that "time or succession is not an element in the Divine existence, is evidently a philosophical rather than a Biblical concept."[34] It represents nothing less than an intrusion of alien ideas into the thinking of the early church.

With these considerations in mind, Olson gives special attention to the attributes of omnipotence and omniscience. The idea of omnipotence means that God has power or energy without limit as far as sheer force is concerned. But it does not mean that God's power has no limits, or is all-determining. For example, God cannot abolish the laws of mathematics, make something be and not be at the same time. Nor can God do things "contrary to himself," things that violate his moral nature. More significant, however, God has choices. He can choose to live with "a restrained sovereignty." That is, he can choose the specific ways in which he wants to exercise his power. If God exercised absolute control, in particular, if God compelled moral beings to act in certain ways, it would "eliminate the reason for their creation." Because he placed the value of a moral world above "an unlimited display of omnipotence,"[35]

Accordingly, he says, it is proper to refer to the Godhead in "both the plural and the singular," in the plural because "there are three Personalities so distinct that 'They' may perform specific functions and actions separately" (*Truth Shall Make You Free*, section 3, 1-3).

[33] Olson, *Truth Shall Make You Free*, section 3, 6.

[34] Olson, *Truth Shall Make You Free*, section 3, 7.

[35] Olson, *Truth Shall Make You Free*, section 3, 22-23.

God grants them the power of self-determination. In creating moral beings, then, beings who have "the power of contrary choice," God rendered himself vulnerable to human obstinacy and disobedience.

When it comes to omniscience, Olson concludes from "a painstaking reading of the Bible"[36] that God's knowledge cannot include "the future choices of moral beings," when "acting in their moral agency," because such events do not exist until they take place. Still, there is a great deal about the future that God does know in advance. God knows "many future choices, actions, and mass reactions of men" and makes his plans accordingly. And as the future acquires a definite shape, God's plans similarly become more definite, moving from mere possibilities, through likelihoods, to future certainties. For example, God worked out the plan of atonement through Christ "as a possibility" before the foundation of the world, and the plan became a certainty in God's mind from the moment humanity sinned.[37]

There are also events that God knows in advance because he decides to bring them about. Olson is a bit tentative here, saying first, they "appear to be associated with the idea of causation," and later, "God can prophesy . . . many things because He has determined to bring them to pass by His direct causation."[38] These include the hardening of Pharaoh's heart, the naming of Cyrus, king of Persia, the seventy-year captivity of the Jews, and remarkably, the insistence of the Jewish leaders of Christ's time that he be executed by crucifixion rather than by stoning.[39]

Many other passages, in contrast, "when taken in their natural meaning," seem to show that God does not have "absolute foreknowledge over all His future actions, nor over all those of His moral creatures." The word *repent* and its derivatives describe God's actions some thirty-three

---

[36]Olson, *Truth Shall Make You Free*, section 3, 13.

[37]Olson, *Truth Shall Make You Free*, section 3, 14-15.

[38]Olson, *Truth Shall Make You Free*, section 3, 15, 17.

[39]Olson, *Truth Shall Make You Free*, section 3, 15-16. Olson gives Jesus' prayer in Gethsemane—"let this cup pass from me"—an unusual interpretation. As he describes it, Jesus prayed, not to be delivered from dying, but from being stoned to death, the customary Hebrew form of capital punishment. And the reason was Jesus' desire to undergo crucifixion instead! Only if Jesus were crucified, a process that typically took extended time, would the agony over sin that the sacred atonement required be clearly visible (Olson, *Truth Shall Make You Free*, section 3, 16).

times in the Old Testament, from God's regret over having created the world, which led to the flood, through his choice of Saul to be king, to the decision to destroy Nineveh. And based on his study of the New Testament, to mention three examples, Olson argues that Judah's betrayal of Jesus was not a foregone conclusion, but a "tragic surprise," that the return of Christ has not happened as soon as God anticipated, and that names can be blotted out from the book of life, which indicates that they must have been written there at some time.[40]

To sum up Olson's conclusions, the biblical evidence requires us to regard God's experiences of creation as an ongoing series of events, not as a timeless, comprehensive act of cognition. God is affected by human decisions and actions, and God takes them into account when making his own decisions. While God's experience of and interaction with his creatures is variable, there are aspects of God that are utterly changeless, namely, the essential features that define God's character. God's goodness, holiness, righteousness, love and truthfulness are ever the same. In short, God is utterly faithful.[41]

HOWARD ROY ELSETH

Another Bible student who devoted detailed attention to specific themes and passages is Howard Roy Elseth, who graduated from a Bible college in Canada and later attended Seattle Pacific College (now Seattle Pacific University). His book, *Did God Know? A Study of the Nature of God*,[42] contains the results of his meticulous Bible study. One of its appendixes, for example, lists "over 11,000 verses that reveal God changes his mind." Another identifies a number of prophecies made to Israel that were not fulfilled. And the final two sections address "explicit verses which show God did not know man's future free choices," along with various occasions on which God changed his mind.

Elseth acknowledges an indebtedness to both McCabe and Olson—he describes McCabe as "a great, yet unrecognized theologian"[43]—and

---

[40]Olson, *Truth Shall Make You Free*, section 3, 18-22.

[41]Olson, *Truth Shall Make You Free*, section 3, 25-29.

[42]Howard Roy Elseth, *Did God Know? A Study of the Nature of God* (St. Paul, MN: Calvary United Church, Inc., 1977).

[43]Elseth, *Did God Know?*, 180.

enthusiastically reiterates a number of their conclusions, often dismissing rejected alternatives with fervent indignation. He is particularly critical of Augustine and Calvin, as well as C. S. Lewis, three figures whose views of divine foreknowledge and predestination make God responsible for all that goes wrong in the world, human sin and suffering included. Elseth bemoans the fact that people who blame God for the tragedies in their lives often wind up hating him as a result. Although he finds extensive evidence in the Bible to support the idea that God's relation to the world is dynamic and interactive, it is the question of divine knowledge, as the title indicates, specifically divine *foreknowledge*, that particularly concerns him.

To set the stage, Elseth insists on the reality of libertarian freedom. If God created humans with moral action, they must have freedom. And "freedom cannot exist without contingencies."[44] This creates a tremendous problem for the traditional concept of divine foreknowledge, because foreknowledge and freedom are utterly incompatible. The popular notion that God's foreknowledge does not affect humanity's freedom leaves one "glaring problem" unanswered. "How is it possible to have 'foreknowledge' without 'predestination'?" If God has absolute knowledge of future events, those events must have been planned by him, and that makes him responsible for everything that happens.[45] In contrast to the futile efforts of theologians to harmonize freedom and foreknowledge, Elseth finds in the Bible "a clear and consistent view of God's knowledge," and with it, a distinct alternative to the view that all reality is present to God at once.[46] To the contrary, as the title of chapter seven puts it, "God lives in time."

Time is not something created by God, it is an integral aspect of the divine experience.[47] And this means that there is a real difference between past and future, not just from our perspective, but from God's perspective too. Because God created beings who are free, God doesn't

---

[44]Elseth, *Did God Know?*, 29.
[45]Elseth, *Did God Know?*, 50.
[46]Elseth, *Did God Know?*, 39, 65.
[47]Elseth, *Did God Know?*, 67.

know everything they're going to do—not because there is something God doesn't know, but because their decisions do not exist until they make them.[48] Consequently, the divine life consists, not in a single timeless moment, but in an eternal duration of successive moments.

Far from diminishing God, Elseth argues, this concept of divine knowledge enhances our view of God. "It doesn't take any power at all for God to deal with what is certain. All He has to do is sit back and watch what is happening, which He always knew would happen." In contrast, "it takes a far superior God to deal with the challenge of that which is not yet known. . . . It takes a far greater being to run a universe that involves changes not known in advance than one that has no unexpected occurrences."[49]

Although Elseth makes a number of logical points, the most notable feature of his project is the careful attention he gives to various biblical passages. For example, he argues that the Greek word for "foreknowledge" means something closer to the English word *prognosis* than "knowledge of something before it happens." In other words, it means to *predict*, rather than to *know*. Accordingly, we should not read the texts where it occurs, such as Romans 8:29 ("For those whom he foreknew he also predestined"), as conveying the idea that God knows the exact choices of free agents.[50]

Elseth also has interesting things to say about the "sand trap" of biblical prophecy. The purpose of all prophecy, he argues, is "to call men to righteousness."[51] Only a small portion of prophecies involve foretelling the future, and these fall into two basic categories: "telic prophecies," which become true "because of God's causation or providential government," and conditional prophecies, whose fulfillment depends on human response, such as Jonah's prophecy of Nineveh's destruction.[52]

---

[48]"Knowing all things does not imply knowledge of what does not exist. A future choice is still contingent, and its outcome does not exist and thus cannot be known. . . . [To quote Albert C. Knudson,] 'For as omnipotence does not imply the power to do the non-doable, so omniscience does not imply the power to know the unknowable'" (Elseth, *Did God Know?*, 75).
[49]Elseth, *Did God Know?*, 79.
[50]Elseth, *Did God Know?*, 57.
[51]Elseth, *Did God Know?*, 107.
[52]Elseth, *Did God Know?*, 111.

A third prophetic category, which Elseth calls "ecbatic" prophecies, includes Old Testament passages New Testament writers apply to certain events with the expression "that the Scriptures might be fulfilled." This phrase should not be understood to say that a particular event had to occur in order for a prediction to be fulfilled. Instead, it simply points to a similar situation, an application or illustration of something that happened before.[53]

Elseth devotes two chapters to verses that pose problems for his view of God, such as Jesus' prediction that Peter would deny him—"The Briars and Thorns," he calls them—and finds ways to harmonize them with his dynamic view of God. Approaching the end of the last chapter, he exclaims, "God knows all that is knowable and is capable of doing all that is possible. God is free! He can change his mind! . . . God is an all-loving God who loves, thinks, creates and who is real and genuine."[54]

Though Elseth's book lacks the trappings of a technical treatise—it abounds in personal appeals and rhetorical questions—it contains a vigorous argument and offers some serious exegetical work. And its underlying motive is evident throughout, namely, a desire to do justice to the full range of biblical descriptions of God.

CONCLUSION

With the exception of Adam Clark, none of the figures discussed above were recognized religious authorities. To my knowledge none of them acquired advanced degrees in philosophy, theology, or biblical studies. They seldom appealed to the work of previous scholars. Their views were not widely known and seem to have attracted little if any serious scholarly attention.

Given their location outside the theological mainstream, one can't help wondering if the "avocational" nature of their interest in these issues freed them to look at God from a perspective unencumbered by the traditional vision of God's essential attributes—eternity, immutability,

---

[53]The use of the subjunctive mood in Greek, rather than the indicative, supports this point (Elseth, *Did God Know?*, 120).
[54]Elseth, *Did God Know?*, 179.

impassibility, and so on. In contrast, the concerns that preoccupied these figures were the freedom, foreknowledge and providence of God. They viewed these topics as a network of related issues, each one of which leads inexorably to the others. And they all insisted on the importance of creaturely contingency and its effects on God's knowledge and experience. Unfettered by the terms and concepts of traditional views of God, they were able to read the Bible in ways that allowed the features of the God-world relation to emerge more clearly.

There's not much evidence that the work of contemporary open theists has been directly influenced by the work of these thinkers. But the positions they propose offer evidence that the picture of God later identified with "open theism"—or certainly some of its features—is one that thoughtful people have found appealing for quite some time, not least because it so nicely comports with the biblical portrayal of God.

CHAPTER TWO

▸▸▸▸▸ EARLY FORMULATIONS ▸▸▸▸▸
▸▸▸▸▸ OF OPEN THEISM ▸▸▸▸▸

TWO BOOKS HAVE BEEN PUBLISHED under the title *The Openness of God,* and by coincidence I was involved in writing both of them.[1] The first appeared in 1980; the second, the one that has generated considerable theological and philosophical discussion, appeared in 1994.

In the summer of 1979 I presented a paper on God's relation to the world at a conference on history and religion held at the campus where I was teaching. Some who heard the paper said the ideas deserved a more extended discussion, so I spent the rest of the summer working up a longer version. I'm not sure just how I came upon the phrase *the openness of God.* I may have been unconsciously influenced by E. L. Mascall's book *The Openness of Being,* which I had read several years before as a graduate student.

Richard Coffen, an editor at Southern Publishing Association, a Seventh-day Adventist operation in Nashville, learned of the project and asked me for a copy of the manuscript, and I soon heard that it had been accepted for publication. Shortly thereafter, however, "Southern Pub" merged operations with the Review and Herald Publishing Association in Washington, DC, not far from denominational headquarters, so *The Openness of God* appeared under the Review and Herald imprint in late 1980. Evidently a number of people in the Adventist church found the

---

[1]Although, unbeknown to me, the expression *openness of God* appeared in a 1969 book by Thomas Torrance, *Space, Time and Incarnation,* to my knowledge I was the first to use it as book title.

ideas in the book troubling, and in response to their objections the RHPA administrative committee voted to withdraw the book from circulation in July 1981.[2] This decision upset a number of other Adventists, however, who felt that the church should be more open to new ideas. Soon the administrative committee reversed itself, and the book became available once again, and sold out rather quickly. When the first run of books was exhausted, the publishers elected not to reprint it.

I thought my first scholarly effort had quietly expired until I received a letter out of the blue one day in April, 1984. It was from Clark Pinnock, a well-known evangelical theologian, who taught at McMaster Divinity College in Hamilton, Ontario, Canada. I recognized his name, of course, from his many articles in *Christianity Today*, but I had no idea why he would be writing to me. His letter began, "This is a shot in the dark," and went on to say that he had read *The Openness of God*, liked it, and wanted to establish contact. He mentioned his transition from Calvinism to Arminianism and indicated that we had work to do. Pinnock also said he had "a heck of a time" getting the book and wondered if the publishers had withdrawn it. When I wrote back and told him what had happened, he suggested contacting Bethany House Publishers in Minneapolis. I did, and the next year they reissued the book, with a couple of minor modifications, under the title *God's Foreknowledge and Man's Free Will*.[3]

The next book to bear the title *The Openness of God* had its beginnings with a conversation between John Sanders and Clark Pinnock at the Wheaton Theology Conference during the summer of 1992. Sanders told Pinnock about a book idea he had on the nature of God and providence. It would draw on the biblical material that Terence Fretheim had done, the philosophical work of William Hasker, and practical theological considerations that David Basinger had published.

When Sanders said he was several years away from getting all the research done, Pinnock suggested that Sanders should see if Hasker and

---

[2] According to Coffen, Neal C. Wilson, President of the General Conference of Seventh-day Adventists, was very upset that the book had been withdrawn from publication. His intention was that it merely be treated with "benign neglect" (*Adventist Today*, Spring 2014, 9-10).

[3] *God's Foreknowledge and Man's Free Will* is now available from Wipf and Stock Publishers of Eugene, OR (2004).

Basinger would be game for coauthoring a book. Sanders had never thought of a collaborative project, so he worked up a chapter outline of the book, sent it to Pinnock, and he liked it. Sanders then contacted Fretheim, Hasker, and Basinger. Fretheim could not participate, so Pinnock contacted me since I had written on the topic several years before.

When it came time to pick a title for our project, Pinnock suggested the original title of my first book. He felt that the word *openness* had a positive ring to it, conveying the ideas that God is open to the creatures and the future is open with multiple possibilities. Moreover, the expression didn't carry any traditional theological baggage. The other contributors agreed and that's how the title of this book originated.

With the 1994 publication of *The Openness of God*, the general perspective that God enjoys a highly interactive relation to the world, that God's creatures have significant freedom, and that the future is indefinite acquired a verbal handle that has become widely used. The expressions *openness of God*, *open theism*, and *openness theology* now frequently appear in theological and philosophical books and articles.

The basic ideas in this theological perspective have been summarized numerous times and can be identified rather easily. Open theism arises from the conviction that love defines the very nature of God. Love is not merely an attribute or an activity of God—something God has or does—it is what God is in his very essence. Love defines God's inner reality, and love characterizes God's relation to all that is not God. In sovereign freedom, God created the world as an expression of the love that God is, and love not only accounts for God's decision to create a world distinct from himself, love also comes to expression in all of God's relations to the world.

Out of love, therefore, God created beings who themselves have the capacity to love—to enjoy loving relationships with God and with each other. In order to make creaturely love possible, God endowed the creatures with the freedom, the ability to respond with love to God's love for them. Since coercion has no place in love, their response to God's love had to be a choice, not an inevitability. It was not something God could unilaterally determine, or decide for them. Having chosen to create beings with a capacity for self-determination, God is not responsible for everything that happens in the world. The decisions and actions of the creatures also contribute to the ongoing course of events.

There are two further features of open theism that its affirmation of divine love involves. One is the fact that God is genuinely related to the creaturely world. God is intimately involved in the affairs of the world, both acting within it and interacting with it. God affects the world, and the creaturely world affects God. Everything that happens has an effect on his experience. Consequently, God's reactions to what happens in the world involve immense variety—from joy and delight through great concern to disappointment and dismay.

At the same time, what happens in the world, indeed, whatever happens and no matter what happens, God's commitment to the world is unconditional. God's love for the creatures is not contingent on their response to his love. God relentlessly pursues his purposes for the world, inviting the creatures to accept his love and join in fulfilling his dreams and achieving his hopes for them.

This interactive portrait of God's relation to the world involves temporality. Open theists express God's temporality in various ways. Although some say that God is "in time," another way—preferable in my view—would be to say, "time is real for God." In other words, God's experience is sequential; "before" and "after" apply to God's inner life.[4] God is "with us" in the going course of events that constitute creaturely reality. And God's decisions and actions make a real difference, not only to the creatures, but also to God.

The concept that God experiences events as they happen, rather than all at once, has important implications for divine knowledge. Since free choices don't exist until they are made, God experiences them as they occur rather than ahead of time, or from all eternity. This concept of divine knowledge—"dynamic omniscience" as John Sanders calls it—enables us to make sense of a wide range of biblical passages, such as those that speak of God testing people; asking questions about the future; being surprised, delighted, and disappointed; experiencing regret and

---

[4]See Sanders, *The God Who Risks: A Theology of Divine Providence*, 2nd ed. (Downers Grove, IL: InterVarsity Academic, 2007), 15.

sorrow; and perhaps most important, changing his mind in response to human decisions and actions.

The open view of God thus provides a paradigm in which the world represents a work in progress, a source of ongoing divine experiences, rather than an object of a single, all-inclusive perception. So, it is better to think of the world as God's adventure rather than God's invention, or as God's project rather than God's product.[5]

With this general sketch in mind, let us look more closely at the version of *The Openness of God* that gave its name to this theological development. Then we'll review three of the proposals from open theists that spell out their positions in more detail.

THE OPENNESS OF GOD, 1994

As the subtitle of this seminal volume makes clear, *A Biblical Challenge to the Traditional Understanding of God*, a primary objective of these essays was to describe the features of open theism that set it apart from the more familiar view of God, which is variously described as "classical," "traditional," and "conventional." And it compares the two in light of historical, theological, philosophical, and practical, as well as biblical, concerns in mind.

As considered by open theists, the various biblical descriptions of God responding to human actions, occasionally reconsidering his decisions, variously expressing joy or regret, are to be taken just as seriously as affirmations of divine eternity, changelessness, and steadfastness. In contrast to traditional interpretations, these descriptions should not be regarded, or disregarded, as mere affectations or figures of speech, that is, as anthropomorphisms or anthropopathisms that characterize God *as if* his decisions, actions, and indeed, feelings, were affected by conditions in the creaturely world, but do not literally do so. Basic to open theism is the conviction that God genuinely, not merely figuratively, interacts with creaturely reality. God not only affects the world, the world has an effect on God.[6]

---

[5]Cf. Sanders, *The God Who Risks*, 37.

[6]In contrast to Thomas Aquinas, for example, for whom creatures are relative to God, but God is not related to creaturely reality, open theism maintains that relational qualities do indeed apply to God himself.

The discussion of biblical support for an interactive view of God reviews statements that describe God as responsive to things that happen in the world—as variously having certain emotions, changing his attitude, or modifying his plans—as well as statements that indicate creaturely freedom, such as divine warnings and promises.[7] It also suggests that we can reconcile passages that describe God as changing with those that describe God as changeless if we apply them to different aspects of the divine reality. Thus, in his existence and character, God is absolutely immutable, through all eternity never other than he is. But in his experience, that is, in his concrete actuality, God is infinitely sensitive to the ongoing course of creaturely events and therefore constantly changing.[8]

In the historical chapter, John Sanders attributes the prominence of immutability, impassibility, timelessness, and simplicity in traditional doctrines of God to the pervasive influence of Greek philosophy on Christian theology. For all the benefits of this "biblical-classical synthesis"[9]—and they were not insignificant—it obscured the personal qualities of God that appear in the biblical portrait, leaving the broad stream of Christian thought, from the church fathers, through Augustine, Aquinas, and the Reformers, to most contemporary evangelicals, with a view of God that lacks the ability for genuine personal relationship.

In the chapter on systematic theology, Clark Pinnock applies the distinction between open and traditional views of God to the familiar list of divine attributes. He notes that the influential models of God as caring parent and aloof monarch both affirm divine sovereignty, but provide contrasting perspectives on the way God governs. Unlike the traditional portrait of God as immutable, all-powerful, and all-determining, the open view of God emphasizes God's sensitivity, responsiveness, and vulnerability. It portrays God as intimately involved in history—rather

---

[7]Clark Pinnock, Richard Rice, John Sanders, William Hasker, and David Basinger, *The Openness of God: A Biblical Challenge to the Traditional Understanding of God* (Downers Grove, IL: Inter-Varsity Press, 1994), 18.

[8]Pinnock et al., *The Openness of God*, 48.

[9]Pinnock et al., *The Openness of God*, 60.

than standing above or apart from it—and as variously delighted and saddened by human decisions and behavior.[10]

As Pinnock describes it, this perspective provides a helpful corrective, drawn from the Bible, to the tendency to emphasize divine transcendence over divine immanence.[11] A social view of the Trinity provides a basis for affirming both God's self-sufficient fullness and God's openness to the world in overflowing love.[12] The difference between them is not whether God is all-powerful, but the way in which God exercises power. Instead of unilaterally determining all that is, God's love is nurturing and empowering. From Pinnock's perspective, "total control is not a higher view of God's power but a diminution of it."[13] God expresses his power by sharing it with some of the creatures.[14]

Open theism thus entails a complex view of God. God is unchanging, immutable, in his essence, but not in his experience, knowledge, and action.[15] Here God is open to the decisions and actions of the creatures and infinitely responsive to their decisions and actions. Accordingly, God takes delight in their joys and sorrows when they suffer. And this means that God is "with us in time, experiencing the succession of events with us."[16] God's knowledge is perfect, in the sense that God knows all there is to know. But since what there is to know changes as events develop in the world, future decisions are not conceivable objects of knowledge.[17] Instead of planning the course of events down to the last detail, God created beings with the capacity to "surprise and delight him." Accordingly, "the open view of God stresses qualities of generosity, sensitivity, vulnerability more than power and control. It allows us to think of God as taking risks."[18]

To provide a philosophical perspective, William Hasker addresses a number of the questions that open theism raises about God's attributes.

---

[10]Pinnock et al., *The Openness of God*, 103, 104.
[11]Pinnock et al., *The Openness of God*, 107.
[12]Pinnock et al., *The Openness of God*, 108.
[13]Pinnock et al., *The Openness of God*, 114.
[14]Pinnock et al., *The Openness of God*, 115.
[15]Pinnock et al., *The Openness of God*, 118.
[16]Pinnock et al., *The Openness of God*, 120.
[17]Pinnock et al., *The Openness of God*, 123.
[18]Pinnock et al., *The Openness of God*, 125.

Properly understood, he argues, both perfection and omniscience are compatible with the open view of God. The idea that God cannot change, because something can change only for the better or the worse, ignores the fact that some changes are neither. Indeed, certain changes are "consistent with and/or required by a constant state of excellence." So, while God is unchanging in "his essential nature, his love and wisdom and power and faithfulness," God is not impassive and unmoved by creation. To the contrary, he opens himself to the possibility of joy and sorrow.[19]

God's knowledge is perfect because at any time God knows everything that it is logically possible to know. The crucial question is whether free decisions and actions are knowable before they occur. Because open theism embraces libertarian freedom its answer to this question is, *No, ahead of time they are not "there to know."* Given this notion of freedom, open theism differs from both Molinism, with its view of counterfactuals of freedom, and from simple foreknowledge, which regards the future as visible to God in all its detail. For open theism, the future is open to various possibilities, depending to a significant degree on the choices and decisions that creatures make. And because its details are nonexistent in the present, it cannot be known in advance.

When it comes to divine power, Hasker distinguishes open theism from both Calvinism and process theology. Calvinism attributes all that happens to the exercise of God's power, while process philosophy maintains that God's influence on the world is entirely "persuasive." God has an influence on all creaturely events, but he never directly or unilaterally causes anything to happen.

For Hasker, an adequate understanding of providence requires that God has general strategies in pursuing his objectives for the world and exercises immense creativity in implementing them. Consequently, the ultimate outcome of history is not "up in the air," as it seems to be for process thought.[20] Nor is the entire course of history determined in

---

[19]Pinnock et al., *The Openness of God*, 133-34.
[20]Contra Alfred North Whitehead's view "that Tennyson's phrase, 'that far-off divine event to which the whole creation moves' presents a fallacious conception of the universe" (*Process and Reality: An Essay in Cosmology* [New York: Free Press], 131).

advance, as it is for Calvinism. Both majestic and intimate, immensely powerful and infinitely responsive, the God who created beings with the freedom to accept or reject his love, accepting the risks this involves, displays "tremendous resourcefulness" in working to achieve his purposes for creation.[21]

In the concluding essay, David Basinger explores the practical implications of the open view of God for a number of issues, including petitionary prayer, discerning God's will, the problem of evil, and the Christian's social and evangelistic responsibilities. Open theism differs from both Calvinism and process philosophy in resisting an either-or approach to the nature of God's action in the world—one that says God is either directly responsible for everything or not directly responsible for anything. For open theism, things are more complicated. In the case of prayer, open theism holds that God has the power to intervene unilaterally, but out of respect for human freedom rarely does so and sometimes waits until invited.[22] When it comes to suffering, open theism does not attribute each instance to some divine plan. In the complex reality that we live in, a good deal of gratuitous evil occurs—suffering that does not contribute to any greater good.[23]

The opening and closing chapters of this seminal work on open theism deal with what for many people are the major attractions of the position. The view of God it presents takes into account the complex portrait of God we find in the Bible and it addresses in helpful ways the needs and intuitions of many believers on a personal level. The Bible indicates in numerous passages and in numerous ways that God is aware of, interested in, and affected by what happens in human history. And believers sense that God is intimately involved in their personal lives—listening to their praise and complaints, offering reassurance and direction. The perspective of open theism thus meets two essential criteria of theological adequacy—biblical faithfulness and practical religious value. Open theists recognize that additional theological concerns deserve

---

[21]Pinnock et al., *The Openness of God*, 153.
[22]Pinnock et al., *The Openness of God*, 161.
[23]Pinnock et al., *The Openness of God*, 169-70.

attention as well, and as this volume demonstrates, they are sensitive to Christian tradition, the central concerns of Christian theology, and the question of its logical coherence. Though the book hardly answers all the questions open theism raises, it makes the case that the open perspective deserves careful consideration.

Within a few years of the 1994 publication, open theists developed its themes further in a number of important ways. Their works include *The God Who Risks: A Theology of Divine Providence* by John Sanders, *God of The Possible: A Biblical Introduction to the Open View of God* by Gregory A. Boyd, and *Most Moved Mover: A Theology of God's Openness* by Clark H. Pinnock.

THE GOD WHO RISKS, 1998, 2007

Appearing four years after *The Openness of God*, Sanders's provocative title, *The God Who Risks: A Theology of Divine Providence*, remains the most extensive discussion of open theism by a single author. The book follows the sequence of topics found in *The Openness of God* and develops its themes more extensively—from Old and New Testament material pertaining to "a relational view of providence," through the theme of divine relationality as it appears in Christian tradition, to an explanation of "a risk view of providence" and the concept of divine sovereignty it entails. Like the final essay in the 1994 volume, Sanders's concluding chapter applies his view of providence to various aspects of the Christian life.

In referring to the view of God he proposes as the "risk model of providence," Sanders emphasizes what to many is the most controversial feature of open theism, namely, its notion that God created a world with an unforeseen future, a world with the potential to delight and disappoint its Creator. In creating the kind of world he did, a world over which he would not exercise complete control, God risked being disappointed that things would not turn out the way he hoped.

As Sanders sees it, this is not only a necessary corollary of creaturely freedom; more fundamentally, it is an expression of the love that God is, a love that seeks genuine relationship with creatures and therefore requires reciprocity, or genuine interaction.

The purpose of Sanders's discussion is to offer a thoroughgoing case for "relational theism" as an "overarching theological model."[24] And to achieve this, he seeks to show that it meets the essential criteria of theological adequacy, namely, "substantial agreement with Scripture, consonance with tradition, conceptual intelligibility, and adequacy for the needs of Christian living."[25] Although Sanders's focus is on the constructive task of fleshing out the open or relational perspective, the more familiar, and more influential, view of divine sovereignty, along with its corollary concepts of immutability and absolute foreknowledge, is always in the background.

The risk model of providence does not diminish God's sovereignty; it expresses the way God decides to exercise his sovereignty. As he puts it, "God sovereignly decides to make his project dependent on his people."[26] From such accounts as the breaking and renewal of the covenant in Exodus 32–34 it is apparent that God does not follow a detailed blueprint in relating to human beings. Rather than exercising "control and domination," he tries different paths with his creatures. In his covenant with Israel, God offers his people a relationship of "love and vulnerability."[27]

Sanders notes the wide variety of statements we find in the Old Testament regarding God's relation to human beings. God is described as sometimes changing his mind or repenting, and sometimes refusing to change it. When God declares that something will happen in the future, there are times when it happens, and times when it doesn't. It appears from the Old Testament that the future is partly settled and partly unsettled—definite in certain respects and indefinite in others. And since the future itself is complex, God's knowledge of the future is correspondingly complex. In place of absolute or exhaustive foreknowledge, Sanders proposes the concept of "dynamic omniscience" to underscore the concept that the content of God's knowledge reflects the ongoing nature of reality. On any account of omniscience, God knows all there is to

---

[24]Sanders, *The God Who Risks*, 173.
[25]Sanders, *The God Who Risks*, 289.
[26]Sanders, *The God Who Risks*, 60.
[27]Sanders, *The God Who Risks*, 71.

know, but since many aspects of the future become definite only as events take place, God knows the yet-to-be settled aspects as unsettled.[28]

When it comes to biblical accounts of God's actions, we find a similar contrast. There are times when God announces that certain events will take place, and they do . . . because he brings them about. There are also times when God says he will do certain things and then he doesn't, because he takes into account the way people respond. The familiar potter-clay analogy found in Jeremiah illustrates the give-and-take in God's relations to his people.[29] To describe the way God exercises his power, Sanders says, "God is sovereign over his sovereignty."[30]

This has significant implications for the kind of world God created and, beyond that, for whether or not God even decided to create. According to Sanders, God did not need to create, nor was God obligated to create the kind of world he did. On a trinitarian concept of God, divine love finds fulfillment within the fullness of God's own life. The creaturely world does not meet some necessity in the divine nature.[31] Nor was God's only option to create a world in which creatures were genuinely free. Had he chosen to do so, he could have planned the world down to the last detail and exercised "meticulous control" over it.[32] However, in harmony with the love that characterizes all that God is and does, he created a world containing creatures who are themselves free and who make decisions without divine dictation. Instead of determining all their actions, God takes great interest in what they do, and he shares in their experiences as they happen. The distinctions *before* and *after*, as well as *past* and *future*, apply not only to creaturely existence itself but to God's experience as well.

All this raises the question, of course, as to how God could achieve his purposes in a world whose inhabitants are free to accept or resist God's desires for them. And this is where open theism entails a "high" view of

---

[28]Sanders, *The God Who Risks*, 83.
[29]To use Walter Brueggemann's expression, God exercises "responsive sovereignty." Sanders, *The God Who Risks*, 91.
[30]Sanders, *The God Who Risks*, 223.
[31]Sanders, *The God Who Risks*, 185.
[32]Sanders, *The God Who Risks*, 189.

divine providence. God desires the best for the creatures, God is responsive to all they experience, God is bitterly disappointed when they reject his love and wreak havoc on his world, but God relentlessly seeks to redeem creation. To quote the concluding sentences of Sanders's work, "God has the wisdom, power, love and perseverance necessary to meet the challenges ahead. God is competent and resourceful in working with us and sometimes in spite of us to bring about the eschatological completion of his creational project. The Father, Son and Holy Spirit embarked on an adventure with us and the triune God of love is not finished with us yet."[33] So while God took genuine risks in creating the sort of world he did, there is no chance that creation will fail to reach his goals for it.

GOD OF THE POSSIBLE: A BIBLICAL INTRODUCTION TO THE OPEN VIEW OF GOD, 2000

Within a few years of Sanders's book on divine risk, other books supporting the open view of God began to appear. In *God of the Possible*, Gregory A. Boyd draws a sharp contrast between the "classical view of divine foreknowledge" and the open view of God, insisting that what divides them is not the nature of divine knowledge but the nature of the future.[34] For the classical view the future is entirely settled; for the open view the future is open—not wide open, but partly settled and partly open—open, that is, to the extent that it is yet to be determined by free agents. On either account, God's knowledge is perfect; he knows all there is to know. The question is what there is for God to know.[35]

The classical view of divine foreknowledge raises a number of "thorny questions," says Boyd. But the most perplexing is its failure to account

---

[33]Sanders, *The God Who Risks*, 291. The second edition (2007) begins with a new chapter titled "Theological Ground Rules." It deals with the nature of figurative language, a topic that Sanders has pursued at some length over the past fifteen years or so. He has studied cognitive linguistics, supported in part with a grant from the Templeton Foundation, and his book, *Theology in the Flesh: How Embodiment and Culture Shape the Way We Think About Morality, Truth, and God*, appeared in 2016 (Minneapolis: Fortress Press).

[34]For this reason, Boyd prefers to speak of the "open view of the future" rather than "the open view of God" (*God of the Possible: A Biblical Introduction to the Open View of God* [Grand Rapids: Baker Books, 2000], 15).

[35]Boyd, *God of the Possible*, 15.

for many biblical passages that express divine regret, surprise, and frustration, as well as those that describe God testing people to know their character.[36] The strongest evidence for the "motif of divine flexibility" appears in passages such as Jeremiah 18, a favorite text of open theists, which describes God as changing his mind in response to human acts and decisions.[37]

We do not have to skirt around the plain meaning of these passages, Boyd argues, if we give up the traditional view that the future is entirely settled in favor of the view that it is partly settled and partly open. Moreover, such a concept of the future fits with our common human experience nicely, and it gives us a basis for attributing both change and changelessness to God. While God's concrete experience changes over time, God's perfect character—his defining attributes—remains eternally the same.[38] With distinctions such as these, the open view of God enjoys the advantages of the traditional view of God, while avoiding its difficulties.

MOST MOVED MOVER:
A THEOLOGY OF GOD'S OPENNESS, 2001

Based on the 2000 Didsbury Lectures, Clark Pinnock's *Most Moved Mover: A Theology of God's Openness* provides another expression of open theism by one of the contributors to the 1994 book. In direct contrast to Aristotle's "unmoved mover," whose utter immutability sets it apart from everything else, the God portrayed in the Bible is better described as the "most moved mover." What distinguishes him from all creaturely reality is the fact that he changes more than anything else. God's experience includes every event that takes place everywhere in the universe. What never changes about God is the generic excellence of his change. His experience is the perfect register of all reality. He alone is most moved by all that happens.

In his first two chapters, Pinnock summarizes the truth of the Christian message; in the remaining two he seeks to give that message a

---

[36]Boyd, *God of the Possible*, 63.
[37]Boyd, *God of the Possible*, 75-87.
[38]Boyd, *God of the Possible*, 136.

contemporary interpretation.[39] As Pinnock interprets it, the Bible portrays God sovereignly and freely deciding to create a world that would express his identity as one of self-giving love, that is, a world containing creatures who were themselves free and self-determined. Like Sanders, Pinnock asserts that the triune God is complete in the intimate fellowship of Father, Son, and Spirit, so God did not create in order to meet some inner necessity or compensate for divine incompleteness. Moreover, God created a world containing personal beings, beings endowed with freedom and self-determination, in other words, beings capable of cooperating with God in achieving his objectives.

Like Sanders, Pinnock attributes to God both temporality and risk. God "operates from within time," says Pinnock. He "remembers the past, interacts with the present and anticipates the future."[40] And since he engages the creatures in dynamic relationships, God does not control the world; he does not exercise "meticulous providence." Consequently, things don't happen just because God wants them to. Since "God goes in for partnerships where the junior partners make a real contribution, . . . history is a drama with profound risks and enormous dynamics."[41] The biblical account of God's dealings with humans is replete with stories of cooperation and resistance, leaving God delighted and disappointed. To give the creatures freedom, Pinnock asserts, "God limited his own freedom. He made room for a partner and accepted a degree of risk."[42]

A further implication of this view of God is "a partly settled future."[43] Instead of knowing the future exhaustively, God knows the future as it is, as partly certain and partly uncertain.[44] Only this concept, he argues, does justice to the biblical descriptions of God as experiencing regret, surprise, as testing people, and as changing his mind. And with this view of divine interaction, we can finally make sense of those biblical passages

---

[39]Clark Pinnock, *Most Moved Mover: A Theology of God's Openness* (Grand Rapids: Baker Academic, 2001), 18.

[40]Pinnock, *Most Moved Mover*, 32. Pinnock also says that God "savors" the present (41).

[41]Pinnock, *Most Moved Mover*, 35.

[42]Pinnock, *Most Moved Mover*, 41.

[43]Pinnock, *Most Moved Mover*, 47.

[44]Pinnock, *Most Moved Mover*, 48-49.

that attribute passion, or "pathos," to God—descriptions of God as suffering because of, with, and for his people.[45]

Pinnock argues that this "integrated reading" of the rich and complex descriptions of God found in the Bible calls for a reconsideration of the attributes of the characteristic of "conventional theism"—divine immutability, impassibility, eternity, sovereignty, and omniscience.[46] The reason conventional theists have a problem with open theism, he insists, is not because it is unscriptural, but because it challenges well-established traditions.[47] And in the second chapter, he attributes these traditions—without mincing words—to "a pagan inheritance." As a number of scholars have shown, the Hellenistic category of changelessness has had enormous influence on Christian thought, generating a package of divine attributes, "leaning in the direction of immobility and hyper-transcendence."[48] Accepting the basic concept that change involves loss, Greek thinkers and their Christian followers held that ultimate reality must be impervious to change, immune to the passage of time, and throughout Christian history influential thinkers such as Augustine and Thomas Aquinas have taken this position. The result is an enduring tension within Christian thought between the dogma that God is changeless and the biblical descriptions of God's connections to the temporal world as creator and sovereign.[49]

To overcome the "biblical-classical synthesis," Pinnock appeals to various biblical descriptions that support "the open nature of God,"[50] including portrayals of God as intimately related to the world, as personal, loving, changeably faithful, wise, and resourceful. We cannot be faithful to the biblical portrait without conceiving of God as temporal. Time, he asserts, is a property God "cannot fail to possess as a personal agent.

---

[45]Pinnock, *Most Moved Mover*, 55-57.

[46]Pinnock, *Most Moved Mover*, 64.

[47]Pinnock, *Most Moved Mover*, 64.

[48]Pinnock, *Most Moved Mover*, 65.

[49]Nor will it do to qualify the concept of God's absolute immutability while retaining such attributes as timelessness, all-controlling sovereignty, and exhaustive omniscience. "The conventional package of attributes," Pinnock insists, is "tightly woven. . . . Tentative changes will not do" (Pinnock, *Most Moved Mover*, 76-77).

[50]Pinnock, *Most Moved Mover*, 79.

Scripture is clear that God experiences temporal duration when he enters into give and take relations with us."[51]

Moreover, temporality is not just a characteristic of God's relation to creation, it is a quality of the divine life itself. The missions of Son and Spirit within the history of salvation "echo eternal processions" within the divine being, and characterize the inner dynamics of the everlasting Trinity as temporal.[52] As a result, past and future are different to God, and the persistent notion of exhaustive divine foreknowledge cannot be sustained. While God knows all there is to know—the entire past, the entire present, and the future to the extent that it can be foreseen—God does not know the entire future, since the future is only partly settled at any one time. As events take place they enter God's experience.[53]

In the second half of his discussion, Pinnock turns to philosophical and practical considerations, arguing that the open view of God is both logically sound and existentially meaningful. The general theme of chapter three, "The Metaphysics of Love," is that theology can use the help of philosophy in solving some of the problems that philosophy has caused.[54] Since conventional theology depends heavily on the classical Greek view of ultimate reality as impervious to change and untouched by anything else, it cannot do justice to the biblical view that God is personal and relational, not only affecting the creaturely world, but affected by it as well.

To portray these aspects of biblical theism, Pinnock argues, theology needs the resources of a philosophy that elevates temporal change and personal relationality—just the sort of things that process thought emphasizes. Unlike the ancient preference for permanence

---

[51]Pinnock, *Most Moved Mover*, 97. Pinnock phrases God's temporality in various ways: "as experiencing past, present, and future successively," as being "related to the world within the structures of time," as being "inside not outside time," as experiencing "successions of events," indeed, as knowing "the passage of time as a dimension of his own endless existence."

[52]Pinnock, *Most Moved Mover*, 96-99.

[53]"Presentism" thus applies to God's experience (Pinnock, *Most Moved Mover*, 106-7). Though associated with Socinians and process theists, Pinnock argues, presentism was independently endorsed by orthodox Christian thinkers such as Lorenzo McCabe and Adam Clark.

[54]"If philosophy played a role in getting theology off track, philosophy may help to restore things" (Pinnock, *Most Moved Mover*, 114).

and changelessness, process philosophy reflects the modern preference for change over permanence. And it provides the basis for a view of God that differs sharply from the qualities central to conventional theism that leave us with a God that is remote and indifferent—pure actuality, immutability, simplicity, and timelessness. Such a view conflicts dramatically with the biblical portrayal of God as acting within human affairs and responding to human actions and decisions. No wonder, then, that it is afflicted with "intellectual contradictions and lack of existential appeal."[55] In its place Pinnock offers a "biblical philosophy," which "teases out" some of the conceptual implications of the portrait of God that open theists find in the Bible. With such a portrait he hopefully suggests, "Christian theism can become intellectually compelling again."[56]

Philosophical reflection provides a basis for understanding God's existence as an explanation for the deep-seated confidence human beings have in "the final worth of their existence."[57] But revelation greatly expands this notion with its portrayal of God as a triune community of love who freely creates beings who have the capacity to appreciate God's love and the freedom to return or reject it.[58] The freedom that creatures have is therefore "real freedom," that is to say, "libertarian or contra-causal freedom."[59]

A world whose inhabitants are free in this way is a "subtle and supple place."[60] Depending on the choices they make, it may go in a variety of different directions. And this affects the nature of God's activity. God

---

[55]Pinnock spells this out this way: "that God is timeless yet acts in time; that God's knowledge is exhaustive yet freedom is real; that God's power is all-controlling yet things happen contrary to his will; that God is unchangeable and yet knows and relates to a changing world" (*Most Moved Mover*, 118).

[56]Pinnock, *Most Moved Mover*, 151.

[57]Pinnock, *Most Moved Mover*, 124. Compare Schubert M. Ogden's argument for the reality of God, which begins with "our basic confidence in the abiding worth of our life" (*The Reality of God and Other Essays* [New York: Harper & Row Publishers, 1966], 37). See also B. A. Gerrish's description of "elemental faith that underlies all human activity: confidence in the intelligibility of the world we experience and of our own existence in it." This sort of faith, Gerrish observes, "is justified not by demonstration but by the recognition that we cannot do without it" (*Christian Faith: Dogmatics in Outline* [Louisville, KY: Westminster John Knox Press, 2015], 9).

[58]It is also Pinnock's view that God does not need the world and is not greater for having created it.

[59]Pinnock, *Most Moved Mover*, 127.

[60]Pinnock, *Most Moved Mover*, 129.

may act unilaterally from time to time, but God also interacts with the creatures. Their choices and actions have an effect on God, and God takes them into account when he responds. Though the course of events often disappoints him, God remains faithful to "the creation project," and his wisdom, power, and resourcefulness guarantee that history will ultimately fulfill his purposes. With all the options at his disposal, "Nothing arises which God does not anticipate and handle," and the eventual fulfillment of his purposes is assured. As Pinnock colorfully puts it, "God knows how to play the game."[61] And in the end, it "will be worth it all."[62]

In view of the similarities between open theism and process thought, Pinnock takes pains to clarify the significant differences between them. He deplores the "guilt by association" that a number of critics have employed, and insists that open theism is not "a thinly disguised version of process theology."[63] True, process philosophy provides a helpful alternative to the static metaphysics that influenced Christianity for much of its history. And its "dialectic" view that God is "necessary and contingent, eternal and temporal, infinite and finite, . . . temporally everlasting rather than timelessly eternal," is certainly helpful.[64] But the process view that God is "ontologically dependent on the world" and that "God's power is always and only persuasive and never coercive or unilateral" leaves "little room for miracles and final victory."[65] Thus, while "process philosophy can be helpful," it "must be refashioned and cannot be adopted wholesale."[66]

In his chapter titled "The Existential Fit," Pinnock notes that many people find open theism attractive because it "makes sense of their lives."[67]

---

[61]Pinnock, *Most Moved Mover*, 139.

[62]Pinnock, *Most Moved Mover*, 140.

[63]Pinnock, *Most Moved Mover*, 141. In the previous chapter, we noted that David Tiessen insists that many of the features of open theism were expressed by Lorenzo McCabe in the 19th century ("The Openness Model of God: An Evangelical Paradigm in Light of Its Nineteenth-Century Wesleyan Precedent," *Didaskalia*, Spring 2000, 77-101).

[64]Pinnock, *Most Moved Mover*, 143.

[65]Pinnock, *Most Moved Mover*, 146.

[66]Pinnock, *Most Moved Mover*, 148.

[67]Pinnock, *Most Moved Mover*, 154.

In fact, people typically live as if open theism were true, whatever their actual theological convictions may be. If we believed that God has determined everything that happens, and the future is settled down to the last detail, we face a number of unsettling questions. If there is really nothing left for us to decide, why should we bother trying to make good decisions or exert ourselves to do the right thing? And what incentive is there for us to ask for divine guidance, if God is utterly unaffected by anything outside himself, including our prayers?

As we noted in the previous chapter, the enduring appeal of open theism is arguably due to the fact that "ordinary Christians untutored in theology" find in it "the view of God that they have picked up through a simple reading of the [biblical] text and makes such good sense of what they experience."[68] It is particularly in prayer that "the practicality of the open view of God shines," for it presupposes that real dialogue takes place with God, that God does not unilaterally decide everything."[69] At the same time, the open view of God resists all false assurances regarding our salvation. It is possible to fall away from grace, to lose our hold on eternal life. That is one of the risks that freedom involves and we should not minimize it in a desire for false security.[70]

PROBLEM BIBLICAL PASSAGES FOR OPEN THEISM?

The distinctiveness of their perspective requires open theists to look carefully at biblical passages that are often cited to support the view that God's will is all-determining and the more widely held view that God sees the entire future in a single glance.[71] For many Christians, biblical prophecies represent forecasts of the future and demonstrate that coming events are entirely foreknown to God. In fact, God's ability to predict the future is often taken as proof of his divinity and the accuracy of its

---

[68]Pinnock, *Most Moved Mover*, 157.

[69]Pinnock, *Most Moved Mover*, 171.

[70]Pinnock, *Most Moved Mover*, 171.

[71]For discussions of these two topics from the perspective of open theism, along with divine providence, see chapters 6 to 8 of Richard Rice, *The Openness of God*, (Washington, DC: Review and Herald Publishing Association, 1980). See also a later edition entitled *God's Foreknowledge and Man's Free Will* (Minneapolis, MN: Bethany House Publishers, 1980).

prophecies as evidence that the Bible is divinely inspired. A passage often cited to support this view is Isaiah 46:9-10: "I am God, and there is no other; I am God, and there is no one like me, declaring the end from the beginning and from ancient times things not yet done."

There are also passages that describe God as "destining" or "predestining" certain events to take place. One of the most familiar is Romans 8:29-30: "For those whom he foreknew he also predestined. . . . And those whom he predestined he also called; and those whom he called he also justified; and those whom he justified he also glorified."[72]

Open theists maintain that, when carefully interpreted, both prophecy and predestination are compatible with an open view of the future. For one thing, biblical prophecies fall into various categories. While some are apparently flat-out predictions—announcements of what will happen no matter what, others describe what may, or may not, happen, depending on circumstances, including the way humans respond to them. The latter are often referred to as "conditional prophecies." These are the sort of prophecies found in Jeremiah 18, which compares the way God treats his people to the way a potter treats the clay he's working with. God's predictions may take the form of a warning or a promise. Whether or not what God predicts comes to pass depends on the way people respond to it.[73] Thus, while certain biblical prophecies may refer to what cannot fail to occur, this is not by any means true of all of them.

When it comes to biblical references to predestination, the guaranteed fulfillment of God's purposes, it is helpful to note the role that corporate identity played in the thinking of ancient people. The fact that God has definite plans for the ultimate destiny of his people as a group does not

---

[72]Another relevant text is Ephesians 1:5, 11. "He destined us for adoption as his children through Jesus Christ, according to the good pleasure of his will. . . . In Christ we have also obtained an inheritance, having been destined according to the purpose of him who accomplishes all things according to his counsel and will."

[73]"Just like the clay in the potter's hand, so are you in my hand, O house of Israel. At one moment I may declare concerning a nation or a kingdom, that I will pluck up and break down and destroy it, but if that nation, concerning which I have spoken, turns from its evil, I will change my mind about the disaster that I intended to bring on it. And at another moment I may declare concerning a nation or a kingdom that I will build and plant it, but if it does evil in my sight, not listening to my voice, then I will change my mind about the good that I had intended to do to it" (Jer 18:6-10).

necessarily mean that the identity of every individual who will ultimately belong to it is determined in advance. Whether or not a specific person enjoys what God has predestined for his people may depend on her decision to join them or not.

The doctrine of providence also pertains to the fulfillment of God's purposes, and this too invites various interpretations. The concept that God's care for creation is ongoing and that God works in, through, and sometimes in spite of events in this world, including human actions, is central to the biblical portrayal of God. A well-known text in this connection is Romans 8:28, which, according to the NRSV, is capable of three different translations: (1) "all things work together for good for those who love God, who are called according to his purpose"; (2) "God makes all things work together for good"; and (3) "in all things God works for good." And they seem to lend support to varying views of providence—from "everything happens the way God wants it to" to "no matter what happens God responds in ways that prove beneficial."

The last construction comports with the open view of God. In the biblical narrative, people undergo difficult circumstances for various reasons—the mistreatment of others (e.g., Joseph), their own mistakes (e.g., Samson), or simply natural misfortune (e.g., Ruth and Naomi). But in each case the story continues. Something positive occurs, thanks to God's continuing care. Instead of unilaterally deciding what happens, God often responds to events brought about by other factors in ways that promote the fulfillment of his purposes.

However persuasive attempts like these to interpret important theological concepts may or may not be, they illustrate the preeminent concern of open theists, namely, to do justice to the richness and complexity of the biblical portrait of God—something the subtitle of the 1994 book underscores.[74]

---

[74]"A Biblical Challenge to the Traditional Understanding of God." For open theists, what Albert Einstein supposedly said about scientific theories arguably applies to theology as well: "Everything should be made as simple as possible, but not simpler."

Though he distinguishes it from open theism, John C. Peckham's "canonical model" of divine love shares many of its concerns, including a highly relational view of God and creation. On his account, the world exists solely as the result of God's decision to create; God is not responsible

CONCLUSION

Pinnock's concluding concern provides a useful note on which to conclude this chapter. For all its practical appeal, and largely because of its practical appeal, we can see why open theism has generated such forceful opposition. For those immersed in traditional views of God, open theism appears to be nothing less than an affront to God's majesty and glory. Indeed, for some, it is nothing less than an idol—a god fashioned in the image of the creature. It violates the radical divide between God and everything that is not God. As they see it, the only way to maintain the glory, the transcendence, the worshipfulness of God is to insist that God is utterly unlike the creatures—self-existent and utterly independent of creation. God would be God, in every essential respect exactly what he is, no matter what happens in the world, or even whether or not the world existed.

To respond to this persistent criticism, open theists draw a fundamental distinction between God's essential nature and God's concrete experience. Those qualities that make God God, the defining characteristics of divinity, are unchanged and unchangeable, independent of any creaturely reality, as absolute as any traditional version of theism maintains. Because God is not a being who stands apart from the world he made, however, a being who is content with splendid isolation, these defining characteristics are not all there is to God. In his concrete experience God is intimately related to the world. Does this make God another version of ourselves? Not for open theists. As Pinnock's title indicates, both the nature and scope of God's relatedness distinguish God's experience from that of all created beings.

First, there is nothing God is unaware of, nothing his knowledge and experience do not take into account. God is intimately acquainted with every aspect of reality, from what happens on our planet to all that happens in the farthest reaches of the cosmos. Second, God's responsiveness to the creatures is unrivaled in its intensity. While we only partially grasp, for example, the qualities of someone else's joy or sorrow,

---

for everything that happens in the world; and God is genuinely affected by it. John C. Peckham, *The Love of God: A Canonical Model* (Downers Grove, IL: IVP Academic, 2015).

God shares the experience completely. It is not just vaguely registered, it is fully appreciated in all its concrete reality. Thus God is affected by everything that exists and everything has a profound effect on God. To rephrase Pinnock's title, for open theists God is at once both the unmoved mover—unmoved in that the scope and excellence of his experience never change—and the most moved mover of all.

CHAPTER THREE

⟩⟩⟩⟩⟩ CRITICS AND CONFLICTS ⟩⟩⟩⟩⟩

NOT THAT LONG AFTER IT APPEARED, *The Openness of God* set off something of a firestorm in conservative Christian circles—much to the surprise of its authors. As Pinnock remarked in 2001, "I did not for a moment imagine in 1994 that our book . . . would create such interest and provoke such controversy, particularly in the evangelical community."[1] There were times when the intensity of people's reaction morphed into open hostility. Fifteen years after the book's publication, Roger Olson, not himself an open theist, described the controversy that surrounded open theism as "the most dismaying and disillusioning thing I have experienced in my fifty-some years of being an evangelical."[2]

The titles of works like these show how shrill some of the objections became: *No Place for Sovereignty: What's Wrong with Freewill Theism*,[3] *God's Lesser Glory: The Diminished God of Open Theism*,[4] *Bound Only Once: The Failure of Open Theism*,[5] *The Battle for God: Responding to the Challenge of Neotheism*,[6] and *Creating God in the Image of Man?*[7]

---

[1]Clark Pinnock, *Most Moved Mover: A Theology of God's Openness* (Grand Rapids: Baker Academic, 2001), ix.

[2]Kevin T. Bauder, R. Albert Mohler Jr., John G. Stackhouse Jr., and Roger E. Olson, *Four Views on the Spectrum of Evangelicalism* (Grand Rapids: Zondervan, 2011), 186.

[3]R. K. McGregor Wright, *No Place for Sovereignty: What's Wrong with Freewill Theism* (Downers Grove, IL: InterVarsity Press, 1996).

[4]Bruce A. Ware, *God's Lesser Glory: The Diminished God of Open Theism* (Wheaton, IL: Crossway Books, 2001).

[5]Douglas Wilson, *Bound Only Once: The Failure of Open Theism* (Moscow, ID: Canon Press, 2001).

[6]Norman L. Geisler and H. Wayne House, *The Battle for God: Responding to the Challenge of Neotheism* (Grand Rapids: Kregel, 2001).

[7]Norman Geisler, *Creating God in the Image of Man?* (Bloomington, MN: Bethany House Publishers, 1997).

To appreciate the issues that open theism raises, it will be helpful to look at the discussion it precipitated within the Evangelical Theological Society and then to review some of the objections of its more outspoken critics.

OPEN THEISM AND THE EVANGELICAL THEOLOGICAL SOCIETY

Open theists anticipated their ideas would raise some questions, and they no doubt looked forward to that. But if they believed their views would be thoughtfully considered and cordially discussed, they were mistaken. Reactions among their fellow evangelicals were typically forceful and occasionally uncompromising. For some, it wasn't just that open theists held views that varied in certain ways from the evangelical mainstream. It was whether their views took them out of the mainstream altogether. This was the question Clark Pinnock and John Sanders had to face as members of the Evangelical Theological Society (ETS).

The openness of God received a good deal of attention at the annual meeting of the Evangelical Theological Society in Colorado Springs in the fall of 2001. About thirty papers were delivered on the topic, only three or four of which were favorable toward it. John Sanders and Bruce Ware presented hour-long lectures on the question, "Is Open Theism Evangelical?" Sanders said it was. Ware said it wasn't and argued that it undermined the inerrancy of Scripture and contradicted the basic tenets of evangelicalism.

At the same meeting ETS members were asked to consider whether or not openness theology falls within "the boundaries of Evangelical thought." After some parliamentary maneuvering, members voted overwhelmingly to approve the following resolution: "We believe the Bible clearly teaches that God has complete, accurate and infallible knowledge of all past, present and future events, including all future decisions and actions of free moral agents."[8] The 2001 meeting turned out to be the first of several to consider open theism and the relation of open theists to the Society.

---

[8]"Reports Relating to the Fifty-Third Annual Meeting of the Society," *Journal of the Evangelical Theological Society* 45, no. 1 (March 2002): 186-87. Hereafter this journal will be abbreviated *JETS*.

The next annual meeting of the ETS took place in Toronto in 2002, and once again open theism was on the agenda. One evening a special business session was held to consider whether the views of Clark Pinnock and John Sanders were compatible with the doctrinal basis of the Society. About eight hundred people met to consider a motion to refer the issue to the executive committee. They voted to ask the committee to consider the merits of the challenge with respect to each theologian, taking into account both accusations and defense, and report their conclusions a year later.[9]

Accordingly, in October, 2003 Pinnock and Sanders were both investigated by a nine-member executive committee, and the following month the committee reported its findings at a special business session during the Society's annual meeting. Each scholar read a prepared statement, followed by an hour's discussion and a vote by secret ballot on whether to sustain the charges against him. In Pinnock's case the vote was 212 in favor to 432 against sustaining the charges. In Sanders's case, the vote was 338 in favor of sustaining the charges to 231 against. Since a two-thirds majority was required for dismissal, both men retained their ETS membership. Although this settled the "membership issue" with respect to Pinnock and Sanders, some members still felt that the Society was facing a potential crisis regarding its doctrinal identity. Therefore, a motion requesting that elected leadership help "us to clarify and preserve the doctrinal integrity of the Society" was passed the following day.[10]

Sanders survived the challenges to his ETS membership, but not the difficulties he encountered as a faculty member at Huntington College (now Huntington University). In spite of glowing reviews of his teaching from both students and school administration, he was removed from a tenure-track position.[11] Representatives of the United Brethren in Christ, which sponsors the school, found his views troubling, according to then

---

[9]"Reports Relating to the Fifty-Fourth Annual Meeting of the Society," *JETS* 46, no. 1 (March 2003): 174.

[10]"Reports Relating to the Fifty-Fifth Annual Meeting of the Society," *JETS* 47, no. 1 (March 2004): 170-72.

[11]Sanders later joined the faculty at Hendrix College in Arkansas, where he is now a tenured professor.

president G. Blair Dowden. There were other open theists on the faculty at the time, including William Hasker, but none had attracted the negative attention Sanders had. Evidently, the problem was not embracing open theism per se, but becoming well known for doing so.[12]

The June 2002 issue of the *Journal of the Evangelical Theological Society* (*JETS*) contains some of the presentations made the previous November in Colorado Springs. In his opening presentation, Bruce Ware focuses his attention on a single issue, the one belief that separates open theists from the broader evangelical and orthodox heritage, including other Arminians, and therefore raises "the boundary question."[13] "The specific denial of exhaustive divine foreknowledge," he asserts, "is embraced in open theism as central and essential to its own identity."[14] Indeed, open theism is "nothing without this doctrine."[15] Open theists may view this notion of foreknowledge as a corollary of libertarian freedom, but it is the denial of foreknowledge that defines the line that separates unacceptable from acceptable versions of evangelicalism.

Give up absolute foreknowledge, Ware insists, and we are left with a Bible devoid of its hundreds of divine predictions regarding future free human actions, a gospel unable to account for God's eternal design, in which he foreknows and purposes to save those who would inevitably sin against him, and a view of Christian faith that exaggerates the human contribution to the future and diminishes God's knowledge, wisdom, and certainty. Most unfortunate of all, the result of denying foreknowledge is a God with truncated knowledge and imperfect wisdom, a God who holds false beliefs about the future, a God who may make mistakes, and whose inability to make accurate predictions reduces him to the level of the idols denounced by the prophet Isaiah.[16]

By its denial of absolute foreknowledge, Ware concludes, open theism "has shown itself to be unacceptable as a viable, legitimate model within

---

[12]Stan Guthrie, "Open or Closed?" *Christianity Today*, December 1, 2004.

[13]Bruce Ware, "Defining Evangelicalism's Boundaries Theologically: Is Open Theism Evangelical?," *JETS* 45, no. 2 (June 2002): 194.

[14]Ware, "Defining Evangelicalism's Boundaries Theologically," 193.

[15]Ware, "Defining Evangelicalism's Boundaries Theologically," 195.

[16]Ware, "Defining Evangelicalism's Boundaries Theologically," 211.

evangelicalism."[17] Deny God's absolute foreknowledge, specifically foreknowledge of future free human actions, and the entire framework of Christian faith collapses. And if open theists argue that he is making too much of this—that foreknowledge was never an issue for earlier generations of Christians—Ware asserts that that was because no one within orthodox Christianity ever doubted that God had absolute foreknowledge until open theists came along.

The same issue of *JETS* followed Ware's forceful critique with responses from three open theists: Clark Pinnock, John Sanders, and Gregory Boyd.

In his reply, "There Is Room for Us," Clark Pinnock seeks to move the discussion beyond a narrow focus on the issue of divine foreknowledge to a more fundamental concern of open theism, namely, its model of divine-human relationship. According to open theism, God in his sovereign freedom chose to create a world whose creatures were significantly free, endowed with the capacity to make their own contributions to the future. God would pursue his objectives in cooperation with them, respecting and responding to their choices along the way. This view of providence involves infinite wisdom, and if anything enhances God's glory rather than diminishing it.[18]

This model also nicely expresses the biblical portrayal of human history as a love story, filled with pathos and drama, not a sequence of events that were settled from eternity, as the concept of exhaustive foreknowledge requires.[19] And it provides a more natural reading of the many biblical passages that describe God as affected by and responding to the decisions and actions of human beings in various ways, from pleasure through bewilderment to regret. It is ironic, says Pinnock, to find people who insist on the inerrancy of the Bible disregarding these descriptions because they don't fit their predetermined system.[20]

---

[17]Ware, "Defining Evangelicalism's Boundaries Theologically," 212.
[18]Clark H. Pinnock, "There Is Room for Us: A Reply to Bruce Ware," *JETS* 45, no. 2 (June 2002): 213-14.
[19]Open theists don't find compatibilist attempts to reconcile foreordination and exhaustive foreknowledge convincing.
[20]Pinnock, "There Is Room for Us," 217.

In his reply to Ware's remarks, John Sanders makes a number of points that touch on Ware's deterministic view of human events. For Ware, Sanders argues, the entire course of history must be definite from God's perspective. Otherwise, we are left with a God who makes errors, entertains false beliefs, and utters false statements. Sanders replies that this view disregards a number of biblical passages according to which God announces that something will happen, such as the destruction of Nineveh, and then it doesn't. It also fails to consider the possibility that some of the biblical predictions that came true were in fact conditional, as well as the possibility that some predictions were indications of what might happen, but not ironclad announcements of what could not fail to happen. In other words, it is perfectly logical that many of the Bible's predictions express the fact that God knows the degree of probability of something happening.[21] But even if God foreknows infallibly what free agents will do, God cannot determine or control their choices since they are already fixed items in his knowledge, and this leaves him without the only sort of control that Ware insists God must exercise: "meticulous providence."

Sanders notes that Ware's criticisms of open theism touch on the fundamental issues that have always divided Calvinists and Arminians, namely, "whether God exercises meticulous or general providence, whether God is absolutely unconditioned by creatures or whether he can respond to us, and whether humans have libertarian or compatibilistic freedom." Since Ware's criticisms of open theism apply just as readily to any version of Arminianism, Arminians, not just open theists, should "beware of Ware."[22]

For Gregory A. Boyd, Ware's criticisms of open theism are cause for dismay. As he sees it, Ware's strategy is not to engage open theists in genuine dialogue, but to bring dialogue to an end. He uses "alarmist and inflammatory language" in order to stir up feelings for his own view, not to deepen understanding of the issues involved, and there are important features of open theism that his one-sidedness overlooks.[23] For one,

---

[21]John Sanders, "Be Wary of Ware: A Reply to Bruce Ware," *JETS* 45, no. 2 (June 2002): 224.
[22]Sanders, "Be Wary of Ware," 231.
[23]Gregory A. Boyd, "Christian Love and Academic Dialogue: A Reply to Bruce Ware," *JETS* 45, no. 2 (June 2002): 243.

open theists do not deny that God's knowledge is coextensive with reality. What they deny is that the future is entirely definite; it cannot, therefore, be exhaustively known.[24] At the same time, open theists have an exalted view of God's intelligence. According to Boyd, God's perspective on the future encompasses the entire range of possibilities, and he sees each one as clearly as if it there were no alternatives.[25] Consequently, God not only knows what cannot fail to come to pass, he knows what *might* come to pass, and he can respond in ways that promote his loving purposes.[26]

This view of God's knowledge provides a basis for refuting the accusation that God holds false beliefs or makes mistakes. When the Bible says that God thought or expected something to happen and it doesn't, this is because highly probable events don't always occur. Free agents can do unlikely things. Similarly, God never makes mistakes, but "the wisest decision can go awry if other agents make poor choices, and this does not diminish the wisdom of the decision. . . . Where free agents are involved, there is no infallible guarantee" that God's best hopes will be fulfilled.[27] If God is disappointed, it isn't because God did not make a wise decision; it's because the creatures thwarted his plans.

When it comes to questions of biblical interpretation, Boyd notes, fairness requires one to consider the full range of statements on a topic. It's not acceptable to pick verses that support a favored position and treat others as relatively insignificant. This is important when it comes to passages such as Isaiah 40–48, which critics of open theism often cite as an indication that God has absolute foreknowledge. These chapters indicate that God's ability to foretell the future separates him from idols, but a careful reading indicates that what really distinguishes God from idols has not to do with what God knows, but with what God does—with

[24]Boyd, "Christian Love and Academic Dialogue," 233.
[25]Boyd, "Christian Love and Academic Dialogue," 235.
[26]Boyd, "Christian Love and Academic Dialogue," 236. Boyd's position is thus similar to Molinism, named after Jesuit theologian Luis de Molina (1535–1600), which affirms that God knows not only all that has occurred and what will occur, but what *might* have occurred in light of human free choice.
[27]Boyd, "Christian Love and Academic Dialogue," 238.

God's power rather than his knowledge. It refers to God's ability to bring about what he announced will happen.[28]

The tone of Ware's rejoinder to these responses is animated, to say the least. He reiterates his concern about the potential damage that this "doctrinal innovation" could have on "our churches and children" and insists that this "serious departure from the historic understanding of Scripture's teaching" places it beyond the bounds of evangelicalism.[29] "Open theism's denial of what Scripture teaches and what all historic views affirm," he argues, "constitutes a departure that is biblically, theologically, and practically so serious in nature, that Christian leaders should declare open theism unacceptable as a viable, legitimate model within evangelicalism."[30]

Ware finds a number of flaws in the reasoning of open theists. He doesn't see how God could hold "mistaken beliefs" about the future, even if these are beliefs about probabilities rather than certainties. "It is hard," he says, "for me to think that because a decision might be 'wise' prospectively while not actually best retrospectively, that is *perfectly wise*."[31] Behind this difficulty is Ware's rejection of any idea that the free actions of creatures could interfere with either God's knowledge or God's actions. For him, anything that detracts from the idea that God knows in precise detail everything that is going to happen and plans with absolute precision exactly what he is going to do is unworthy of consideration. Its theological and practical consequences are utterly unacceptable.

Ware is willing to grant that open theists rightly emphasize God's sensitivity to his creatures, but he insists that this is perfectly compatible with absolute foreknowledge and a completely definite future. Anything that even hints at change in God will have disastrous consequences for Christian faith and life. It diminishes God beyond recognition.

---

[28]Boyd, "Christian Love and Academic Dialogue," 239. Cf. "I am God, and there is no one like me, declaring the end from the beginning and from ancient times things not yet done, saying, 'My purpose shall stand, and I will fulfill my intention.'... I have spoken, and I will bring it to pass; I have planned, and I will do it" (Is 46:9-11).

[29]Bruce A. Ware, "Rejoinder to Replies by Clark H. Pinnock, John Sanders, and Gregory A. Boyd," *JETS* 45, no. 2 (June 2002): 245-47.

[30]Ware, "Rejoinder," 251.

[31]Ware, "Rejoinder," 253.

MORE CRITICISMS

As Ware's comments illustrate, the most vigorous objections to open theism arise from the perception that it lessens God's power and denies God's omniscience. Unless God's power is all-determining—unless God decides everything—opponents argue, God is less than what God could and should be. In an interview titled "God at Risk," for example, Royce Gruenler insisted that open theism limits God to a mere percentage of power. "Does he have 20 percent and the advancing world has the other 80 percent? Is it 30/70? And if that's the case, why is he worth worshiping?"[32] Others complain that open theism is just another version of process philosophy. As one put it, "The open view of God has developed as a direct result of Whitehead's influence on American Protestantism," and embraces "the Whiteheadian, rather than biblical, view of divine knowledge."[33]

From the urgency of their comments it is clear that many of its earlier critics view open theism with genuine alarm. For the authors of *God Under Fire: Modern Scholarship Reinvents God*, as for Ware, open theism poses a serious threat to Christian faith. The title of the first chapter, "Should the God of Historic Christianity Be Replaced?" sets the tone for those that follow. In contrast to historic Christianity, its authors remark, "open theists claim that God does not have exhaustive, infallible knowledge of the future, God changes his mind, and God does not exercise providential control over most events."[34] Their emphasis on "incompatibilist or libertarian freedom" leads open theists to regard God as "a temporal being." Since God does not have exhaustive knowledge of the future, he learns of events as they occur and may be genuinely surprised or disappointed when unexpected things happen.[35]

---

[32]*Christianity Today*, March 5, 2001, 56. A number of open theists replied to the Gruenler interview in "Truth at Risk," in the Reader's Forum of *Christianity Today*, April 23, 2001, 103.

[33]Fernando Canale, *Handbook of Seventh-Day Adventist Theology* (Hagerstown, MD: Review and Herald, 2000), 148. In the same vein, Norman Gulley describes the openness of God as "a modified version of process theology" (*Christ Is Coming! A Christ-Centered Approach to Last-Day Events* [Hagerstown, MD: Review and Herald, 1998], 56n21).

[34]Eric L. Johnson and Douglas S. Huffman, "Should the God of Historic Christianity Be Replaced?," in *God Under Fire: Modern Scholarship Reinvents God*, ed. Douglas S. Huffman and Eric L. Johnson (Grand Rapids, Zondervan, 2002), 27.

[35]Johnson and Huffman, "Should the God of Historic Christianity," 26.

It is this "strictly temporal" view of God, they argue, with its idea that God develops in the "quality of his relationships with others as he comes to know them better," that sets open theism apart from historic Christianity. While Christianity "has always strongly affirmed God's relationality and his genuine, concerned love of his creation," the idea of God actually developing would have been inconceivable within the Christian tradition from the first to the nineteenth and twentieth centuries.[36]

Although open theism is "a recently developed, novel view of God"—one of several such views, actually—its proponents claim to be evangelicals and to embrace historic Christianity, and their concept of God appears to be closer to traditional Christianity than the "other models of alternate Christian theologians." But these very factors are what makes the challenge it poses particularly insidious. For despite any appearances to contrary, open theism at bottom is nothing other than an attack on the God of historic Christian theism and as such poses a threat to the very essence of Christianity.[37]

The military allusions in the book's title and the confrontational language of the first chapter set the tone for the discussions that follow. The answer Paul Helm gives to the title question of chapter five, "Is God Bound by Time?" is, obviously, no. "The idea that God is in time is incompatible with divine sovereignty, with divine perfection, and with that fullness of being that is essential to God."[38] Unlike his time-bound creation, God himself "does not exist in time at all."[39] From our perspective, past and future are different because time carries us along, but there is no before or after from God's. Since God exists as a complete unity, "his existence is not spread out in time and space," but is "all at once."[40] God eternally wills the events that take place in time, and though these events are temporally distinct, there is no temporality in the divine willing itself. "Every moment of the temporal order is eternally present to God."[41]

---

[36]Johnson and Huffman, "Should the God of Historic Christianity," 27.
[37]Johnson and Huffman, "Should the God of Historic Christianity," 38.
[38]Paul Helm, "Is God Bound by Time?," in Huffman and Johnson, *God Under Fire*, 122.
[39]Helm, "Is God Bound by Time?," 121.
[40]Helm, "Is God Bound by Time?," 121.
[41]Helm, "Is God Bound by Time?," 135.

Although Helm is emphatic in denying divine temporality, he doesn't say much about divine timelessness, and appeals to God's ineffability as an excuse. "Is it not improper," he asks, "for us to try to imagine what the life of God is like? How could we, whose minds are designed to function in space and time, come to understand the nature of the one who exists outside space and time?" We are better off trying to say "what divine eternity *is not* rather than to attempt a comprehensive understanding of what it is."[42]

And even though influential figures in Christian history like Augustine and Aquinas support a timeless view of God, Helm admits that it is difficult to find it in the Bible,[43] especially in light of the numerous passages that apply the language of time and change to God and describe God as acting and reacting in time. Such statements are not to be taken literally, however. They only demonstrate that God accommodates himself to the human condition. To communicate with beings who exist in space and time, God "must represent himself to them in ways that are not literally true."[44] And even though the Bible speaks of God as acting, which seems to suggest "bringing about a state of affairs that was not there before," Helm insists, "God's action is causal but not temporal."[45]

Helm's emphatic denial of divine temporality sets the stage for three other questions that serve as chapter titles: "Does God Take Risks?" "Does God Have Emotions?" and "Does God Change?" In contrast to open theists, whose answer to all three questions is yes, the authors of these chapters say no.

In evaluating the idea that God takes risks, James S. Spiegel compares two views of divine providence. Important Christian thinkers from Augustine to Luther, Calvin, and Jonathan Edwards present us with a "strong" view of providence. On this view, God knows the entire future and cannot be taken by surprise, controls the world absolutely, guarantees the

---

[42]Helm, "Is God Bound by Time?," 126.

[43]While passages like Ps 90:1-2 do not entail divine timelessness, he says, they strongly suggest it (Helm, "Is God Bound by Time?," 123).

[44]Helm, "Is God Bound by Time?," 128-29.

[45]Helm, "Is God Bound by Time?," 131.

ultimate fulfillment of his plans. Nothing, including human suffering and immorality, lies outside his sovereignty.[46]

Compared to this view of providence, Spiegel finds the view open theists favor decidedly weak. Since "a risky act is one that might result in unforeseeable and uncontrollable misfortune,"[47] open theists are seriously mistaken in embracing it. According to their "time-bound" view of God, God does not have exhaustive knowledge of the future, and if God does not know in advance what human beings will do, there is no guarantee that his purposes will be fulfilled. If God can accomplish his goals for them only if they cooperate, their failure to do so can leave God frustrated and disappointed.[48]

Spiegel compares the biblical passages to which proponents of each view of providence appeal. The strong view of providence finds support in biblical affirmations that God's sovereignty extends over the entire cosmos, including human history, human choices, and individual human lives, including suffering and even moral evil, such as the hardening of Pharaoh's heart. Most impressive is the abundance of predictive prophecies,[49] which clearly show that God sees the future in detail and support God's absolute trustworthiness. In contrast, open theists appeal to conditional ("if-then") statements describing God's possible reaction to human decisions; expressions of divine regret and relenting; the effects of petitionary prayer; and descriptions of divine ignorance and error.[50] Another reason he gives for preferring the strong view of providence is the fact that it rests on "didactic" passages in the Bible, while "the risk model rests predominantly on historical narrative."[51]

Though he rejects the risk model of providence, Spiegel concedes that there are lessons to be learned from open theism, especially its emphasis on divine relationality. Open theists call attention to God's care for creation, his personal involvement in our lives, his compassion for us. Instead

---

[46]James S. Spiegel, "Does God Take Risks?," in Huffman and Johnson, *God Under Fire*, 188-89.
[47]Spiegel, "Does God Take Risks?," 192.
[48]Spiegel, "Does God Take Risks?," 196-97.
[49]Spiegel, "Does God Take Risks?," 200-203.
[50]Spiegel, "Does God Take Risks?," 201.
[51]Spiegel, "Does God Take Risks?," 207.

of overemphasizing divine impassibility, he suggests, it would be preferable to think of God as omnipathic, since "God is experientially acquainted with all creaturely feelings." Spiegel concludes that God is both loving and caring *and* sovereign, directing history according to his perfect will. Then he makes this striking statement: "The Scriptures might not show us *how*, but they plainly teach *that* both of these claims are true, and, thus, fundamentally compatible. The biblically informed Christian, then, must affirm both divine relationality and divine sovereignty, without allowing either of these doctrines to undermine a commitment to the other."[52] Open theists would heartily agree. An adequate view of God must do justice to the full range of biblical testimony.

Spiegel's conclusion that open theists don't have a way to attribute both supreme sovereignty and tender compassion to God is curious, since he is well aware that open theism proposes a way of doing that. He notes that open theists believe that "God's nature may be conceived as both 'actual' and 'potential.' God is not only absolute, necessary, eternal, and changeless, but *also* relative, contingent, temporal and changing, insofar as he relates and responds to his creation."[53] But rather than reflect on this observation, he relegates it to a footnote and gives it no further consideration.[54]

Another reason people object to open theism is its affirmation of divine temporality. As temporal beings, we are subject to the passage of time, so our lives are not complete at any one moment, but this is why we cannot attribute temporality to God. It renders God "incomplete." As Patrick Lee puts it, "That which changes has its existence spread out over time, broken up, as it were." Since temporality involves a continuous transition from the present to the past, a temporal being cannot exist wholly in any one moment, but is "spread out over time and must be composed of parts." Since it depends on its parts, whatever is temporal is dependent, and God, of course, is essentially

---

[52]Spiegel, "Does God Take Risks?," 210.
[53]Spiegel, "Does God Take Risks?," 196n37.
[54]By distinguishing between two aspects of the divine reality, one changing, the other unchanging, one absolute, the other relative, the one temporal, the other eternal, open theists believe that their view of God nicely accommodates the contrasting biblical statements regarding God's nature and experience.

independent.[55] Unless God is everything he is capable of being at all times he could not be perfect. God must be pure actuality, as classic theism insists.

Like Siegel, Lee notes the questions to his position that arise from certain biblical passages. If a perfect being cannot change, or be changed by anything, how are we to interpret biblical descriptions of God as repenting, rejoicing, becoming angry?[56] According to Lee, they apply to God only indirectly or analogically. "Even concepts that properly apply to ourselves—such as *understanding, willing* and *love*—cannot be directly applied to God in the sense that they apply to ourselves."[57] Indeed, "thinking that the language about God in Scripture is a straightforward description of God's essence overestimates our cognitive grasp of God. . . . God's being or nature is incomprehensible and ineffable. To think that we understand what God is in himself is to compromise his transcendence, to carve him down to something much less than he is."[58]

According to Lee, any attempt to apply human categories to God is fraught with difficulty. Although our creaturely cognitive limitations prevent us from taking a biblical description of God literally, it will not do to affirm a contrary property, either. For example, if we deny that God literally suffers, we are not allowed to say that God is aloof and indifferent.[59] "To say that God is immutable is not to say that God is static. To say that God is impassible is not to say that God is indifferent. Rather, in each case both contrary properties should be denied of the Creator."[60] In line with the classic apophatic tradition, Lee seems to accept the view that what we deny of God is far more reliable that what we assert.

Lee also rejects the suggestion that there may be differing yet complementary aspects of God's being, the idea that God is necessary and uncaused in one aspect yet contingent in another.[61] Nevertheless, we can

---

[55]Patrick Lee, "Does God Have Emotions?," in Huffman and Johnson, *God Under Fire*, 217-18.
[56]See Lee, "Does God Have Emotions?," 214.
[57]Lee, "Does God Have Emotions?," 222.
[58]Lee, "Does God Have Emotions?," 225, 224.
[59]Lee, "Does God Have Emotions?," 226.
[60]Lee, "Does God Have Emotions?," 227.
[61]This, he insists, involves the unacceptable view that God is a composite being (Lee, "Does God Have Emotions?," 222).

think of God as having emotions. For example, we can say that God is pleased or angry with us "in a relational sense," that is to say, "we are related to God as one who pleases is related to the one who is pleased and that God has what is necessary to be related to in this way." And he says this tells us something "indirectly" about God, but exactly what it tells us is something Lee does not make clear.[62]

The difficulty of affirming certain divine qualities without accepting their logical implications is particularly evident in Charles E. Gutenson's response to the question, "Does God Change?" He holds that there is no need to abandon the traditional attribute of immutability, but then he goes to considerable lengths to show that divine changelessness does not compromise God's relationality. True, he admits, there are persistent tensions "inherent in affirming that God is immutable and yet profoundly relational," and the attempts of early church fathers to reconcile them are varied.[63]

Still, he insists, it is possible to come up with a coherent affirmation of both. He stipulates, to start with, that there is no change in divine knowledge, divine will, or divine disposition. Unlike the "fragmentedness experienced by humans"—an interesting characterization—God enjoys "temporal omnipresence." Past, present, and future are equally known to him. God has all there is to know in one timeless cognitive experience.[64] While God "possesses the wholeness of time in actual presence," however, he still knows "the chronological sequence in which they [*sic*] exist for us." Past, present, and future do not carry *temporal* significance for God, but "they bear something of *logical* significance." God's eternity "contains the actual life and the cumulative result of the free choices instantiated within the lives of free creatures."[65] What we experience as a series of acts, God experiences as "a single eternal act." The divine eternity "easily involves *all* of the 'nows' of linear temporal existence."[66]

---

[62]Lee, "Does God Have Emotions?," 229-30.
[63]Charles E. Gutenson, "Does God Change?," in Huffman and Johnson, *God Under Fire*, 251.
[64]Gutenson, "Does God Change?," 243.
[65]Gutenson, "Does God Change?," 244.
[66]Gutenson, "Does God Change?," 245.

This view of divine knowledge clearly elevates the static above the dynamic. To know something eternally is higher than, more praiseworthy than, coming to know it. This view also involves what we might call a "spatializing of time." It envisions time as an extension that may be experienced in two ways, successively or simultaneously—by moving along it in successive moments of experience or by viewing it in its entirety all at once. Dynamic experience is inferior to static experience. Coming to know something—learning—is inferior to knowing it all along. For Gutenson, nothing enters God's experience for the first time. If God knows something, then God has always known it. He never learns anything.

Gutenson also asserts that there is no change in the divine will either, in spite of biblical passages that describe God as repenting, or changing his mind in response to human actions.[67] Similarly, there is no change in the divine disposition, that is, in God's being pleased or dismayed by human beings. Here again, the range of God's dispositions, from pleasure to disapproval, as in God's attitude toward King Saul, can be conceived as "an eternal, single act."[68]

When it comes to divine love, we might wonder if God is sensitive to the variations of our experiences, if he really responds to our joys and disappointments, our highs and our lows. But here again, God is changeless. Not only is God unchangingly committed to our welfare, but divine love "is always fully engaged, . . . purely actualized without any elements of potentiality."[69] Within the human sphere, love involves compassion, and compassion involves suffering as those one loves suffer, but this is not true of divine love.[70] God's love exhibits none of the potentially negative features of human love.

In the last and longest chapter of the book, D. A. Carson addresses the challenge of reconciling the love of God with the transcendent sovereignty of God. He begins, as do many critics of open theism, by mentioning

---

[67]It is possible, he argues, to build responsiveness "into the possible expressions of divine will" (Gutenson, "Does God Change?," 247).

[68]Gutenson, "Does God Change?," 245.

[69]Gutenson, "Does God Change?," 249.

[70]Gutenson, "Does God Change?," 250-51.

their view of divine foreknowledge, which he characterizes as a "relative ignorance" of the future.[71] Although open theism aligns itself with some strands of classical theism that espouse libertarian freedom, he says, it does so by denying God's exhaustive foreknowledge and losing his sovereign control.[72]

To support this assessment, Carson turns to a number of specific biblical passages that deal with God's knowledge or control. Some of them, like a dozen statements in Isaiah 40–49, assert that the true God is distinguished from idols because he can predict the future. In fact, they identify this ability as the test of true deity (Is 41:23). Then there are a number of passages where wicked agents fulfill God's intentions. The clearest example is Genesis 50:19-20, where Joseph says of his brothers' act of selling him into slavery, "Even though you intended to do harm to me, God intended it for good." According to Carson, this is not a case where God brought good out of evil; it demonstrates that in certain instances God intends evil to happen in order to bring about good. Thus, "it preserves both God's goodness and God's knowledge and sovereignty."[73] Here, and in other passages, such as the Assyrians' attack on God's covenant people, the suffering Satan inflicts on Job, and the promised punishment of Israel by the Chaldeans in the book of Habakkuk, God not only uses the evil that occurs but deliberately intends for it to happen.[74]

We must be very careful, Carson insists, in the way we read different biblical passages. Their "obvious" meanings may not be the most reliable, nor do they always provide "literal" descriptions of God. It would be ridiculous, for example to conclude from God's asking Adam, "Where are you?" that God did not know his whereabouts, and from the description in Hosea of God taking Ephraim in his arms, that God has two upper limbs. Analogy and metaphor play a central role in biblical descriptions of God, and it takes careful work to reconcile any one passage with others that have a bearing on the issue. So when we speak of God as having

---

[71]D. A. Carson, "How Can We Reconcile the Love and the Transcendent Sovereignty of God?," in Huffman and Johnson, *God Under Fire*, 283.
[72]Carson, "How Can We Reconcile," 294.
[73]Carson, "How Can We Reconcile," 300.
[74]Carson, "How Can We Reconcile," 301.

emotions, we cannot take the statement too literally. While God does exhibit love, there are many aspects of human love that cannot meaningfully apply to God.[75]

Carson is similarly forceful in rejecting open theism's view of divine knowledge. The idea that the future is partly open and partly closed—partly open because God cannot know our future free decisions, and partly closed because God knows what he is going to do—results in "massive ignorance on God's part."[76]

The fundamental problem Carson has with open theism is the way its proponents apply the Bible's contrasting descriptions of God to different aspects of the divine reality. As he sees it, open theists domesticate one side of the biblical portrait of God, the view that God is sovereign and transcendent, with the other, the view that God is personal and loving. The result is a picture of God who is "tamed by doctrinaire presuppositions that cannot themselves be tested or corrected by Scripture."[77] In effect, then, open theists force God into the narrow framework of their presuppositions, ignore the full scope and complexity of the biblical portrayals of God, and caricature the classical view of God. All this leaves them with a diminished view of the divine reality.

Working through the various contributions to *God Under Fire*, one is increasingly impressed with the sensitivity of the authors to the concerns that lie behind open theism, in spite of the book's inflammatory title. There is a consistent emphasis among the contributors on the importance of God's relationality, God's intimate connection with and tender care for human beings. In fact, as Spiegel's essay indicates, there is a pervasive insistence that this is just as important to the biblical view of God as the concept of divine sovereignty. They concede that it is not easy to affirm both and that attempts to do so in Christian tradition are quite varied. The authors also acknowledge the important similarities between open theism and conservative Christianity in general. As the opening essay states, "With historic Christianity, open theists believe God is the

---

[75]Carson, "How Can We Reconcile," 304-8.
[76]Carson, "How Can We Reconcile," 309.
[77]Carson, "How Can We Reconcile," 310.

self-existent, personal, all-powerful Creator of the universe, who can and does act in the world and who has given humans the power of free choice." Open theists also have a "high view of Scripture and believe God freely created *ex nihilo* and has the power to override human decisions if he wishes."[78]

From the perspective of open theists, divine relationality, and the temporality that goes with it, are essentially positive. They involve dependence, but it is God's prerogative to create a world to which he opens his experience. God could be complete in himself, immune to any contribution of anything else, but he decided not to be. His creative generosity, his openness to his creatures, renders God responsive to, indeed vulnerable to, their decisions and actions. He is genuinely affected by what they do. This allows for a more natural interpretation of numerous biblical passages. And it allows us to attribute to God the positive dimensions of temporal passage. The view that God has all the value of the world at once denies God the ability to enjoy the distinctive quality of momentary experience, such as the surprise, satisfaction, and delight that comes from seeing the spontaneous reactions and decisions of his creatures.

Like the contributors to *God Under Fire*, the various authors of another symposium, *Beyond the Bounds*, are willing to concede that open theism calls attention to some underemphasized themes in contemporary conservative theology, but they too dismiss it as biblically uninformed and theologically misleading, as well as a threat to the personal lives of those who find it attractive. Indeed, for them, open theism not only lies beyond the pale of acceptable theological options. They believe that its advocates should be formally excluded from teaching Christian theology and roundly criticize the circumstances that permit them to do so.

Along with its title, "Grounds for Dismay: The Error and Injury of Open Theism," the final sentences of the last article could hardly be more forceful. Writes John Piper, "I see open theism as theologically ruinous,

---

[78]Johnson and Huffman, "Should the God of Historic Christianity," 25.

dishonoring to God, belittling to Christ, and pastorally hurtful. My prayer is that Christian leaders will come to see it this way, and thus love the church by counting open theism beyond the bounds of orthodox Christian teaching."[79]

In another contribution to the book, William C. Davis explains why, in his view, this has not happened yet and "why open theism is flourishing now." Along with the "freedom-intoxicated, authority-distrusting age" in which we live,[80] it is due to the "emergence of extra-ecclesial Christianity," represented by groups such as InterVarsity Christian Fellowship and Campus Crusade for Christ.[81] When members of such organizations regard them as a spiritual home, they are left without the "ordained spiritual oversight" that a local church and a specific denomination provides.[82] Similarly, Christian scholars often function in professional associations like the American Academy of Religion and the Society of Christian Philosophers in relative freedom from denominational control.[83]

What we need when it comes to developments like open theism, Davis asserts, is "guidance by exclusion." As an example, he cites a resolution passed in June 2000 by the Baptist General Conference, where the delegates "affirm that God's knowledge of all past, present and future events is exhaustive," and "that the 'openness' view of God's foreknowledge is contrary to our fellowship's historic understanding of God's omniscience." At the same session, however, another resolution passed allowing that the views of open theist Gregory A. Boyd "did not warrant his termination as a member of the Bethel College faculty and by inference that his views fall within the accepted bounds of the evangelical spectrum."[84]

---

[79]John Piper, "Grounds for Dismay: The Error and Injury of Open Theism," in *Beyond the Bounds: Open Theism and the Undermining of Biblical Christianity*, ed. John Piper, Justin Taylor, and Paul Kjoss Helseth (Wheaton, IL: Crossway, 2003), 384.

[80]William C. Davis, "Why Open Theism Is Flourishing Now," in Piper, Taylor, and Helseth, *Beyond the Bounds*, 145.

[81]Neither Intervarsity Christian Fellowship nor Campus Crusade for Christ is technically a "church." In general, their participants are also members of specific Christian communities or denominations.

[82]Davis, "Why Open Theism," 128.

[83]Davis, "Why Open Theism," 128, 131.

[84]Davis, "Why Open Theism," 135.

John Piper vigorously dissented from this "Solomonic" decision in a blog post he wrote the following month titled, "We Took a Good Stand and Made a Bad Mistake: Reflections on the Baptist General Conference Annual Meeting at St Paul." "In order for the two resolutions to cohere, open theism must be viewed as an insignificant aberration from the Biblical norm. But this is a profound mistake in theological and historical judgment, for open theism is a massive re-visioning of God." Then follows this dire warning: "If the Baptist General Conference does not wake up to the magnitude of the distortion of God being powerfully promoted in the writings and classrooms of one of Bethel's most popular teachers [a reference to Greg Boyd], the Conference of fifty years from now will probably not be the faithful evangelical institution it is today."[85]

In 2001 the Southern Baptist Convention passed a more straightforward resolution regarding divine omniscience, affirming that it "extends to all creation and throughout all time, to all things actual and potential even to the thoughts and actions of his conscious creatures, past, present, and future."[86] According to Davis and Piper, open theism is a threat, a serious, insidious threat to Christian faith and life, and it must be met decisively by denominational authorities. Not surprisingly, Boyd no longer teaches at Bethel University.

FROM CONTROVERSY TO CONVERSATION

Clark Pinnock concludes his book *Most Moved Mover* by commenting on the harsh and angry responses open theism encountered in evangelical circles, including "the hostility of certain Calvinists and the suspicion of many Arminians."[87] He finds it hard to understand why he has been "so savagely attacked" when his objectives were to take the Bible seriously, think more profoundly, and address important questions about our relationship with God.[88] And he expresses the hope that open theism

---

[85]John Piper, "We Took a Good Stand and Made a Bad Mistake: Reflections on the Baptist General Conference Annual Meeting at St Paul," *Desiring God* (blog), July 5, 2000, www.desiringgod.org /articles/we-took-a-good-stand-and-made-a-bad-mistake.

[86]Davis, "Why Open Theism," 136.

[87]Pinnock, *Most Moved Mover*, 185.

[88]Pinnock, *Most Moved Mover*, 180.

might be accepted by evangelicals as a "valid option," or at least as "a research program, not a settled model."[89] He grants that conventional theism is "a brilliant interpretation and intellectual achievement of greatest magnitude," but insists that it has some conspicuous inadequacies and this may account for the "vehemence against the open view." Perhaps its critics sense that their preferred view is not only "vulnerable," but "precarious."[90] At the time of his writing, Pinnock hoped that discussion among evangelicals will be allowed to continue and a "vociferous minority" will not be allowed to call all the shots.[91]

In time Pinnock's hope was fulfilled, at least partially. Not all the treatments of open theism were as heated as some of those we have considered, and among some in the evangelical community the tone of criticisms lightened up considerably. Later accounts of open theism placed it within the mainstream of conservative theology, its distinctive emphases notwithstanding.

Open theism has also attracted a measure of appreciation from a variety of sources. Occasionally even its detractors concede that open theism has made important contributions to theological discussion despite its alleged deficiencies. According to Barthian scholar Bruce L. McCormack, for example, "what is valuable in the open theistic proposal is its critique of a putative divine impassibility and timelessness."[92] And, rather surprisingly, one of the contributors to the book *God Under Fire* lists several "lessons to be learned from open theism," including the importance of affirming the relationality of God and reevaluating the doctrine of divine impassibility.[93]

Some of the discussions that *The Openness of God* generated did reflect the spirit that Pinnock hoped for. One example of a more measured approach is the cover story of *Christianity Today* in its May 2001 issue.

---

[89] Pinnock, *Most Moved Mover*, 179.
[90] Pinnock, *Most Moved Mover*, 184-85.
[91] Pinnock, *Most Moved Mover*, 185.
[92] Bruce L. McCormack, "The Actuality of God: Karl Barth in Conversation with Open Theism," in *Engaging the Doctrine of God: Contemporary Protestant Perspectives*, ed. Bruce L. McCormack (Grand Rapids: Baker Academic, 2008), 209.
[93] Spiegel, "Does God Take Risks?," 210.

Titled "An Openness Debate," this article, and a second that appeared the following month, featured a series of nine exchanges between John Sanders, an early supporter of open theism, and Christopher A. Hall, who raises questions about it.[94]

The two continued to discuss their views and in 2003 their letters were published in a book of thirty-seven short chapters titled, *Does God Have a Future? A Debate on Divine Providence.*[95] The tone of the conversation is cordial throughout in spite of the distinct differences in their views. In the preface they describe their correspondence as "a small part of the testing and sifting process any theological model must undergo if it is to be wisely and safely offered to the church."[96] And their jointly authored postscript reiterates the need for respectful dialogue even when participants have sharply different views. Noting that "the rhetoric against open theism is often mean-spirited and filled with caricatures," they call on readers to avoid polar perspectives in expressing their views and pursue "dialogical virtues."[97]

The conversational exchanges touch on a number of the topics that open theism raises, with Hall typically asking questions and Sanders responding. Sanders begins by summarizing the essential points of open theism—God's sovereign decision to create beings who were free to return his love, his respect for their decisions and actions, his exercise of general rather than meticulous providence, and the temporal nature of his experience. Past and future are different to God, and he sees the future as partly settled and partly unsettled.[98]

In response to the idea that the future does not yet exist, Hall expresses his conviction that God "views all times as eternal now." Consequently,

---

[94]Surrounding the title on the cover of the May 21, 2001, issue was a list of provocative questions, each printed in a different color: *Does God change his mind? Will God ever change his mind in response to our prayers? Does he know your next move? If God knows it all, are we truly free? Does God know the future? Was God taking a risk in making the human race? What does God know and when does he know it?*

[95]Christopher A. Hall and John Sanders, *Does God Have a Future? A Debate on Divine Providence* (Grand Rapids: Baker Academic, 2003).

[96]Hall and Sanders, *Does God Have a Future?*, 9.

[97]Hall and Sanders, *Does God Have a Future?*, 200.

[98]Hall and Sanders, *Does God Have a Future?*, 12.

future events are not future for God, "but simply present."[99] Then the two turn to three biblical instances where, according to Hall, people make decisions that are apparently known in advance—Abraham's willingness to sacrifice Isaac, Judas's betrayal of Jesus, and Peter's denial. Sanders replies that if Abraham was truly tested by God's request, then his character could not have been fully formed until his faithfulness was graphically demonstrated. After all, he had a record of both trusting and distrusting God. In Peter's case, Jesus could have known that his loyalty would not survive the challenge it would face. And in Judas's case, we need to note that the New Testament writers sometimes speak of Scriptures being "fulfilled" that are not predictions as such, but demonstrate that "what happened in the past is happening again."[100] Knowing Judas as he did, Jesus could see that he was set on a treacherous course of action.

One of the more interesting exchanges involves the role of antinomies in theology and the larger question of the nature of theological language. While some antinomies are merely verbal, Sanders observes, others can be resolved by making a distinction, and still others present us with a contradiction that should be eliminated. How then should we view the contrast involved in asserting that God determines everything and that humans are morally responsible for their actions? Sanders maintains that this is not an "antinomy" but a contradiction and therefore meaningless.[101] He also argues that our language about God is essentially metaphorical rather than literally descriptive of God, and that a good deal of it consists of "conceptual metaphors," which is how we should construe words like *immutable*, *impassible*, and *sovereign*. Thus, human language about God is "adequate, though not perfect," for understanding God.[102] But this does not justify picking and choosing among biblical descriptions and arbitrarily dispensing with those that don't neatly fit our doctrinal preferences.

This leads Hall to comment on divine passibility, which some biblical statements seem to assert (cf. Eph 4:30). He sides with those, however,

---

[99]Hall and Sanders, *Does God Have a Future?*, 17.
[100]Hall and Sanders, *Does God Have a Future?*, 31.
[101]Hall and Sanders, *Does God Have a Future?*, 49.
[102]Hall and Sanders, *Does God Have a Future?*, 59.

who view such language as an accommodation to human understanding and affirms the traditional view that "God remains ineffably impassible and immutable."[103]

In reply, Sanders observes that the concept of impassibility has been going out of favor in recent years and is no longer the majority view of theologians. What open theists say is not that God had to suffer, but that God freely decided to create a world where he delegated some responsibility to the creatures and would therefore be affected by their decisions and actions. "God can suffer because God opens himself in his love to us to allow us to affect him. The self-sufficient God opens himself to include others even to the point of being . . . vulnerable to disappointment when we fail to love."[104] As for statements asserting that God does not change, they should be interpreted as affirmations of God's reliability and steadfastness, not as unqualified assertions of complete immutability.[105]

The question of divine omniscience, particularly God's knowledge of the future, is a persistent source of disagreement in their exchanges. Hall finds evidence that God knows the future in detail because there are so many predictions that came to fulfillment, particularly those involving the redemptive life and death of Jesus. And he is troubled by the thought that God could have mistaken beliefs about the future. Sanders counters that he is not saying that God makes mistakes, but that God's expectations may be disappointed—something quite different. When it comes to predictions, Sanders reasons, there are different kinds of predictions.

Turning to the topic of immutability, Sanders cites the ways different people resolve the apparent contradiction in biblical statements regarding divine change. Granted, there are texts that affirm that God does not change: Malachi 3:6, Numbers 23:19; 1 Samuel 15:29. But there are also passages that say that God does change: Genesis 6:6, Exodus 32:14. One solution is to take one set literally and regard the other as "anthropomorphisms," as Paul Helm does in *The Providence of God*. But Sanders argues that we can affirm both sets if we hold that God is unchanging in

---

[103]Hall and Sanders, *Does God Have a Future?*, 63.
[104]Hall and Sanders, *Does God Have a Future?*, 67.
[105]Hall and Sanders, *Does God Have a Future?*, 69.

some ways and changing in others—unchanging in his nature, for example, but changing in his thoughts, will, and emotions.[106]

As Hall sees it, "the openness model offers two significant challenges
to the traditional understanding of God's nature and providence." It
holds that "God knows only the past, present and those aspects of the
future that God has foreordained will occur." And it "contends that
God can make mistakes on the basis of God's limited knowledge of the
future actions of free agents." These limitations on God's omniscience
and the predication of divine error "weigh too heavily against the
acceptance of the model," when we measure it against the Christian
tradition. Representative figures within the tradition who affirmed libertarian freedom and exhaustive divine foreknowledge accepted the
incomprehensibility of divine providence rather than choose between
the two.[107]

We could go on, but it is fairly clear from these exchanges what open
theism proposes and why people find it problematic. The open view
varies from some of the most familiar things most Christians have been
saying about God for centuries. It raises questions across a waterfront of
areas, from the meaning of time-honored divine attributes to the interpretation of a number of passages in the Bible. Hall is unconvinced by
Sanders's explanations, but their exchanges reflect mutual respect for
each other's positions.

As we have seen, there is quite a variation in tone among those who
have responded to open theism. Their most persistent sources of
concern are its revisionary view of divine foreknowledge and its departure from the traditional concept of divine immutability. At the
same time, those who are critical of open theism often indicate that
they have a good grasp of its central tenets and even appreciate its
basic concerns. And they share with open theists a desire to do justice
to the contrasts we find in biblical descriptions of God. Yet it is precisely the similarity of open theism to their own understanding of
Christianity that leads many to view it as a threat. As a church historian

---

[106]Hall and Sanders, *Does God Have a Future?*, 125-27.
[107]Hall and Sanders, *Does God Have a Future?*, 182.

once observed, "Nothing divides so bitterly as common convictions held with a difference."[108]

With time the furor that arose following the publication of *The Openness of God* subsided and a more measured tone emerged. Today open theism is no longer dismissed as a mere variation of process thought, nor just another version of classical theism. For example, John Cooper of Calvin College describes open theism as a form of "voluntary relational panentheism," and maintains that it is not a species of process thought.[109] Instead, he says, it should be viewed as "revised classical theism," since it retains "a supernatural view of God's existence, power, revelation, and acts in history."[110] In the same vein, Steven C. Roy describes open theism as "a variation on classical Arminian theology."[111]

For their part, open theists have provided pertinent, thoughtful responses to their critics, and in the process their views have emerged as a distinct theological perspective. Growing numbers of philosophers and theologians have taken note of it. The expression *open theism* and its variants appear regularly in books on philosophy of religion.[112] And philosophical journals often contain articles analyzing its various aspects.[113]

Thanks to the influence of two prominent figures in American theology, Clark H. Pinnock and John B. Cobb Jr., and the energetic work of Thomas Jay Oord, the consultation on Open and Relational Theologies,

---

[108]Gerald R. Cragg, *Freedom and Authority* (Santa Ana, CA: Westminster Press, 1975), 222; quoted in Walter B. Shurden, ed., *The Struggle for the Soul of the SBC: Moderate Responses to the Fundamentalist Movement* (Macon, GA: Mercer University Press, 1993), 282.

[109]Cooper, *Panentheism*, 192.

[110]Cooper, *Panentheism*, 343-44. He also notes that the tone of some of open theism's critics is not as helpful as their arguments (344n21).

[111]Roy, *How Much Does God Foreknow?*.

[112]Charles Taliaferro notes the openness view of divine omniscience in his textbook, *Contemporary Philosophy of Religion* (Malden, MA: Blackwell, 1998), 121. See also Michael Peterson et. al., *Reason and Religious Belief: An Introduction to the Philosophy of Religion*, 3rd ed. (New York: Oxford University Press, 2003), 167-69; and Chad Meister, *Introducing Philosophy of Religion* (New York: Routledge, 2009), 56.

[113]See, for example, these articles in *Faith and Philosophy: Journal of the Society of Christian Philosophers* (*FP*): Donald Wayne Viney, "Jules Lequyer and the Openness of God," *FP* 14, no. 2 (April 1997): 212-35; Dale Tuggy, "Three Roads to Open Theism," *FP* 24, no. 1 (January 2007): 28-51; Alexander R. Pruss, "Probability and the Open Future View," *FP* 27, no. 2 (April 2010): 190-96; and Alan R. Rhoda, "Probability, Truth, and the Openness of the Future: A Reply to Pruss," *FP* 27, no. 2 (April 2010): 197-204.

which was introduced in 2004, is now a regular part of the annual meeting of American Academy of Religion. Oord has also been active in developing the Center for Open & Relational Theology, which began in 2019.

Open theism has also generated appreciation from a variety of sources. As we noted, even detractors like Bruce McCormack and Steven Roy concede that despite its alleged deficiencies, open theism has made discernible contributions to theology.[114] And others, who do not identify themselves as open theists, nevertheless embrace some of its ideas. Philip Clayton, for example, describes his own position as "open panentheism," since it modifies the tenets of process thought with some of the features of open theism.[115]

In sum, open theism has taken a position of its own on the theological landscape. As David Basinger noted in 2013, "What was less than 20 years ago a theological perspective of interest primarily to conservative Protestant Christians is now a theological perspective widely discussed in both mainstream theological and philosophical circles."[116]

The give and take between proponents of the openness of God and its critics is only part of the story. With the passage of time, open theists have expanded their reflections in a number of directions. And along the way, some interesting differences among them have emerged, as we shall see in the next two chapters.

---

[114]Bruce L. McCormack, "The Actuality of God: Karl Barth in Conversation with Open Theism," in *Engaging the Doctrine of God: Contemporary Protestant Perspectives*, ed. Bruce L. McCormack (Grand Rapids: Baker Academic, 2008), 209. Steven C. Roy, *How Much Does God Foreknow? A Comprehensive Biblical Study* (Downers Grove, IL: InterVarsity Press, 2006), 16.

[115]Philip Clayton, *Adventures in the Spirit: God, World, Divine Action* (Minneapolis: Fortress, 2008), 175.

[116]David Basinger, "Introduction to Open Theism," in *Models of God and Alternative Ultimate Realities*, ed. Jeanine Diller and Asa Kasher (New York: Springer, 2013), 274.

CHAPTER FOUR

▸▸▸▸▸▸▸▸▸ PHILOSOPHICAL ▸▸▸▸▸▸▸▸
▸▸▸▸▸▸▸▸▸ DISCUSSIONS OF ▸▸▸▸▸▸▸▸
▸▸▸▸▸▸▸▸▸ OPEN THEISM ▸▸▸▸▸▸▸▸

WHILE THE OPENNESS OF GOD began as the expression of a theological perspective, in time it attracted a good deal of philosophical attention as well. A few years ago, one philosopher observed that open theism has been "embraced by a sizable and growing minority of theistic philosophers and is now recognized as a major player in philosophical discussions of the nature of God and of divine providence."[1] Discussions of open theism now regularly appear alongside more venerable views of God in standard textbooks in philosophy of religion.[2] One of the thirteen parts in the large collection *Models of God and Alternative Ultimate Realities* is devoted to "Open Theism."[3] And symposium volumes devoted to specific topics like divine providence, divine foreknowledge, and the problem of evil often place open theists in conversation with advocates of other positions.[4]

---

[1]Alan R. Rhoda, "Open Theism and Other Models of Divine Providence," in *Models of God and Alternative Ultimate Realities*, ed. Janine Diller and Asa Kasher (New York: Springer, 2013), 287.

[2]See for example, Michael Peterson, William Hasker, Bruce Reichenbach, and David Basinger, eds., *Reason & Religious Belief: An Introduction to the Philosophy of Religion*, 5th ed. (New York: Oxford University Press, 2012); and William Hasker, "The Openness of God," in *The Philosophy of Religion Reader*, ed. Chad Meister (New York: Routledge, 2008), 146-60.

[3]Diller and Kasher, *Models of God and Alternative Ultimate Realities*. Part 4, the section of essays on open theism, follows the parts titled "Classical Theism" and "Neo-classical Theism," and directly precedes those titled "Process Theology" and "Panentheism."

[4]James K. Beilby and Paul R. Eddy, eds., *Divine Foreknowledge: Four Views* (Downers Grove, IL: IVP Academic, 2001); Dennis Jowers, ed., *Four View of Divine Providence* (Grand Rapids:

In the summer of 2007 twenty scholars met at Eastern Nazarene College for a three-week conference sponsored by the John Templeton Foundation in order to consider the relation between open theism and science. They listened to a variety of lecturers and developed topics for further research. The following April the same group met at Azusa Pacific University to present the results of their investigations. The subsequent publication of two books contained a number of articles based on these presentations: *Creation Made Free: Open Theology Engaging Science*,[5] and *God in an Open Universe: Science, Metaphysics, and Open Theism*.[6] The contents covered a wide range of topics all the way from cosmology, relativity, time, and evolution to religious language, forgiveness, and prayer.

Open theism's basic vision of Creator and creation raises a cluster of interrelated questions of a philosophical nature. The presentations at the conferences in 2007 and 2008, along with the publications that followed, demonstrated that open theism has generated a good deal of rather sophisticated reflection. And in a growing number of books and articles ever since, both supporters and critics have refined and amplified their arguments. Along the way, open theists themselves have developed a variety of answers to some of the philosophical questions to which the open view of God gives rise.

DIVINE FOREKNOWLEDGE

Though it is not by any means the only concern of open theism, nor for open theists themselves the most important aspect of their view of God, no facet of the open view of God has stimulated more discussion than its view of divine knowledge. Whenever people consider open theism, it seems, they typically identify it with a reference to divine foreknowledge.[7]

Zondervan, 2011); Chad V. Meister and James K. Dew, eds., *Perspectives on the Problem of Evil: Five Views* (Downers Grove, IL: IVP Academic, 2017).

[5]Thomas Jay Oord, ed., *Creation Made Free: Open Theology Engaging Science* (Eugene, OR: Pickwick Publications, 2009).

[6]William Hasker, Thomas Jay Oord, and Dean Zimmerman, eds., *God in an Open Universe: Science, Metaphysics, and Open Theism* (Eugene, OR: Pickwick Publications, 2011).

[7]When Bethany House Publishers reissued my first book, *The Openness of God*, it was published in 1985 under the title, *God's Foreknowledge and Man's Free Will*.

For example, an article appeared in 2004 in the *Chronicle of Higher Education* describing the difficulties that advocates of open theism were facing in certain Evangelical institutions. Its title was "Can God See the Future?"[8] And when another article on the same topic appeared a few months later in *Christian Century*, it was titled, "What God Knows: The Debate on 'Open Theism.'"[9]

Open theists are not by any means distinctive in devoting attention to divine foreknowledge. After all, omniscience is one of the perfections uniformly attributed to God, and this attribute inevitably raises questions concerning the extent to which God knows the future. Indeed, it would be hard to come up with a question that has generated more diverse or more strongly held opinions than this one: *If God infallibly knows that a person will choose to perform a particular action in the future, how could that person be free to do anything else?* Despite centuries of reflection, scholars remain as divided on the issue as they ever were. There is no consensus regarding the question of freedom and foreknowledge and not a little frustration that none of the proposed answers seems to work.

Linda Zagzebski, for example, concludes her book *The Dilemma of Freedom and Foreknowledge* on a note of resignation and regret. "The divine foreknowledge dilemma is so disturbing, it has motivated a significant amount of philosophical work on the relation between God and human beings since at least the fifth century. A really good solution should lay to rest the gripping worries that have motivated all this work. Sadly, none of the solutions I have proposed in this book really do that, and I have never heard of one that does."[10] In his article "The Foreknowledge Conundrum," William Hasker makes a similar assessment. After considering three "minor" solutions to the problem and four "major" ones, as well as a more recent proposal, he finds none of them satisfactory.[11]

---

[8]Burton Bollag, "Can God See the Future?," *Chronicle of Higher Education*, November 26, 2004.

[9]James K. A. Smith, "What God Knows," *Christian Century*, July 12, 2005, 30-32.

[10]Linda Zagzebski, *The Dilemma of Freedom and Foreknowledge* (New York: Oxford University Press, 1991), 180.

[11]William Hasker, "The Foreknowledge Conundrum," *International Journal for Philosophy of Religion* 50 (2001): 97-114.

Put the topic of foreknowledge on the table, and a number of others follow in quick succession. What, exactly, is the nature of the future? Are past, present, and future essentially the same, that is, do they have the same ontological status? Are they equally definite, or are they significantly different? Then too what is the nature of time? Is time more accurately conceived as linear, or as progressive? And just what is God's relation to time? Is God inside time, outside time, or what?

For many scholars, questions regarding the future easily merge with linguistic considerations. What, for example, is the nature of our language about the future? What is the status of propositions that certain events "will" or "will not" happen? What concept of the future do such statements reflect? Or do they in some way determine our concept of the future?

Open theists are drawn into this discussion because they affirm an open future as a necessary corollary of libertarian freedom. Instead of trying to resolve the dilemma of freedom and foreknowledge by recasting our views of the future, or by redirecting our attention to language about the future, open theists accept "theological incompatibilism." They reject the idea that "comprehensive, infallible divine foreknowledge is compatible with libertarian free will for human beings."[12] The result is the belief that "God does not possess complete, infallible knowledge of the future," a view that Hasker acknowledged, in what certainly proved to be an understatement, is "quite likely to raise theological hackles."[13]

Moreover, the discussion of any of these topics quickly descends—or ascends, depending on your perspective—into technical language, a good deal of it too complex for our purposes here. At the very least, however, it is clear that open theism has stimulated a good deal of serious conversation and that its supporters have given careful consideration to a wide range of the issues it raises. What follows, then is a representative account, a mere sample, actually, of some of the particular questions that philosophers interested in open theism have pursued.

---

[12]Hasker, "The Foreknowledge Conundrum," 98-99.
[13]Hasker, "The Foreknowledge Conundrum," 110.

Are divine foreknowledge and genuine human freedom compatible? In an article titled "Three Roads to Open Theism,"[14] Dale Tuggy explores several ways in which open theists explain why exhaustive divine foreknowledge is incompatible with genuine human freedom, "the narrow road, the wide road, and the shortcut," he calls them. Those who take "the wide road," the one more traveled by than the others, and the one Tuggy prefers, hold that "some claims about future contingents presently fail to be either true or false."[15] Whenever there is a free decision to be made, there are different possibilities to be realized, and until the decision is made, its outcome is indefinite, not something to which either label "true" or "false" now applies.

For those who accept incompatibilist freedom, therefore, past, present, and future do not represent segments or points on a single line. There is no complete set of events, some past and some future—all of which are possible objects of knowledge. And since more than one possible series of events could occur, their view of the future is "branching" rather than linear.[16]

The unknowability of the future thus results from the nature of the future, not from the limitations of our knowledge. The branches in this view of time reflect "real, objective indeterminism in a dynamic universe." To be precise, they represent facts about the present, possible outcomes that depend on the course of time up till now. To be even more precise, "there is now no future—no *complete* future world-segment or branch which is now such that it will be."[17]

This view of time requires us to modify our view of the past as well, and the result is a position known as "presentism," the concept that future and past "branch-segments" are not to be thought of as realities, but rather as "events which have been real, and events which will become or might become real."[18] So, despite our conventional language—our

---

[14]Dale Tuggy, "Three Roads to Open Theism," *Faith and Philosophy* 24, no. 1 (January 2007): 28-51.
[15]In more technical language, the principle of bivalence, according to which all propositions are either true or if not true, then, false, does not apply to some statements about the future. Tuggy, "Three Roads to Open Theism," 31.
[16]Tuggy, "Three Roads to Open Theism," 32.
[17]Tuggy, "Three Roads to Open Theism," 33.
[18]Tuggy, "Three Roads to Open Theism," 50n35. Alan Rhoda argues to the same conclusion. Because God chose to create a world in which creatures have significant freedom, there is no such

tendency to speak of "the future," as if it were already entirely definite—the future does not consist of a single course of events. Strictly speaking, in fact, the future does not literally exist.

In another article on the future, Alan R. Rhoda, along with Gregory A. Boyd and Thomas G. Belt, develops both semantic and metaphysical arguments for the "incompatibility thesis," the idea that a settled future is incompatible with future contingency.[19] Their metaphysical argument distinguishes presentism from eternalism. For eternalism, past, present, and future are equally real. But for presentism, "all of reality exists now, in the present; the past is no more, the future is not yet."[20] Accordingly, propositions about the past and future can be true only by virtue of their relation to the present—only if they are true now. Because it *now* obtains, for example, that Caesar crossed the Rubicon, the assertion that he did so is true, and the statement that humans will land on Mars is true in case *going to land on Mars* now obtains.[21]

Though open theists share the view that the future is not settled, there are differences among them when it comes to the status of statements about the future. As we have seen, Tuggy rejects the applicability of "bivalence" to statements about the future, that is, the position that such statements are either true or false, one or the other. In contrast, Hasker accepts it, as do Rhoda, Boyd, and Belt. Hasker, however, maintains there are true statements about the future that God is not in a position to know. Rhoda, Boyd, and Belt conclude that the open view of the future does not require us to reject bivalence, provided we construe the disjunction *will* and *will not* statements as contraries (both false) rather than contradictories (if one is true the other is false).[22]

---

thing as a completely settled future for God to know. In other words, there is no sequence of events subsequent to the present that is going to be *the* actual future. "Instead, there is a branching array of possible futures." ("Beyond the Chess Master Analogy: Game Theory and Divine Providence," in Oord, *Creation Made Free*, 151).

[19]Alan R. Rhoda, Gregory A. Boyd, and Thomas G. Belt, "Open Theism, Omniscience, and the Nature of the Future," *Faith and Philosophy* 23, no. 4 (October 2006): 432-59.

[20]Rhoda, Boyd, and Belt, "Open Theism, Omniscience, and the Nature of the Future," 446.

[21]Rhoda, Boyd, and Belt, "Open Theism, Omniscience, and the Nature of the Future," 447.

[22]Rhoda, Boyd, and Belt, "Open Theism, Omniscience, and the Nature of the Future," 454-55.

To the surprise of no one familiar with philosophical arguments, opponents of open theism find none of this convincing. In their article "Perils of the Open Road,"[23] William Lane Craig and David P. Hunt review in detail the various arguments for the incompatibility thesis presented by Tuggy and by Rhoda, Boyd, and Belt and reject them all, from the branch theory of possibilities through the semantic and metaphysical considerations. For Craig and Hunt, none of them effectively establishes that exhaustive divine foreknowledge conflicts with the reality of future contingent truths.[24] In language rather dramatic for philosophical discussion, they say they find the "trend toward open theism lamentable, indeed, baffling,"[25] and they believe "the wide road to open theism" leads to "logical and metaphysical (not to mention theological) ruin."[26]

But just as there are divisions among open theists on certain issues, the same is true of their critics. Although Craig and Hunt agree that open theists are mistaken in rejecting absolute foreknowledge, their own accounts of foreknowledge are quite different. Among the available options, Hunt prefers "simple foreknowledge," while Craig is a well-known proponent of middle knowledge, or "Molinism."[27] To simplify Hunt's position, the less we try to explain foreknowledge, the better. He believes that God knows future free decisions, but he doesn't know what free agency is or how God knows the future.[28]

"By his middle knowledge," as Craig explains it in an earlier work, "God knows all the various possible worlds that he could create and what every free creature would do in all the various circumstances of those possible worlds."[29] And since God knows which of these possible worlds is the actual one, he knows this world's entire future, including all the

---

[23]William Lane Craig and David P. Hunt, "Perils of the Open Road," *Faith and Philosophy* 30, no. 1 (January 2013): 49-71.

[24]Craig and Hunt, "Perils of the Open Road," 49.

[25]Craig and Hunt, "Perils of the Open Road," 49.

[26]Craig and Hunt, "Perils of the Open Road," 71.

[27]See their respective contributions to *Divine Foreknowledge: Four Views*, ed. James K. Beilby and Paul R. Eddy (Downers Grove, IL: InterVarsity Academic, 2001).

[28]David Hunt, "The Simple-Foreknowledge View," in Beilby and Eddy, *Divine Foreknowledge*, 101-2.

[29]William Lane Craig, *The Only Wise God: The Compatibility of Divine Foreknowledge and Human Freedom* (Grand Rapids: Baker, 1987), 133.

free choices it contains. So the future is entirely known to God, even though it is not, strictly speaking, determined by God.

For open theists, Craig misconstrues the nature of the present world. The flaw in his theory, as Richard Creel puts it, "is its assumption that God can know which possible world is the actual world."[30] If creatures are genuinely free to do otherwise, their decisions are not definite, and therefore not knowable, until they make them. Or, to put it another way, if God's creatures are genuinely free, the course of events in this world is not due to God's creative power alone. It owes its content to God-and-the-creatures.[31]

From the lines of thought Tuggy and Craig pursue it appears that they come to different conclusions regarding freedom and foreknowledge because their arguments proceed in opposite directions. Because bivalence applies to statements about the future, Craig argues—because statements about the future have truth value—the future is definite, and God, being omniscient, knows all true statements including those about the future. In contrast, Tuggy argues that genuine creaturely freedom entails a future that is indeterminate and therefore cannot be an object of knowledge, even for God. Consequently, there are certain statements about the future to which we cannot assign truth value. What appears to be nonnegotiable for Tuggy is creaturely freedom, while for Craig, it is exhaustive foreknowledge.

What is the nature of the future? Alan R. Rhoda gives extensive attention to different ways of understanding the future from an open theist perspective.[32] He notes that open and classical theists both view God as existing necessarily and possessing the qualities of perfect power, knowledge, and goodness. Both also believe that God created the world *ex nihilo* and "can unilaterally intervene in it as he pleases."[33] Unlike

---

[30]Richard Creel, *Divine Impassibility: An Essay in Philosophical Theology* (Cambridge: Cambridge University Press, 1986), 90.

[31]See my essay "Divine Foreknowledge and Free-Will Theism," in *The Grace of God, the Will of Man: A Case for Arminianism*, ed. Clark H. Pinnock (Grand Rapids: Zondervan Academic, 1989), 127.

[32]Alan R. Rhoda, "Generic Open Theism and Some Varieties Thereof," *Religious Studies* 44 (2008): 225-34.

[33]Rhoda, "Generic Open Theism," 226.

classical theists, however, open theists view the future as both causally and epistemically open to God. In other words, there are contingent events in the future and God does not know them in advance.[34]

Within the framework of these shared convictions, however, open theists construct different accounts of God's relation to the future. For a few—William Hasker is the best known—God knows all that can conceivably be known, but there are truths about the future that are inaccessible even to him.[35] To put it another way, Hasker sees the future as epistemically open for God, even though it is "alethically settled."[36] If the future is alethically settled, then statements about some future event are either true or false. But if the future is epistemically open to God, then there are things about the future that God does not know, because they cannot be known.

Rhoda divides other open theists into two camps, depending on whether they advocate "bivalentist" or "non-bivalentist omniscience." In contrast to Hasker, those in both groups agree that the future is alethically as well as epistemically open to God. But they differ when it comes to the status of "will" and "will not" propositions. For the "non-bivalentists" "will and will not" propositions about future contingencies represent "contradictories," that is, statements that are either true or false. And because statements about future contingencies are neither true nor false, bivalence must be rejected.[37] For those who accept the "bivalentist" version of open theism, "will" and "will not" propositions about the future are not contradictories, but contraries. Instead of one being true and the other false, both may be false. And if that is the case, then the statement that something *might and might not* occur in the future is true.[38] So, while all open theists accept an open future, they find different ways to account for God's relation to it.[39]

---

[34]Rhoda, "Generic Open Theism," 227.

[35]Rhoda, "Generic Open Theism," 229-30.

[36]The word *alethic* is related to *alētheia*, the Greek word for "truth."

[37]Rhoda, "Generic Open Theism," 231.

[38]Rhoda, "Generic Open Theism," 231.

[39]Consequently, Rhoda insists, both defenders and critics should make it clear whether they have in mind the features that identify open theism in general or one of its specific versions. Rhoda, "Generic Open Theism," 232.

In an essay that appeared a few years later,[40] Rhoda extended the number of senses in which the future could be thought of as open to five, adding to *alethic* and *epistemic* openness *causal, ontic,* and *providential* openness.

To describe the future as causally open is to say there are various possible "extensions of the actual past," in other words, there are "future contingents."[41] If the future is "ontically" open, there is no one, complete series of events that it comprises.[42] If the future is alethically open—as we just noted—there is no "one complete true story" that covers the actual future.[43] If the future is epistemically open, then it cannot be infallibly known, even by God.[44] And if the future is providentially open, God cannot act unilaterally to achieve his plans, and the actual course of events may not fulfill his objectives in every detail.[45] After identifying five ways in which the future might be open, Rhoda explores the possible relations among them and comes to the conclusion that the logical possibilities are limited to two, theological determinism and open theism. If the former is true, we play the role that God has designed for us. But if open theism is true, then there are a number of different ways in which God might fulfill his objectives.[46] Simply put, if the future is causally open, as open theism requires, then it is open in *all five* senses.[47]

As these discussions indicate, once open theists embrace the idea that the future differs from the past in being open in a significant way, indeed, open to God as well as to humans, a number of challenging questions arise. And that is arguably true of any attempt to account

---

[40] Alan R. Rhoda, "The Fivefold Openness of the Future," in Hasker, Oord, and Zimmerman, *God in an Open Universe,* 69-93.

[41] Rhoda, "The Fivefold Openness of the Future," 73.

[42] Rhoda, "The Fivefold Openness of the Future," 74. According to "presentism," as we have seen, there is only one world state, namely, the present one, and the future does not yet exist.

[43] Rhoda also suggests that open theists are, in effect, committed to the "Piercean" rather than the "Ockhamist" system of "tense logic." In other words, they believe that the grounding for all truths lies in the present. So, if the statement, "There will be a sea battle tomorrow," is true now, it is because there are sufficient conditions now to ensure that the battle will occur ("Generic Open Theism," 230).

[44] Rhoda, "The Fivefold Openness of the Future," 75.

[45] Rhoda, "The Fivefold Openness of the Future," 76.

[46] Rhoda, "The Fivefold Openness of the Future," 93.

[47] Rhoda, "The Fivefold Openness of the Future," 70.

for temporal experience. To some observers, proposals like the ones above will bring to mind Augustine's famous observation that he knew what time was if no one asked him. But if asked about time, he found he was unable to explain it. At the same time, these various proposals demonstrate that open theists take very seriously the challenge of providing an adequate conceptual account of one of their basic convictions.

DIVINE PROVIDENCE

When theologians consider the future, the question of divine providence inevitably arises. And for many people, at least on a personal level, this issue is more pressing than that of divine foreknowledge. Just how does God work through events in the world to fulfill his purposes? And what assurance do we have that his goals will ultimately be realized? These topics have attracted extensive scholarly attention. And as in the case of divine foreknowledge, the range of opinions is vast, the distinctions are often subtle, much of the terminology is technical, and disagreements are often vigorously expressed.

According to open theism, the world owes its existence entirely to God, and God has the power to determine the entire course of events. Instead of doing so, however, God gave certain creatures the freedom to accept or resist God's intentions for them, and the ultimate fulfillment of his purposes requires their cooperation. The reality of creaturely freedom means that God cannot achieve his purposes unilaterally.[48] This raises an important question for open theists. Can we be sure that God's purposes for creation will ultimately be realized? Or does the reality of creaturely freedom—libertarian freedom—entail the risk that God's plans could fail? In other words, just how much is at risk for "the God who risks"?[49] As the subtitle of Sanders's book suggests, providence is a central concern for open theists, and they have developed

---

[48]Alan R. Rhoda, "Open Theism and Other Models of Divine Providence," in Diller and Kasher, *Models of God and Alternative Ultimate Realities*, 296-97.

[49]The centrality of providence to the concerns of open theism is apparent from the title of Sanders's well-known book, *The God Who Risks: A Theology of Divine Providence*, rev. ed. (Downers Grove, IL: IVP Academic, 2007).

rather distinctive views of the topic. We'll look at two that provide an interesting contrast.

Along with his careful analysis of foreknowledge, Alan Rhoda has noted various ways in which God's providential activity can be conceived. In one essay, he notes how divine determinism, Molinism, process theism, and open theism envision the manner, scope, and limits of God's providential activity.[50] As he analyzes it, open theism is both similar to and different from each of these alternatives in distinctive ways, but in summary, God's power is essentially unconstrained for open theists, it is both efficacious at times and persuasive at others, and God exercises general rather than meticulous providence.

Providence and game theory. In another essay, Rhoda proposes a way of describing God's providential activity that he finds to be superior to the Chess Master analogy, which many open theists find helpful.[51] Just as a grand master will inevitably defeat a mere novice at chess, the reasoning goes, God will surely achieve his purposes, no matter what the creatures decide to do. For Rhoda, this analogy is simplistic. In chess, there are only two players, the moves are strictly sequential, the rules and objectives are the same for both players, and finally, chess is a zero-sum game—one player wins at the other's expense.[52]

In contrast, the features of other games include "overlapping factors," such as strategic complexity, artistic elegance, significant and diverse outcomes, and uncertainty.[53] Suppose we think of God's relation to the world in terms of a "Creation Game"? In this case, there would be a high degree of complexity and a large number of players who are free and who have a wide variety of skills. God would want creation to have a "high degree of artistic elegance," so the participants could cohere in beautiful ways. And he would want the game to have high stakes and some degree of risk.[54]

---

[50]Rhoda, "Open Theism and Other Models."

[51]The analogy is often attributed to William James. See Richard Rice, *God's Foreknowledge and Man's Free Will* (Eugene, OR: Wipf and Stock, 2004), 66.

[52]Alan R. Rhoda, "Beyond the Chess Master Analogy: Game Theory and Divine Providence," in Oord, *Creation Made Free*, 155.

[53]Rhoda, "Beyond the Chess Master Analogy," 171.

[54]Rhoda, "Beyond the Chess Master Analogy," 173-74.

Rhoda finds a biblical precedent for his analogy in passages such as Jeremiah 18:7-10, where God outlines his strategy for dealing with his people in a series of "if-then" statements. If God threatens to destroy a nation and the nation repents, then God will relent from punishing. And if God promises to build up a nation, and it does evil and disobeys, then God will retract his promise. So God adjusts his strategy from blessing to punishing (or vice versa) in reaction to a nation's response to his announcement.[55]

Though game theory does not provide a single concrete model for divine providence, Rhoda argues, it does give us a "systematic framework for thinking about interactive decision making," which can be adjusted to the complexities of various situations.[56] And this could be helpful in addressing one of the most perplexing questions related to the problem of evil. *Why does God choose to intervene in some cases of suffering, but not in others? Why doesn't he respond to comparable situations in exactly the same way?*[57] Game theory suggests that God's strategy may vary from one situation to another. In view of complex "value preferences" and his "overall optimum strategy," God sometimes decides to intervene and sometimes chooses not to.[58]

Game theory also illustrates another way in which open theism is superior to its familiar alternatives. If God infallibly knew the outcome of the creation game in advance—as both classical theism and Molinism require—it is hard to understand why God would create at all. After all, it is the very possibility of different outcomes that makes a game interesting, and by this standard an utterly risk-free world—a game whose outcome is a foregone conclusion—would have nothing to interest God. With its affirmation of an open future and divine risk, however, "the sort of Creation Game Open theists envisage is the very sort of game that God would choose to play."[59]

For Rhoda, game theory illustrates the priority that open theism places on love, freedom, and creativity. For open theism, the path creation takes

---

[55]Rhoda, "Beyond the Chess Master Analogy," 163.
[56]Rhoda, "Beyond the Chess Master Analogy," 168.
[57]David R. Larson refers to this as "the morality of selective intervention."
[58]Rhoda, "Beyond the Chess Master Analogy," 168.
[59]Rhoda, "Beyond the Chess Master Analogy," 175.

is not one decided entirely by God, nor one whose events were known to him entirely in advance. Instead, God created a world whose future was indefinite, suspenseful, even mysterious. And he committed himself to pursue his goals for the world no matter what happened. Consequently, the ultimate fulfillment of God's purposes represents a genuine achievement—something God works for—not a foregone conclusion. For other views of providence, the future is entirely predictable and the fulfillment of God's purposes is inevitable. In contrast, the open view offers adventure, suspense, and ultimate achievement.

Providence and divine love. In a symposium volume comparing four views of providence, Gregory Boyd presents his version under the title, "God Limits His Control." From a christocentric starting point, he identifies four criteria by which to evaluate his position: the reality of spiritual warfare (a favorite theme of Boyd's), God's reliance on his superior power and wisdom, God's "other-oriented love"—the kingpin of Boyd's position—and, finally, God's ability to bring good out of evil, which ensures the certainty of God's victory. Boyd then lays out the "open model of providence" and evaluates it in light of these criteria.

For Boyd, as for others, the heart of open theism is the conviction that love is central to God's identity. As revealed in Jesus, God's "eternal nature is other-oriented, self-sacrificial love." This love characterizes God's inner reality as "a loving community of three divine persons," and, most significantly for a doctrine of providence, this love "empowers humans genuinely to affect him." The cross underscores both the form that God's self-sacrificing love characteristically takes and the extent to which this love was willing to go. And it is this love, as well, that establishes the certainty of God's final victory over his "cosmic foes" and the fulfillment of his ultimate purposes for creation.[60]

Because everything God does is motivated by love, God created the world as "an expression of his love and for the purpose of inviting others to share in his love."[61] Though God possessed the inherent power to create a world whose inhabitants would do exactly what he directed

---

[60]Gregory A. Boyd, "God Limits His Control," in Jowers, *Four Views of Divine Providence*, 186-87.
[61]Boyd, "God Limits His Control," 188.

them to do, their response to God would not be one of genuine love unless it was truly *their* response, a response they freely chose. In order for us genuinely to love God, therefore, "he must create us with the capacity to choose to love *or not*."[62] "God gave us the capacity freely to reject his loving will *because it was necessary for love*."[63]

Once having decided to grant creaturely agents free will, says Boyd, God can neither meticulously control it nor revoke it.[64] What creatures decide to do therefore makes an indelible contribution to the scheme of things. This does not mean that God does nothing in response to their decisions. To the contrary, God is extensively involved in the ongoing course of events, reacting to and seeking to influence their choices. "But the one thing God cannot do, by definition, is meticulously control or unilaterally revoke a free will once given."[65]

Given the freedom God grants his creatures, the future is open to a variety of different possibilities, from God's viewpoint as well as from ours. And where history goes depends both on what creatures decide and on God's responses to their decisions. This explains why the Bible describes God as variously surprised, delighted, and disappointed by what takes place. And it also supports a complex view of divine providence. Because God is a God of perfect love, "God does not meticulously control everything."[66]

To illustrate his view of providence Boyd refers to a children's book series titled Choose Your Own Adventure. Instead of laying out a single story line, the author gives readers the opportunity to decide at various points how the story should proceed. What happens in the story depends in part on the choices they make. In a somewhat similar way, Boyd suggests, the future is partly settled and partly open. God, the author of "the adventure of creation," predetermines the overall structure, the possible story lines, and all the possible endings. In addition, God predestines certain events to take place *if* certain story lines

---

[62]Boyd "God Limits His Control," 189, italics original.
[63]Boyd, "God Limits His Control," 190, italics original.
[64]Boyd, "God Limits His Control," 191.
[65]Boyd, "God Limits His Control," 192.
[66]Boyd, "God Limits His Control," 204.

are followed and others to take place *regardless of* which story lines are chosen.[67] Unlike the author of the book, however, God is an active participant in the adventure of creation. He is both present and "passionately involved" in every decision, though he "lovingly refrains" from ever coercing the creaturely agents.[68]

Given the freedom that God grants the creatures in his otherdirected love, the achievement of God's purposes requires their cooperation; God cannot bring them about unilaterally. And this raises the prospect that God's plans could ultimately fail. Since God gives creatures freedom and always respects their decisions, what would happen if none of them decided to cooperate with him? Is that possible . . . at least theoretically?[69]

According to Boyd, this could never happen. We can be absolutely confident that God's purposes will reach fulfillment. For one thing, God has infinite intelligence. He knows from all eternity every possible future event and he is prepared to meet any eventuality. Indeed, God sees every possible future as clearly as if it were a certainty— every possible story line "as though it was the only story line creation could take."[70] And from eternity God has prepared an appropriate response for each possibility. From this perspective, "the God of open theism knows the future just as effectively as the God of classical theism, who faces an eternally settled future." Only, for the God of open theism, the future he knows is an immense variety of possible futures, each one of which he has perfectly envisioned and is fully prepared to meet.[71]

With this picture of divine foresight, it is certain that God's objectives for creation will ultimately be realized. "We should have no more difficulty trusting that God can bring good out of evil and triumph in the end when

---

[67]Boyd, "God Limits His Control," 199-200.
[68]Boyd, "God Limits His Control," 200-201.
[69]Some critics cite this prospect as one of open theism's telling failures. Boyd cites Bruce Ware, for example, who describes the God of open theism as a "passive, handwringing God" who can do little more than guess about the future and hope for the best (Boyd, "God Limits His Control," 206).
[70]Boyd, "God Limits His Control," 206.
[71]Boyd, "God Limits His Control," 207.

he faces a partly open future than if he faced an exhaustively settled future." And if we need further assurance, Boyd has this to offer. Given God's ability to foresee all possible future worlds, we can be confident that he will eliminate any story lines "that could not result in God's bringing good out of evil. . . . The Author of the adventure of creation would simply exclude them from the adventure."[72]

For Boyd, then, we can be sure that God's purposes will be fulfilled. Because God knows all possibilities—as clearly as if they were definite actualities—God can eliminate those that would thwart the realization of his plans. Consequently, there is virtually no risk, despite the freedom of the creatures to accept or reject God's will, that God's will will not prevail.

Others are not so sure. In an article responding to both Boyd's view of providence and Rhoda's game theory analogy, Johannes Grossol and Leigh Vicens argue that neither effectively eliminates the risk that God's ultimate purposes may never be achieved.[73] To begin with, they distinguish between high-risk and low-risk versions of open theism. For high-risk open theists, like John Sanders and William Hasker, everyone who has the capacity and the opportunity to choose or reject a loving relationship with God could theoretically reject it, so there is a genuine risk that God's creative purposes could fail, even though they think this possibility is so improbable as to be negligible.[74]

In contrast, according to Boyd's "limited risk open theism," God can guarantee the general outcome of creation without "determining particular outcomes." He can achieve his general goal, despite the reality of libertarian freedom, thanks to his ability to eliminate possible futures where he doesn't.[75] In the judgment of Grossol and Vicens, however, this "low-risk" proposal won't work. Since all creatures who enjoy libertarian freedom will have the option of rejecting God, and God cannot eliminate this option without withdrawing their freedom, Boyd's "low risk open

---

[72]Boyd, "God Limits His Control," 207.

[73]Johannes Grossol and Leigh Vicens, "Closing the Door on Limited-Risk Open Theism," *Faith and Philosophy* 31, no. 4 (October 2014): 475-85.

[74]Grossol and Vicens, "Closing the Door," 477.

[75]Grossol and Vicens, "Closing the Door," 478.

theism," turns out to be "high risk" after all. The possibility remains that God's purposes could be thwarted.[76]

Moreover, as they see it, the popular chess master analogy won't work because it doesn't apply to what God hopes to achieve. The chess master wins the game no matter what moves the novice chooses to make. But if God's objective is that at least some of his creatures freely choose to return his love, the choices must be theirs, and not something God could infallibly bring about.[77]

Furthermore, they argue, the idea that there is a statistical probability that at least some of God's creatures will choose to return his love still falls short of a guarantee. Even if the risk of universal rejection is "negligibly small," they argue, it is substantial nonetheless.[78] Hence, Boyd's claim that God can infallibly know that at least some of his creatures will accept his offer of love conflicts in principle with the libertarian freedom that open theism affirms.[79]

Grossol and Vicens bring their article to a close with an intriguing footnote. If we think of God's "higher-order will" as the creation of a world containing the possibility of creaturely loyalty and his "lower-order will" as the actuality of this loyalty, then we can view creation as fulfilling God's high-order will even if his lower order will is not fulfilled. To this effect, they quote John Sanders: "If God wants a world in which the possibility exists that God may not get everything he wants, then in an ultimate sense the divine will is not thwarted."[80]

RESPONSIBLE RISK?

This raises the question of what makes a risk "responsible." In its most basic sense, a risk involves making a decision or taking an action that involves a potential loss and whose outcome is unknown in advance. What makes a risk worth taking? When the likelihood of failure is low and the potential benefit is high. When is a risk not worth

---

[76]Grossol and Vicens, "Closing the Door," 480.
[77]Grossol and Vicens, "Closing the Door," 481.
[78]Grossol and Vicens, "Closing the Door," 483, 484.
[79]Grossol and Vicens, "Closing the Door," 484.
[80]Grossol and Vicens, "Closing the Door," 485 (see Sanders, *The God Who Risks*, 243).

taking? When the potential benefit is low and the likelihood of failure is high.

After a typical day on campus, I head for home on the freeway. Is there a risk I'll never make it? Well, yes. Accidents frequently happen, and some of them are fatal, but I'll be careful and the chances I won't survive the trip are very low. At the same time, the benefits of getting home—enjoying a good dinner and a restful night's sleep—are relatively high. So, I'll risk the road for an evening at home.

On the other hand, consider the risk of sky-diving without a parachute. What would almost certainly be a deadly plunge to the earth is hardly worth whatever excitement one had during the fall. Lake Elsinore, California, is a popular location for skydiving, and every now and then there are reports of people who survive a fall even when their parachutes fail to open. The reason they make the news, of course, is because their good fortune is so unlikely.

But what do we do with risks that are more complex? People suffering with a terminal condition often undergo aggressive therapy if that is their only hope of continuing to live. The benefits are great enough to justify a treatment that may have serious side effects.

So we have different sorts of risk, depending on the various relationships between "likelihood of failure" and "level of benefit." There are (1) low likelihood/high benefit risks; (2) high likelihood/low benefit risks; (3) high likelihood/high benefit risks; and (4) low likelihood/low benefit risks.

When it comes to identifying the risk that God took in creating a world with freedom in it, we can dispense with 2 and 4. Surely, the stakes are high, since they involve the blessings of loyalty or the consequences of rebellion. That leaves us with 1 and 3. Most theodicies seem to offer a version of 3. The benefits of freedom are immense—only if creatures are genuinely free can there be genuine love—but the chances of rebellion are great as well. This is why God prepares a plan of salvation, knowing that it will certainly, or almost certainly, be needed. But there is another possibility. Suppose the chances that creatures would rebel were very low, perhaps infinitesimally low.

Since they are convinced that God's essential nature is one of love, open theists believe that God created a world with inhabitants who could return his love. And this required endowing them with libertarian freedom. In creating such a world, however, God took a significant risk. Beings who were genuinely free could decide to reject God's love for them. But God valued the prospect of loving relationships with his creatures so highly that he was willing to accept the chance that they would do that. Sadly, that's what happened.

Like Boyd, most open theists regard the creaturely rebellion that occurred as virtually inevitable. Sooner or later, it seems, *someone* endowed with the freedom to give or withhold loyalty to God was bound to take the second option. Then the question becomes one of determining whether or not the risk was worth it, that is, whether the benefits that followed balanced out the loss. Boyd's position seems to be that they do, or that in the long run they will.

Perhaps there is another way to envision the risk that God took. Suppose the rebellion of the creatures was not only not inevitable, but highly unlikely as well. Perhaps, as God anticipated the kind of world he wanted, a world containing creatures who had the freedom to return his love, he knew that they could reject his love, but there was only a slim, perhaps infinitesimal, chance that they would actually do so. Why infinitesimal? Because, first of all, God placed in them a profound capacity, indeed, a deep natural desire, to love and be loved by God. And then God did everything possible to cultivate their love for him, all the while respecting their freedom to reject him. In other words, God did everything he possibly could to minimize the risk, short of eliminating it. Endowed with this natural disposition and placed in this environment, the most natural thing in the world, then, would be for God's creatures to respond exactly as God hoped they would—return God's love and join God in pursuing his purposes for creation.

Unfortunately, events took a different direction. God's beloved creatures rebelled and history followed a different path. But even though that's what actually happened, it may nevertheless have been unlikely, indeed highly unlikely, that it would. When we consider the past, it easy for us to get the impression that what happened was somehow meant to happen. There is only one past, after all, and we sometimes feel as if that is the only one there could have been. The postulate that creatures were truly free, however, entails the possibility that they could have made a different choice when it came to their response to God and that creaturely rebellion would never have occurred.

So this line of reflection allows for the belief that when God decided to create a world containing creatures who were genuinely free, he took a very low risk, indeed, a minimal risk. Though it was possible that the creatures could rebel, there was only a slight chance that they actually would, and God did everything possible, while respecting their freedom, to ensure that they wouldn't. True, God's children still rebelled, and the results have arguably been disastrous. But this doesn't exclude the possibility that the likelihood of rebellion was extremely small, while the benefits of freedom were great, and the only way to realize them was to accept the risk.

Boyd's "providential" formulations raise questions of another sort as well. He asserts that God sees possibilities with the same degree of definiteness as he sees actualities and guarantees the outcome of his objectives for creation by pruning away the possibilities that would prevent it. This view of entirely definite *possible* futures bears a certain resemblance to both classical and Molinist accounts of divine foreknowledge. It seems to eliminate any difference between God's experience of an actual event and God's knowledge of a possible event. If God knows the possible future as fully and as clearly as if it were an actuality, what would its actual occurrence contribute to God's experience?

As is typically the case when philosophical issues are under consideration, every examination of open theism, or any of its facets, serves as a basis for yet further exchanges, rather than bringing discussion to a close. There are numerous aspects of open theism that raise significant questions among those who are favorable to it, as well as those who are critical—more than we have even hinted at here. And as is typically the case with philosophical exchanges, few people change their minds in the process. At the very least, however, two things seem clear. There are differences not only between open theists and their critics, but among open theists themselves, and their vision of God generates a number of thoughtful, stimulating conversations. While exchanges of the sort we have touched on here seldom lead to changes in one's position, all participants agree that the central ideas of open theism merit careful exploration.

 VARIETIES OF OPEN THEISM

IN CHAPTER FOUR, we looked at some of the ways open theists differ from other thinkers, and sometimes among themselves, on topics of a philosophical variety, such as the future, divine action, and even the nature of time. From the give and take among its supporters and critics, it is apparent that open theism has generated a good deal of thoughtful discussion and assumed some interesting variations. Another significant feature of open theism is the emergence of differences in the way its supporters approach certain theological topics.

While open theists share the view that there is genuine interaction between God and the world (arguably the most fundamental feature of the openness of God), they sometimes differ in the ways they construe this interaction. For example, open theists all affirm God's ontological independence from the world, God's active involvement in the world, and the temporal nature of divine experience. Yet there are variations among them concerning all of these points.

Some open theists accept the concept of creation *ex nihilo*, and hold that the world had a beginning, while others maintain that there was never a time when God was without a world. Some believe that God occasionally intervenes, or plays a direct role, in the course of creaturely events. Others hold that God never directly controls, or overrides, creaturely actions and decisions. And some hold that God's life is characterized by everlasting temporality, while others believe that God's temporal experience began with the first moment of creation.[1]

Thomas J. Oord has generated a lot of discussion in recent years for insisting that God's action is never coercive. This follows from the conviction that love is indeed God's most fundamental attribute and his analysis that genuine love is necessarily, not accidentally or intermittently, uncontrolling. Oord maintains that God never overrides the freedom of his creatures, and never unilaterally imposes his will on them.[2] In response, other open theists, including John Sanders, question Oord's categorical rejection of divine control and find Oord's attempt to account for exceptional events like miracles unconvincing.

There are other areas too where open theists take notably contrasting views. One involves the problem of evil. With their commitment to libertarian freedom, open theists uniformly accept a version of the free will defense.

Many are attracted to the open view of God because they find it helpful in responding to the problem of evil, traditionally the most formidable challenge to belief in God. With their strong view of libertarian freedom, open theists as a group embrace the free will defense.[3] For the most part, they believe that evil and suffering were not part of God's plan for his creatures, but originated in a willful rejection of God's love. They also hold that this rebellion was not a foregone conclusion, since future free decisions are not there to be known in advance. Beyond these basic points of agreement, certain open theists entertain markedly different approaches to evil and suffering. There are striking contrasts, for example, in the way Boyd and Hasker deal with the phenomenon of natural evil.

---

[1] David Basinger, "Introduction to Open Theism," in *Models of God and Alternative Ultimate Realities*, ed. Janine Diller and Asa Kasher (New York: Springer, 2013), 273. Compare the view of Old Testament scholar Terence E. Fretheim: "At least since the creation, the divine life is temporally ordered. God has chosen to enter into the time of the world. God is not above the flow of time and history" (*The Suffering of God: An Old Testament Perspective* [Philadelphia: Fortress Press, 1984], 43).

[2] *The Uncontrolling Love of God: An Open and Relational Account of Providence* (Downers Grove, IL: IVP Academic, 2014).

[3] As we shall see, William Hasker notes both similarities and differences between his natural-order theodicy and the free will defense. I believe that it remains a version of the latter in spite of its distinctive features. See *The Triumph of God over Evil: Theodicy for a World of Suffering* (Downers Grove, IL: IVP Academic, 2008), 162-66.

THE PROBLEM OF EVIL

Cosmic conflict. According to the central concept in Gregory Boyd's theodicy, there is a battle raging in the universe, and demonic forces are ultimately responsible for the factors in nature that wreak havoc on human lives—from earthquakes and tidal waves to the manifold variety of diseases that afflict us. And supreme among these powers stands Lucifer, the fallen angel, God's archenemy. As Boyd describes their relation, then, natural evil is subsequent to and derivative from moral evil.

In his essay "Evolution as Cosmic Warfare," Boyd presents what he calls "A Biblical Perspective on Satan and 'Natural' Evil."[4] On this account, human suffering results from the influences of "malevolent cosmic powers" on the natural world.[5] Once we accept the biblical depictions of Satan and demonic powers, "there is no categorical difference between 'natural' evil and moral evil. In *both* cases we can appeal to the free will of created agents," in this case "spirit agents."[6] The evolutionary process is characterized by *chaoskampf*, a motif found in the Old Testament according to which God struggles with the forces of evil and/or chaos.[7] The world we live in, characterized as it is by "parasites, viruses, diseases, deformities, and natural disaster," does not reflect the Creator's benevolent intentions. "They are, rather, the result of Satan and forces of evil corrupting the creative work of the benevolent Creator."[8]

---

[4]Gregory A. Boyd, "Evolution as Cosmic Warfare: A Biblical Perspective on Satan and 'Natural' Evil," in *Creation Made Free: Open Theology Engaging Science*, ed. Thomas Jay Oord (Eugene, OR: Wipf and Stock, 2009), 125-45. Boyd develops his cosmic conflict theodicy in a number of books, including *God at War: The Bible and Spiritual Conflict* (Downers Grove, IL: InterVarsity Press, 1997); *Satan and the Problem of Evil: Constructing a Trinitarian Warfare Theodicy* (Downers Grove, IL: InterVarsity Press, 2001). The purpose of both volumes, Boyd states, "Is to explore the significance of the biblical portrait of Satan for a contemporary theodicy." The purpose of *God at War* is to show that the biblical writers held a warfare worldview. The purpose of *Satan and the Problem of Evil* is to show how the early church lost sight of the warfare worldview and then to demonstrate that it provides for a theodicy that is superior to all alternatives (*God at War*, 22-23).

[5]Boyd, "Evolution as Cosmic Warfare," 127.

[6]Boyd, "Evolution as Cosmic Warfare," 130.

[7]Boyd, "Evolution as Cosmic Warfare," 134.

[8]Boyd, "Evolution as Cosmic Warfare," 138.

To the question, "Is God to blame?" Boyd responds with an emphatic no![9] And the reason, as he explains in several different books, is that God has enemies, these enemies have great power, and they account for the world's sorrows and woes. Satan and his cohort of once angelic, now demonic, followers are the forces behind the strife and bloodshed that riddle human history.[10] And their interference with the processes of nature has transformed the world from the perfect home God intends it to be into an ominous and threatening environment, marked by pain, disease, and death.[11]

Boyd draws a sharp distinction between the warfare worldview and the picture of God that has prevailed through most of Christian history. In the "classical-philosophical portrait," as he calls it, God is the one supreme power in the universe, and his sovereign will is perfectly fulfilled throughout creation.[12] This "divine blueprint view," the view that God is directly responsible for everything that happens, generates the "problem of evil" in its classic formulation: *If God is perfect in goodness and power, why does evil exist? Wouldn't a supremely good and powerful Being want to prevent it?* And this, in turn, imposes a deeply troubling question on anyone who suffers. *Why does God want me to suffer? Just what is my suffering supposed to accomplish?*

According to Boyd, both questions—*Why?* and *Why me?*—dissolve when we replace the classic picture of the God-world relation with the warfare worldview. The pervasiveness of suffering was not bewildering to those who lived during the eras of biblical history, nor to those in the centuries that directly followed. To the contrary, they were keenly aware of the presence of evil powers, and they attributed

---

[9]Gregory A. Boyd, *Is God to Blame? Beyond Pat Answers to the Problem of Suffering* (Downers Grove, IL: InterVarsity Press, 2003).

[10]Portions of this paragraph, and the three paragraphs that follow, also appear in Richard Rice, *Suffering and the Search for Meaning: Contemporary Responses to the Problem of Pain* (Downers Grove, IL: InterVarsity Press, 2015), 78-79.

[11]Asserts Boyd, "There is no such thing as 'natural' evil. Nature in its present state, I believe, is not as the Creator created it to be. . . . When nature exhibits diabolical features that are not the result of human wills, it is the direct or indirect result of the influence of diabolic forces" (*Satan and the Problem of Evil*, 247).

[12]Boyd, *God at War*, 69.

the ills of life to them, not to God. If the universe is populated by a host of beings opposed to God and bent on wreaking death and destruction, it is hardly surprising that we suffer; it would be surprising if we didn't.

From the perspective of cosmic conflict theodicy, then, we do not suffer because God wants us to—God's role is to relieve suffering.[13] We suffer because we live in a war zone. We suffer because God's enemies are active in the world, and we have made ourselves vulnerable to violence.[14] So, it is futile to look for a specific reason or purpose for individual instances of suffering.

A warfare theodicy naturally raises the question of its ultimate resolution, and on this point Boyd is unequivocal. The war waged in the evolutionary process and throughout human history, culminating in Christ's life, death, and resurrection will not go on forever. "God's kingdom will come."[15] "The will of the Lord cannot ultimately be defeated." In the meantime, God works "in, through, and (when necessary) against" both "rebellious spirits" and "rebellious humans" by overcoming evil "with good and by bringing good out of evil." Thus, we find in both nature and the history two factors at work—"the beautiful, creative intelligence of an all-good God as well as the ugly, malevolent intelligence of Satan and other forces of evil."[16]

Natural evil. In *The Triumph of God Over Evil*,[17] William Hasker takes an approach that differs from Boyd's in a number of ways. For Hasker, natural evil is not the result of demonic interference in the world God created. Instead, it is a natural consequence of the sort of world God decided to create—a world in which creatures would face challenges, and in facing them, would grow in a number of significant ways and develop into the sort of persons that God hoped they would become.

---

[13]"As he walked along, he saw a man blind from birth. His disciples asked him, 'Rabbi, who sinned, this man or his parents, that he was born blind?' Jesus answered, 'Neither this man nor his parents sinned; he was born blind so that God's works might be revealed in him'" (Jn 9:1-3).

[14]"By our own rebellion, we are caught in the crossfire of a cosmic war, and we suffer accordingly" (Boyd, *Is God to Blame?* 105).

[15]Boyd, "Evolution as Cosmic Warfare," 145.

[16]Boyd, "Evolution as Cosmic Warfare," 143.

[17]Hasker, *Triumph of God.*

From this perspective, the world we live in is "complex, multileveled, and evolving," and its entities—some of them "sentient and rational"—"act and interact in accordance with their inherent causal powers."[18] As a result, "the universe as a whole, as well as its component systems, develop from within, utilizing their inherent powers and potentialities."[19] Instead of manipulating the world's internal components and structures, or micromanaging their interactions, God lets them develop to a significant degree on their own, and the actual content of the world emerges from their interactions. In other words, God lets the world be the world.[20]

According to Hasker, then, natural evil is not only unavoidable, it is purposeful. The kind of world where natural evil occurs is the only kind of world in which certain values could be realized. Cataclysmic phenomena like earthquakes, volcanic eruptions, tsunamis—the sort of thing we call "natural disasters"—are essential to the development of life forms. The same is true of hurricanes, tornadoes and drought. The atmospheric conditions they create contribute to the growth of living creatures over the long haul. Similar explanations apply to the emergence of various life forms, from predators, parasites, and disease organisms. All these factors have a role to play in an environment conducive to the development of those features that matter most to us—the complex characteristics that define human life.

According to Hasker's "natural-order theodicy," then, "natural evil, in the form of suffering, pain and death, is the result of the overall order of the cosmos, an order which, taken as a whole, is good and admirable."[21] While the fact that we are part of this order means that we are not exempt from suffering, it does not mean that pain and suffering are not evil. Nor does it mean that every instance of suffering somehow fulfills a specific

---

[18]Hasker, *Triumph of God*, 123.

[19]Hasker, *Triumph of God*, 125.

[20]As Terence E. Fretheim puts it, "Israel's God is intensely and pervasively present in the created order but in such a way that God allows the creation to be what it was created to be without strict divine control" (*God and World in the Old Testament: A Relational Theology of Creation* [Nashville: Abingdon Press, 2005], 23).

[21]Hasker, *Triumph of God*, 140.

purpose.[22] No, the evolutionary process itself, Hasker suggests, may be "nonmoral," that is to say, "unintelligent and without intrinsic purpose, even though purposed by divine wisdom to perform the function of engendering a rich array of biological life." God's wisdom and goodness are beyond question. "But he is not a *tame* God, and he has not given us a tame world."[23]

Is the world thus described an ideal state of affairs? Is it all we have to look forward to? No, Hasker replies. He has faith in heaven as a place where the pain and sufferings of this world will be absent, but he says we can't know much about it and there is no way to take it as a model for what life should be like here and now.[24]

In contrast to Boyd, who subsumes natural evil within moral evil, Hasker sharply distinguishes the two. While there is "no compelling reason to suppose that there is something fundamentally amiss with the system of nature," he says, "there is every reason to suppose . . . that there is something deeply disordered about the lives of human beings."[25] Indeed, when we contemplate the horrible things human beings perpetrate, we encounter "the problem of evil in its most troubling form."[26] And this is where the free will defense figures in Hasker's thinking. "A libertarian view of free will," he insists, "is essential for any adequate solution of the problem of moral evil."[27] While it is true that free will is "an essential characteristic of human beings as such," and that "individuals without free will would not, in the true sense, be human beings at all,"[28] it is free will, or rather, the misuse of free will, that accounts for the most egregious forms of human suffering.

While Hasker acknowledges that there are differences between his natural-order theodicy and free will theodicy, he also notes they have important similarities as well. Neither provides justification for particular

---

[22]Hasker, *Triumph of God*, 140.
[23]Hasker, *Triumph of God*, 146.
[24]Hasker, *Triumph of God*, 129, 132-33.
[25]Hasker, *Triumph of God*, 160-61.
[26]Hasker, *Triumph of God*, 148.
[27]Hasker, *Triumph of God*, 152.
[28]Hasker, *Triumph of God*, 156.

evils. Nor on either account should specific instances of suffering be viewed as a means to a moral or spiritual good, or as punishment for sins.[29]

Hasker embraces the basic conviction of open theism that God acted decisively in the life, death, and resurrection of Jesus to counteract and bring about the ultimate defeat of evil. As he sees it, this does not mean that all evils will necessarily be defeated, in the sense that every sin ultimately contributes something positive to a person's relationship with God.[30] Nor does it mean that every person will ultimately be saved. But there is a world to come, and in that world the evils God's people have suffered in this one will be "engulfed in the experience of intimacy with God." They will enjoy a world of "fulfilled human lives, freedom from suffering, death and evil, and permeated with the knowledge and love of God."[31]

GOD AND THE WORLD

Besides taking different approaches to the problem of evil, open theists also look at certain aspects of God's relation to the world in different ways. Basic to open theism are the concepts that the future is open to God—and therefore not exhaustively foreknowable—and that God is genuinely affected by the decisions and actions of the creatures. Most open theists also share the traditional view that God's existence does not require the existence of a world and that God has the power to act within the natural course of things in dramatic ways if and when he chooses. In other words, God is not only open to the world, the world is open to God.

Creation. When it comes to the particular nature of God's relation to the world, however, open theists differ among themselves in a couple of interesting ways. A number of open theists accept the traditional concept of creation *ex nihilo.* The world owes its existence entirely to God, so creation is a gift but not a necessity for God. God's loving nature finds fulfillment in the love that defines God's very being, that is, in God's

---

[29]Hasker, *Triumph of God,* 165.
[30]Hasker, *Triumph of God,* 217.
[31]Hasker, *Triumph of God,* 224.

intratrinitarian being. Thus, the creation of the world represents an expression of God's loving nature, but it is not something that God needs to do for either metaphysical or moral reasons. For other open theists, God's existence as such may not depend on a creaturely world, but God's loving nature makes the creation of a world inevitable. God may not be metaphysically required to create, but he is morally bound to do so. If God is essentially loving, God must have a world to love and care for, and God has never been without one.

David Basinger addresses this topic in his description of open theism in *Models of God and Alternative Ultimate Realities*. Did God create out of freedom or necessity? Says Basinger, there is no simple answer. The concept of creation *ex nihilo* involves the idea that God alone is truly necessary and therefore not dependent on any coeternal or created reality, but this still leaves open the question of whether or not God is "necessarily creative." And for Basinger, the idea that God is by nature creative leads to the conclusion that God is "compelled to create 'something,'" sooner or later, but not that God was obligated to create this, or any other, particular world, or to create at any specific time. "At the very least," he concludes, "I think this to be an issue for legitimate debate among open theists."[32] And the fact is, the issue is debated, and open theists take strikingly different positions on it.

Among open theists who accept a "traditional" view of divine creation are John Sanders and William Hasker. According to Sanders, "God did not have to create. It is the divine wisdom in freedom that brings into existence something that is not God." Thus, "creation is contingent, not necessary."[33] God enjoys libertarian freedom, Hasker argues, so God might have decided to not create at all.[34] Because God exists throughout eternity as a threefold communion of love, God was not dependent on the existence of a creaturely world to find fulfillment.[35] And having

---

[32]Basinger, "Introduction to Open Theism," 274.
[33]John Sanders, *The God Who Risks: A Theology of Divine Providence*, 1st ed. (Downers Grove, IL: InterVarsity Press, 1998), 41.
[34]Hasker, *Triumph of God*, 90-91, 76.
[35]Hasker, *Triumph of God*, 97. And "since God's life is infinitely satisfying . . . the satisfaction cannot be increased by anything that might be added by a created order" (*Triumph of God*, 98).

decided to create, Hasker adds, God was free to decide what kind of world he wanted. There was no one "creatable world"—no best of all possible worlds—that he was obligated to bring into existence.[36]

It is my view as well that God could exist without the creatures, but he chooses not to, so the world owes its existence to God's free choice. Indeed, I believe, "unless the world owes its existence to God's free choice, divine love is a vacuous concept."[37] But the fact that creation was something God freely chose to do does not mean that his creative activity is "purely arbitrary or that creation is merely incidental to God's life or that the value of the world is negligible."[38] Instead of diminishing the value of the world to God, the concept of creation *ex nihilo* enhances its significance as the object of divine love.

Other open theists take a different tack. For Thomas Jay Oord and Michael Lodahl, God has always had a world, not because he is metaphysically dependent on a world, but because the existence of a creaturely world is necessary to the fulfillment of God's character.[39] Since God's essential character is one of *kenotic love*, God must have always had a world to love. Instead of *creatio ex nihilo*, therefore, they propose the concept of *creatio ex amore*.[40] Says Oord, "God does not create ex nihilo. . . . Because God's very nature is self-giving love, God is always creating and relating to, and loving creaturely others."[41] Since God has been everlastingly creative, he has never been without a creation. Although this particular world is not, strictly speaking, necessary, there must always have been some world or other if God is truly a God of love.

Kenotic love. Closely related to the idea that God has always had a world to love is Oord's specific—and among open theists, rather distinctive—view

---

[36]Hasker, *Triumph of God*, 138.

[37]Richard Rice, "Process Theism and the Open View of God: The Crucial Difference," in *Searching for an Adequate God: A Dialogue Between Process and Free Will Theists*, ed. John B. Cobb Jr. and Clark H. Pinnock (Grand Rapids: Eerdmans, 2000), 185.

[38]Richard Rice, "*Creatio ex Nihilo*: It's Not About Nothing," in *Theologies of Creation: Creatio ex Nihilo and Its New Rivals*, ed. Thomas Jay Oord (New York: Routledge, 2015), 95.

[39]Such a position might be regarded as a form of panentheism.

[40]See Thomas Jay Oord, "An Open Theology Doctrine of Creation and Solution to the Problem of Evil," in Oord, *Creation Made Free*, 28-52.

[41]Oord, "Open Theology Doctrine," 52.

of the only sort of relation that a truly loving God could have with the world. It is a relation in which God never exercises direct control over his creatures. Hence the title of his much-discussed book, *The Uncontrolling Love of God: An Open and Relational Account of Providence*.[42]

Central to Oord's proposal is the idea of *kenotic love*. The expression derives from the Greek word *kenosis*—a variation of the key word in the famous New Testament passage that speaks of Christ Jesus who, though in the form of God, "emptied himself, taking the form of a slave," humbled himself, and became obedient to the point of death on a cross (Phil 2:5-8).

Along with the idea that God has always had a world to love, therefore, Oord also insists that there is only one way in which an essentially loving God can act in the world, namely, by "self-giving, others-empowering love."[43] As Oord explains it, "essential kenosis" means that God's activity with this world is without exception "uncontrolling," that is to say, exclusively persuasive. Kenotic love means that God respects his creatures' integrity to such a degree that he never overrides their capacity for self-determination. As a result, nothing that happens in the world is ever due directly, exclusively to divine activity.

Oord sharpens the contours of his position by underscoring its differences from that of John Sanders, whose book *The God Who Risks*, he notes, is "a benchmark contribution to the theology of providence."[44] While warmly approving of Sanders's accounts of divine risk and dynamic omniscience, Oord faults Sanders for holding that God allows or permits evil he has the power to prevent. For Sanders, God created

---

[42]Thomas Jay Oord, *The Uncontrolling Love of God: An Open and Relational Account of Providence* (Downers Grove, IL: InterVarsity Press, 2015).

[43]Oord, *Uncontrolling Love of God*, 133, 159. Oord prefers this interpretation to either "self-emptying, self-withdrawing or voluntary self-limitation" (158). Others who endorse a "kenotic" view of God's relation to the world as a key to interpreting the creaturely suffering involved in the long history of evolution include Nancey Murphy, George F. R. Ellis, and John Haught. See Ellis and Murphy, *On the Moral Nature of the Universe: Cosmology, Theology, and Ethics* (Minneapolis: Fortress Press, 1996); and Haught, *God After Darwin: A Theology of Evolution* (Boulder, CO: Westview Press, 2000). For a discussion of their views, see Richard Rice, "Creation, Evolution, and Evil," in *Understanding Genesis: Contemporary Adventist Perspectives*, ed. Brian Bull, Fritz Guy, and Ervin Taylor (Riverside, CA: Adventist Today Foundation, 2006).

[44]Oord, *Uncontrolling Love of God*, 133.

beings who are genuinely free and exercises voluntary self-restraint out of respect for their freedom. Although it pains God to see his creatures suffer, he respects the creational structures he made and seldom intervenes to prevent it.[45]

To Oord, this account of suffering is unacceptable. If God has the power to veto specific evil acts, then he should prevent them and is morally culpable for not doing so: "The God who could prevent any genuine evil unilaterally is responsible for *allowing* genuine evil."[46] But Oord does not deny that God has the essential power to intervene, so what is it that prevents him from doing so? It is the fact that God's most fundamental characteristic is love, not power. God's loving nature forbids him to control the creatures, and this is why he cannot prevent evil from occurring.

The problem with Sanders's position, Oord argues, is putting power above love among God's attributes. For Sanders, God has the power to create various kinds of worlds, and chooses to create this world rather than one over which he exercised complete control. In contrast, says Oord, God's loving nature requires him to create the kind of world he did. He has no alternative. "If love comes first, God *cannot* exercise meticulous providence or determine everything." God's love "requires God to create a world with creatures he cannot control."[47]

For Oord, there is something else about God that accounts for the fact that he not only does not, but cannot, intervene to prevent specific events from happening in the physical world. And this is the fact that God is an omnipresent spirit rather than a localized body.[48] According to Oord, without the qualities of a physical body, God does not have the ability to intervene in the world in a physical way. Thus, God cannot stop rocks from falling or bullets from reaching their target.

Oord's view of God's relation to the world bears a number of similarities to that of process philosophy. For process thinkers, God is characterized by world-embracing love, uniformly involved in every aspect

---

[45]Sanders, *The God Who Risks: A Theology of Divine Providence,* 2nd ed. (Downers Grove, IL: IVP Academic, 2007), 241; cited in Oord, *Uncontrolling Love of God,* 140.

[46]Oord, *Uncontrolling Love of God,* 142.

[47]Oord, *Uncontrolling Love of God,* 144, 145.

[48]Oord, *Uncontrolling Love of God,* 179.

of reality through persuasive influence, and not directly, unilaterally responsible for any specific event. There is no place for miracles in such a perspective, that is, exceptional events that are due directly to divine agency. But at this point, Oord makes a striking departure from process thought. For in spite of his insistence that God never directly controls things, he accepts the biblical accounts of extraordinary events, or miracles, from the parting of the Red Sea to the bodily resurrection of Jesus.

Oord defines a miracle as "an unusual and good event that occurs through God's special action in relation to creation,"[49] and says, "Miracles are possible when God provides good and unusual forms of existence."[50] Even so, "miracles are neither coercive interventions nor the result of natural causes alone."[51] Such statements bring to mind the biblical accounts of healings that required the exercise of faith as one of their conditions. But Oord insists that "essential kenosis can make sense of genuine nature miracles."[52] "When random or spontaneous events occur and the conditions provide for it, God can act in special ways to offer forms and possibilities in relation to creation that result in miracles."[53]

Oord's willingness to grant the possibility of miracles while insisting on the uncontrolling nature of divine love raises questions. On the one hand, as he describes it, uncontrolling love seems to require that God be equally involved in every aspect of reality. On the other, he says that God is uniquely active in some events, which implies that he is less involved in others. And this raises the very question he poses to Sanders. If God acts in special and unusual ways at certain times, what prevents him from doing so at other times in order to prevent or alleviate suffering?

In his article "Why Oord's Essential Kenosis Model Fails to Solve the Problem of Evil While Retaining Miracles,"[54] Sanders faults a number of

---

[49]Oord, *Uncontrolling Love of God*, 196.
[50]Oord, *Uncontrolling Love of God*, 199.
[51]Oord, *Uncontrolling Love of God*, 200.
[52]Oord, *Uncontrolling Love of God*, 207.
[53]Oord, *Uncontrolling Love of God*, 209.
[54]John Sanders, "Why Oord's Essential Kenosis Model Fails to Solve the Problem of Evil While Retaining Miracles," *Wesleyan Theological Journal* 51, no. 2 (Fall 2016): 174-87.

things in Oord's proposal, including the deficiency referred to in the title. He grants that Oord's view of God's uncontrolling love effectively relieves God of responsibility for evil, but then goes on to note a number of problems with his formulations.

While Oord insists that love and control are incompatible—"love never controls," he says repeatedly—he nevertheless grants that love can be controlling at times, as when a parent puts a resisting child in her crib. And in spite of all his emphasis on love as essentially uncontrolling, it turns out that the real reason that God doesn't or can't intervene to prevent physical instances of suffering and evil turns out to be the fact that God is a spirit with no localized, physical body.[55] So, it turns out that there are two elements in Oord's theodicy: "God is essentially loving which rules out metaphysical control and God is incorporeal which excludes physical control."[56]

Sanders finds several problems with Oord's rejection of God's metaphysical control. For one, Oord does not show why metaphysical control is incompatible with the occasional exercise of physical control. Placing a toddler in a crib may be an example of physical coercion, but it hardly constitutes metaphysical control. The child is still free to object! So why if God did something similar would that constitute metaphysical control? Another is Oord's view that uncontrolling love requires God to love all entities equally, including cancer cells and genetic mutations. No favoritism allowed.[57]

But for Sanders the most important problem with Oord's position is his inability to provide a convincing account of miracles, given his rejection of anything resembling metaphysical divine control. He doesn't see how Oord can claim that essential kenosis relieves God of responsibility for evil and assert at the same time that God can author miracles. The prospect that God can exercise physical control on occasion, though not metaphysical control, makes his view vulnerable to the very objection he raises against open theists in general. Why doesn't God do it more often?[58]

---

[55]Sanders, "Why Oord's Essential Kenosis Model Fails," 179.
[56]Sanders, "Why Oord's Essential Kenosis Model Fails," 179.
[57]Sanders, "Why Oord's Essential Kenosis Model Fails," 180.
[58]Sanders, "Why Oord's Essential Kenosis Model Fails," 186.

Says Sanders, "Oord cannot have it both ways." To relieve God of any responsibility for evil and suffering he affirms God's uncontrolling love. God by virtue of his very nature does not have, or cannot exercise, the power to intervene in the course of natural, finite events. But in order to account for miracles, he suggests that God is indeed more directly involved in bringing about certain events than he is in others.

From my own perspective, Oord's proposal seems suspiciously close to a process view of God's relation to the world. Process thought envisions a close relationship, indeed an interdependent relationship, between God and world. It views ultimate reality as God-and-world, not God alone. It also envisions God as intimately related to the world, influencing and influenced by every aspect of reality, down to its ultimate, infinitesimal constituents, which are variously identified as "actual entities" and "actual occasions."[59] Consequently, it is appropriate to describe God's relation to the world in terms of love. God cares deeply for the whole of reality and for every single event that contributes to it. Yet, while God exercises an influence on the emergence of every actual entity, each one of them has a capacity for self-determination as well, and this means that God is not directly, or unilaterally, responsible for any specific event or development in the world.[60] In one sense, everything is an act of God in that God has a role in bringing it about. In another sense, nothing is an "act of God" in that God acts alone in bringing it about. Process thought represents a naturalistic metaphysics and a naturalistic theism. There are no interruptions in the regularities that apply throughout the universe, and God does not have the power to intervene in the natural course of things. God is therefore involved in all the world's events but unilaterally responsible for none of them.

It seems, then, that Oord has appropriated a process view of God, since the uncontrolling love he attributes to God aptly describes the God of process thought as well. However, Oord backs away from the process

---

[59]See Alfred North Whitehead, *Process and Reality* (New York: Macmillan, 1957).

[60]Charles Hartshorne puts it this way: "It is the existence of many decision makers that produces everything, whether good or ill" (*Omnipotence and Other Theological Mistakes* [Albany, NY: State University of New York Press, 1984], 18).

view that God is not uniquely involved in, or responsible for, any specific finite event. So, in spite of his insistence that divine love never controls, he still wants to attribute some important events in the biblical record to exceptional divine participation.

My reservations with Oord's proposal concern the limited applicability of the process model of love. The genius of process thought is its selection of features from human experience that are capable of unrestricted generality and can therefore serve as principles of unlimited applicability.[61] So, when process thinkers employ a concept such as love—which has great personal significance and many different facets on the human scale—to construct their metaphysics of the God-world relation, they extract certain aspects from it, ones that are applicable to all levels of reality, such as "care for the other's well-being," "respect for the other's integrity," and a "preference for persuasion rather than control."

To function as a metaphysical category, however, the content of "love" must be shorn of a good deal of its original interpersonal significance. But if we then take this "process distilled" version of love and reapply it to personal relationships, we run into problems. A good deal of the original interpersonal qualities of human love will be missing. As generally thought of, human relationships will exhibit all the features of love that apply to everything else, of course, but they involve a good deal more

---

[61] As Charles Hartshorne explains in his essay "Whitehead's Generalizing Power," Whitehead holds that "nature is intelligible if, and only if, the specific traits which emerge are special cases of more general principles which do not emerge but are found all the way down" (*Whitehead's Philosophy: Selected Essays, 1935–1970* [Lincoln, NE: University of Nebraska Press, 1972], 131). Yet, while ultimate metaphysical principles apply to all levels of reality, they are much more accessible to us on the higher levels, specifically, in our own experience, than on lower ones. So the key to identifying such principles is to find aspects of human experience that are capable of unrestricted generalization and are therefore applicable to all possible forms of individual existence. One such aspect is love. Love is obviously an important element of human experience and, when the distinctive features of its human manifestations are set aside, we can see that in other respects it applies to all reality, from the lowest levels of existence to the highest. As we know, love involves awareness of, responsiveness to, and concern for others. We see these in our own experience, we can discern them among other forms of life, and we can apply them with appropriate modifications to all levels of reality, including the highest. In fact, it is, only on the highest level of reality, viz., the divine, that we find them manifested literally, that is, without qualification. Thus, Hartshorne, citing Charles Wesley's expression, "pure unbounded love," asserts that "love, defined as social awareness, taken literally, is God" (*The Divine Relativity: A Social Conception of God* [New Haven, CT: Yale University Press, 1948], 36).

as well. In human relationships, there is certainly a place for "loving control," or "controlling love." As an expression of love, people sometimes do extraordinary things in hopes of achieving extraordinary results. In hazardous circumstances, people will sometimes place their lives in danger in order to save someone else's. And while loving parents will respect and encourage the capacity of children to make decisions, they will insist on occasion that their decisions must be accepted by their children, whether willingly or not.

In many respects, of course, God's love is not controlling in the sense Oord has in mind. Having set up the conditions under which the world functions, God lets the natural course of things play out. As finite creatures, we are dependent on the environment in which we live and we are inevitably affected by decisions and choices of others. As it turns out, we don't deserve all the bad things that may come to us, nor for that matter, a good deal of the goods we experience. And for open theists, as for Arminians in general, God does not exercise unilateral control when it comes to the ultimate destiny of individual humans. He does not determine the way humans respond to his love. But all this does not mean that God does not, and cannot, act directly or unilaterally at times in order to promote his objectives.

Just as there is more to parent-child relationships than mere persuasion, however important that may be, there is more to the biblical portrayal of divine love than mere persuasion. While God is the ultimate source and sustainer of all reality, and while God cares for every aspect of creation, as portrayed in the Bible God also acts in distinctive, sometimes exceptional, ways—sometimes in ways for which the word *control* is appropriate. I doubt, however, that these alternatives exhaust the options available to God. For open theism the possible ways in which God may choose to act within the world, and to interact with human beings, are much richer and far more subtle than either mere persuasion or dominating control.[62] Various biblical passages suggest that God exercises his

---

[62]A recent symposium volume presenting different approaches to the problem of evil includes "An Open Theist View," by William Hasker, and "An Essential Kenosis View," by Thomas Jay Oord (Chad Meister and James K. Dew Jr., ed., *God and the Problem of Evil: Five Views* [Downers Grove,

sovereign love in ways we cannot begin to imagine. One is the Apostle's use of these dramatic words halfway through the letter to the Ephesians: "Now to him who by the power at work within us is able to accomplish abundantly far more than all we can ask or imagine . . ." (Eph 3:20).

The diversity of views we have observed in the last two chapters demonstrates that there are a great many questions left open by the paradigm of divine openness. At the same time, they show that its basic vision of God's interactive relation to the world can provide a way for us to look at a number of time-honored issues from a new perspective.

IL: IVP Academic, 2017]). The fact that the two are presented as different positions strongly suggests that Oord's concept of God's love represents a departure from that of open theism in general.

PART II

THEMES OF OPEN THEISM

CHAPTER SIX

DOES OPEN THEISM LIMIT GOD?

ACCORDING TO F. SCOTT FITZGERALD, there are no second acts in American lives. Is the same true of open theism? Some observers wonder why open theists don't say more; others wonder if they have anything more to say. In 2008 Bruce McCormack described open theism as "pretty much what it was in its origins: a highly aggressive, missionary movement in theology which seeks to convert the evangelical churches to what it alleges to be a more 'biblical' understanding of God. Underneath it all," he continued, "open theism is a rather narrowly defined project . . . to a large degree, parasitic upon classical theism." In McCormack's view, the interests of openness theologians reduce to two things: "the will of God as it relates to free rational creatures and the question of what God knows and when he knows it." They make no attempt to offer "a fully integrated doctrine of God."[1] So, has open theism stalled, concluded, or is it just getting started?

If McCormack has a point, it may be due to the relentless criticism open theists encountered early on. With the change of tone among its observers and the extensive discussion of its ideas in various circles, open theism may now have reached a "postapologetic" phase of its development. There are also indications that others are interested in hearing

---

[1]Bruce L. McCormack, "The Actuality of God: Karl Barth in Conversation with Open Theism," in *Engaging the Doctrine of God*, ed. Bruce L. McCormack (Grand Rapids: Baker Academic, 2008), 189-90.

more from open theists. For Michael Zbaraschuk, process theologians have had a good deal to say about Christology, but "there are no specific treatments of Christ from any of the leading open and relational theologians."[2] He calls for open theists to "revisit their theological reflection, making Christ the center, rather than the periphery, of their ongoing thinking on these and other important theological issues."[3]

Open theism was attractive to its original proponents, not just because it was biblically faithful and religiously helpful, but also because they found it theologically profound. In *Most Moved Mover*, Clark H. Pinnock states almost wistfully that he wants to play offense, not defense, as an open theist, "because the open view of God offers the church such a treasure. It accentuates, not diminishes, how truly glorious God is."[4] And in more recent years a number of open theists have turned their attention from the subsiding complaints of their detractors to the constructive potential of their ideas.

Following the precedent of the 1994 publication, discussions of open theism have typically focused on the doctrine of God. But both critics and supporters note that its essential insights have ramifications for the Christian vision of things as a whole. And if open theism represents more than a corrective, however helpful, to certain positions within traditional Christian theology, these possibilities deserve further exploration. As I indicated earlier, my own view is that the openness of God can be viewed as a paradigm shift, a perspective that potentially puts a new light on the entire scope of Christian faith.

Our objective in this and the chapters that follow is to relate open theism to the central doctrines of Christian faith—God, humanity, salvation, church, and last things. We won't attempt a comprehensive treatment of any of the doctrines, nor, of course, anything like a theological system. But looking briefly at selected aspects of these doctrines from an open perspective may sharpen the contours of open theism and

---

[2]Michael Zbaraschuk, "Process Theology Resources for an Open and Relational Christology," in *Wesleyan Theological Journal* 44 (Fall 2009): 155.
[3]Zbaraschuk, "Process Theology Resources," 167.
[4]Clark Pinnock, *Most Moved Mover: A Theology of God's Openness* (Grand Rapids: Baker Academic, 2001), 18.

flesh out some of its implications. In previous chapters, we've taken notice of the views of various open theists. In what follows, the subjects discussed will be those of particular interest to me and the views expressed will largely be my own. So, as I stated in the introduction, I'll be speaking as an open theist, but not for open theists generally.

The order of topics in this section follows the standard sequence found in systematic theologies—from the doctrine of God to the doctrine of last things. In each case I have looked for particular ways in which the concerns of open theism impact or relate to that doctrine. The result is a series of discussions that are not tightly organized. I have found that the issues open theism raises vary from one doctrine to another, and it seemed more natural to address these questions specifically rather than pursue the same issue or follow the same organizational pattern in each case. This goes against my penchant as a systematic theologian to be, well, more systematic, but I think it will make for a more interesting discussion. The upshot, of course, is that a well-integrated theology from the perspective of open theism remains to be achieved.

At any rate, these are some of the questions that the following chapters address.

Doctrine of God. Open theism affirms that God interacts with the temporal world and that God's experience of the world itself is temporal. This raises an important question regarding God's essential nature. Does temporality describe only God's relations to the world, or does God's inner life comprise an ongoing series of experiences?

Doctrine of humanity. For open theists, an essential characteristic of human beings is libertarian freedom, the freedom "to do otherwise." Both modern science and traditional theology raise serious questions about the reality and the scope of freedom. What evidence is there that we are genuinely free? And what effects does sin have on our freedom?

Doctrine of salvation. For Christians in general, Jesus is the definitive expression of God's love in human history and is appropriately described as both human and divine. From the perspective of open theism, the question of Jesus' freedom, particularly in relation to his temptations, becomes important. Was Jesus' success in meeting the challenges that he faced a foregone conclusion, or was it a genuine achievement?

Doctrine of the church. The emphasis on human freedom characteristic of open theism potentially raises questions concerning the value and even the possibility of genuine Christian community. If we are individually responsible for our response to God, what purpose does Christian community serve? What is there about human nature that makes community desirable?

Doctrine of last things. For open theists, Christian hope includes the expectation of a future beyond this life in which God's purposes for creation reach their ultimate fulfillment. But there are different views regarding the nature of the life to come. Will the saved experience God's fellowship in a single, timeless moment or through an unending succession of experiences?

THE LIMITATIONS OF "LIMITS"

Before we can turn to these doctrinal reflections, however, another task awaits us. Unless we set aside a familiar way of characterizing open theism, it will be next to impossible to give the perspective it provides adequate attention. There is a pervasive tendency on the part of both supporters and critics to refer to open theism as presenting a "limited" view of God. The very idea of God as somehow limited—in fact, the very use of the word *limited* with reference to God—inevitably puts people off. Any mention of God as having limited power, or limited foreknowledge, invites just the sort of objections that have absorbed so much of the discussion. And the effect is to prevent people from looking at open theism from any other direction. Accordingly, I believe that open theists should avoid "limit" language altogether in describing their view of God and employ more positive terminology.

To clear the way for the discussion to follow, therefore, we need to show that there are good reasons to dispense with limit language when considering open theism and employ more positive terminology. For, far from limiting or diminishing God, open theists believe, a dynamic, interactive view of God's relation to the world actually enhances our picture of God. As they see it, the portrait that open theism provides is so rich and inspiring that by comparison it is the traditional view of God that appears limited and restrictive. But whenever open theism is under discussion, it seems, whether it is viewed favorably or unfavorably, some variation of the word *limit* almost always appears.

This is certainly true of open theism's critics. In "Does God Take Risks?," an essay in *God Under Fire*, James Spiegel's summary of the open view of providence includes the statement that "God's power is limited by human freedom."[5] In *What Does God Know and When Does He Know It?*, Calvinist theologian Millard Erickson characterizes open theism as endorsing "limited foreknowledge," rather than "the traditional view of exhaustive divine foreknowledge."[6] According to Barthian scholar Bruce L. McCormack, "limited divine foreknowledge" is foundational to open theism. Open theists abandon the ideas of divine timelessness and impassibility, he asserts, as a logical consequence of "limited divine foreknowledge and a mode of relating to the world that is characterized by affectivity and reciprocity."[7]

Less critical observers follow the same practice. Historian Gary Dorrien attributes to proponents of the openness of God "the classical Arminian position, in which God is viewed has having limited God's power in relation to the world in order to give God's creatures freedom to live and flourish within it."[8] In an online piece titled "God's Self-Limitation," Roger Olson, an Arminian theologian, says that the idea that God limits himself in creation as in incarnation is "an important presupposition of classical Arminian theology and of open theism." God's power is limited, Olson argues, because God chooses to limit it. Although God could exercise omnipotence, God elects not to "for the sake of having real, rather than imaginary, relations with human persons." Moreover,

---

[5]James S. Spiegel, "Does God Take Risks?," in *God Under Fire: Modern Scholarship Reinvents God*, ed. Douglas S. Huffman and Eric L. Johnson (Grand Rapids: Zondervan, 2002), 196.

[6]Millard J. Erickson, *What Does God Know and When Does He Know It? The Current Controversy over Divine Foreknowledge* (Grand Rapids: Zondervan, 2003), 256.

[7]McCormack, "The Actuality of God," 198.

[8]Gary Dorrien, *The Remaking of Evangelical Theology* (Louisville, KY: Westminster John Knox Press, 1998), 176.

only if God "limits his power in relation to creation" can God avoid responsibility for evil.[9]

Even those sympathetic to open theism employ the language of limits. Philip Clayton embraces a position he calls "open panentheism," which shares a number of features with open theism, including "creation *ex nihilo* and the free self-limitation of God."[10]

Clark Pinnock, one of the best-known proponents of open theism, used limit language in order to show the similarities between open theism and other theological positions. The openness model, he says, is "not alone in positing libertarian freedom or divine self-limitation of power to make room for the creature." The openness model, he also notes, "echoes many themes of the theology of hope, which recognizes a God who limits himself in creating a world which has the capacity to affect him."[11] Not surprisingly, the sixth edition of Pojman and Rea's *Philosophy of Religion: An Anthology* introduces a selection from Pinnock by describing open theism as "a view that stands in contrast to 'classical theism' and maintains that God is, among other things, temporal, subject to change and passion, and limited in his knowledge of the future."[12]

In summary, both critics and supporters employ limit language when describing the open view of God. Open theists hold that God created beings who enjoy genuine, or "radical," freedom and that God acquires knowledge of their decisions when and as they are actually made, but not before. In creating such a world, as they often phrase it, God limits both his power and knowledge. For its supporters, these characteristics constitute a self-limitation on God's part: God expresses kenotic love by voluntarily restricting the range of his power and knowledge. For its critics, these aspects of open theism impose unacceptable restrictions on God. Calvinists reject the notion that either God's power or knowledge

---

[9]Roger E. Olson, "God's Self-Limitation," *Society of Evangelical Arminians* (blog), September 9, 2010, http://evangelicalarminians.org/gods-self-limitation/.

[10]Philip Clayton, *Adventures in the Spirit: God, World, Divine Action* (Minneapolis: Fortress Press, 2008), 210.

[11]Pinnock, *Most Moved Mover*, 12.

[12]Louis Pojman and Michael Rea, eds., *Philosophy of Religion: An Anthology*, 6th ed. (Boston: Wadsworth, 2012), 22.

is limited. Traditional Arminians accept a limited view of divine power, but they reject the notion that God's knowledge is limited. Like Calvinists, they affirm exhaustive divine foreknowledge.

The use of limit language when describing God is both unnecessary and misleading. Open theists can make their points effectively without invoking the notion of limits. More important, the use of such language inevitably obscures the positive features of the divine reality open theism seeks to emphasize. Here are five reasons why we should eliminate limit language entirely when considering the open view of God.

1. The connotations of "limit" language. First of all, the very word *limit* carries negative connotations. To describe something as "limited" suggests that it is inferior to, or less than, it could be. When applied to God, the word *limits* or *limited* conjures up a God who is restricted, hampered, in what he can do and know, a God who is decidedly inferior to the more robust alternatives that most Christians embrace. If we think of God along traditional lines as "the greatest conceivable being," the very notion of a "limited God" will seem oxymoronic. When open theists use limit language for their view of God, therefore, when they describe God's power and knowledge as limited, they invite the criticism that open theism suffers in comparison to the view that God has unlimited power and absolute foreknowledge. It is little wonder that classical theists find their view of God superior.

When critics of open theism and when open theists themselves describe the open view of God in terms of limits they imply, intentionally in the one case, no doubt unintentionally in the other, that the God of open theism is somehow less than, or diminished in comparison with, the God of traditional theism.

2. The logic of omniscience. Turning to more substantive reasons to reject limit language, we come to the most widespread objection to open theism, namely, its view of divine foreknowledge. One of the most prevalent descriptions of open theism may also be the least accurate: the idea that it limits God's knowledge, or holds to the concept of "limited foreknowledge."

The question of divine foreknowledge has perplexed Arminians from the time of Arminius himself. Arminius departed from Calvinism with his affirmation of human freedom, but he had no coherent alternative to the Calvinist account of divine foreknowledge. According to Calvin, God knows the future infallibly because he determines it exhaustively. Nothing happens outside God's eternal decrees, God's perfect plan. Since God "foresees future events only by reason of the fact that he decreed that they take place," "it is clear that all things take place . . . by [God's] determination and bidding."[13] Like Calvin, Arminius affirms God's absolute foreknowledge, but unlike Calvin, he has no way to account for it. "The knowledge of God," he states, "is eternal, immutable and infinite, and . . . extends to all things, both necessary and contingent. . . . But I do not understand the mode in which [God] knows future contingencies, and especially those which belong to the free-will of creatures."[14] Arminius rejected divine determinism but affirmed exhaustive divine foreknowledge. But if humans enjoy libertarian freedom, freedom to do otherwise, how could God know their decisions in advance? Arminius admitted that he didn't know.

Arminius's problem has perplexed Arminians ever since. How can God infallibly foresee the content of future free decisions? And, while this is not the place to review them, none of the proposed attempts to affirm coherently both free will and absolute divine foreknowledge has proved satisfying.[15] One is the familiar view that God stands outside time, so past, present, and future are all alike to him. Another is middle knowledge, or Molinism, according to which God knows not only all actualities and all possibilities, he also knows "conditional future contingent events." That is to say, he knows everything each individual *would* do in all conceivable circumstances. And because God has decided to create a particular world, or actualize a particular set of circumstances, he knows all the future decisions of the beings it contains. And a third

---

[13]John Calvin, *Institutes of the Christian Religion*, ed. John T. McNeill, trans. Ford Lewis Battles, 2 vols. (Philadelphia: The Westminster Press, 1960), 3.23.6 (pp. 954-55).

[14]*The Works of James Arminius*, trans. James Nichols and William Nichols, 3 vols. (Grand Rapids: Baker Book House, 1986), 3:64-66.

[15]See Richard Rice, "Divine Foreknowledge and Free Will Theism," in *The Grace of God, the Will of Man: A Case for Arminianism*, ed. Clark H. Pinnock (Grand Rapids: Zondervan Academic, 1989), 121-39.

response is simply to deny that the question of divine foreknowledge and human freedom really requires an answer. If my knowledge of past events doesn't cause them, why should God's knowledge of future events mean that they are somehow caused, or inevitable?

For open theists, the best response to the problem of freedom and foreknowledge is not to solve it, but to dissolve it, to show that there is no such problem. If future free decisions do not become real, or do not exist, until they occur, there is no need to explain how God could know them, because prior to their occurrence there is nothing there to know. And to those who maintain that this constitutes an unacceptable truncation of divine knowledge, open theists respond that omniscience, perfect knowledge, includes every possible object of knowledge. So, the question is not the scope, let alone the excellence of divine knowledge, but the status of future free decisions. If they are "knowable," then God knows them, period. But if they are not "there to know" until they occur, it implies no deficiency in God's knowledge to say that it does not include them.

For open theists, the logic of omniscience is parallel to that of omnipotence. Most theologians who attribute omnipotence to God—from Thomas Aquinas to C. S. Lewis—define it, not as the ability to do anything, period (fill in the blank with anything you please) but as the ability to do things that fall within the range of logical possibility. This avoids attributing nonsense to God, along the lines of drawing square circles, creating married bachelors, or making two and two equal five. According to the generally accepted view of omnipotence, God cannot do such things—not because he lacks the power to do so—but because these expressions do not refer to anything "do-able." They are logical absurdities.

If it makes good sense to define omnipotence in terms of logical possibility, it makes good sense to define omniscience the same way. Omnipotence does not include what is logically undoable; omniscience does not include what is logically unknowable. To quote John Sanders, "If omnipotence, following Aquinas, is defined as the ability to do all that is logically possible, and if this is not an attenuated understanding of divine power, then why should omniscience, defined as knowing all that is logically possible to know, be an attenuated view of divine knowledge?"[16] It is misleading, then, to describe open theism as endorsing a concept of limited foreknowledge, let alone as resting on it. On the open view of God, there is nothing limited about God's knowledge. His knowledge is perfect; it includes all there is to know.

3. The logic of decision. Another reason to avoid limit language to describe open theism is the fact that it denotes nothing distinctive about open theism. There is an important sense in which the notion of limits applies just as well to other views of God, including the Calvinist view.

Open theists believe that God had a choice when it came to creation. God could have created a world in which God determines everything that happens. But open theists believe that God also had the option of creating a world in which (at least some of) the creatures would make choices of their own, undetermined by God. In other words, God could create a world in which there are creatures who enjoy libertarian freedom and whose choices are not foreknown to God.[17] In the one world, God decides everything. In the other, both God and the creatures make decisions. If both worlds are possible, then which of them actually exists depends on God's sovereign choice. As John Sanders puts it, "God is the sovereign determiner of the sort of sovereignty he will exercise. God is free to sovereignly decide not to determine everything that happens in history."[18]

It is also important to note that the choice between these options is genuine only if the two worlds are significantly different. A significant choice presupposes genuine alternatives, and real alternatives involve different consequences. After all, not all goods are "compossible," or simultaneously realizable. In choosing between these options, therefore,

---

[16]John Sanders, *The God Who Risks: A Theology of Divine Providence*, 2nd ed. (Downers Grove, IL: InterVarsity Press, 2007), 208.

[17]For Molinists, as we noted in a previous chapter, future free decisions are known to God because he has decided to create this particular world and knows everything that will ever happen in it (see Thomas V. Morris, *Our Idea of God: An Introduction to Philosophical Theology* [Downers Grove, IL: InterVarsity Press, 1991], 95-96). So there is a sense in which God brings it about that creatures make the free decisions they do. For others, including open theists, this is inherently contradictory.

[18]Sanders, *The God Who Risks*, 174.

God embraces the values available in one world but not the other. Either way, God's decision involves a "limitation" of sorts. The values in a divinely determined world are not available in a world where the creatures are free to make undetermined choices. By the same token, the values available in a world where the creatures have the freedom to make such choices would not be available in a world where God's decisions, or decrees, apply to everything that happens. The question that divides Calvinists (and other divine determinists) from open theists is, Which of these two worlds did God create? But either way, limitations are involved.

An interesting question is whether the world of open theism represents a genuine possibility. Could God, if God chose, create a world containing creatures whose decisions become known only when they make them? If the answer is no, then we have identified something that God lacks the ability to do. And unless such a world is as logically contradictory as a square circle—a flat-out logical impossibility—God's inability to create it represents a significant "limitation" to God's power.

On the other hand, if the answer is yes, that is, if God indeed has the power to create a world with an open future—a future unknown to God—then the question that separates open theism from other views of God is not, What sort of power does God have?, or What sort of world *could* God create? The real question that divides them is this: What sort of world *did* God create? And why *would* God create this particular world rather than the other?

4. The subtlety of divine power. A further reason for open theists to avoid limit language concerns the nature of divine power. According to open theism, God endows the creatures with the capacity to exercise freedom, to make choices, to contribute to the ongoing course of events. As it is sometimes put, God shares God's power with the creatures, or makes room in his life for their experience. And this is often expressed as a self-limitation on God's part: he gives up a certain part of his power, so the creatures can have a measure of their own.

There are several problems with this construal of divine and creaturely power. For one thing, it presupposes a zero-sum distribution of power in the world, according to which there is only so much power to go around.

Consequently, God can only grant the creatures power by giving up some of his own. And the more power God lets the creatures have, the less power he keeps for himself. But why should we think of power this way? We don't think of God as limiting his happiness or his love, for example, by creating beings who are capable of these qualities. What compels us to think of power this way?

Then there is the way in which God manifests power in a world where other agents too have power. There are good reasons to think that such a world involves a greater display of divine power than one in which God determines everything. First of all, such a world may express God's nature more fully and adequately than one in which God decides everything unilaterally. It requires a greater manifestation of power, or a higher kind of power, for God to accomplish his purposes in a world where the creatures' choices are genuinely their own than in a world where God's creative decision includes all that happens. In an open reality, a world whose future is not foreknown, God manifests divine power by pursuing his objectives in response to the decisions of the creatures. Their decisions are truly theirs, but God creatively responds to their choices in ways that serve his purposes.

Joseph's betrayal at the hands of his brothers provides a helpful illustration of this phenomenon. When they begged Joseph to forgive their "crime," he replied in a way that acknowledged both the evil that they had done, *and* the beneficial use that God made of their actions. "Even though you intended to do harm to me, God intended it for good, in order to preserve a numerous people, as he is doing today" (Gen 50:20).

Then too there is the important distinction between exerting power over others, and empowering others to exert themselves. Instead of a limitation of power, it may represent a manifestation of power, indeed, a manifestation that deserves, if anything, greater admiration. Consider, for example, the shift of emphasis in contemporary philosophy of education from teaching to learning. According to this revisionary approach, the instructor's role is not to impart information to his or her intellectual subordinates, but to inspire and enable—empower—students to make their own discoveries, to acquire information and insights for themselves.

As many teachers have found, it can be more challenging to devise learning experience for students than to display one's own knowledge of a subject. It's harder to generate a fruitful discussion than to give a lecture.

In a similar way, it conceivably entails a higher form of power for God to empower his creatures to act and to inspire them to cooperate with him than for God to achieve his objectives unilaterally. If so, it seems inappropriate to describe open theism as limiting God's power. Far from limiting God's power, the creation of a world that contains beings who are genuinely free uniquely expresses it.

5. The richness of divine experience. A final reason for avoiding limit language involves a concern that is more important to open theists than either God's knowledge or God's power, and that is the richness of divine experience. To some extent this emphasis was obscured when my original book entitled *The Openness of God* was republished under the title *God's Foreknowledge and Man's Free Will.*[19] The revised title suggests that the book's principal concern was to provide yet another discussion of a well-known, and well-worn, problem in philosophical theology. What is really at stake in open theism is much more sweeping, however. Open theism seeks to recapture the biblical portrait of a God who is intimately acquainted with, acutely sensitive to, profoundly affected by, and dynamically interactive with the creatures who bear the divine image.

The various aspects of this portrait to which open theists appeal are well-known. They include a broad sweep of biblical passages in which God is described as variously experiencing joy and delight, disappointment and regret, as learning from events in the world, such as the actions of God's people, and as "repenting," that is, as changing God's mind, or altering God's plans, in response to the decisions and actions of human beings, as well as in response to their direct petitions to him. Terence Fretheim succinctly summarized the Old Testament evidence for an interactive view of God under the headings, "The Divine Perhaps," "The Divine If," "The Divine Consultation," and "The

---

[19]Richard Rice, *The Openness of God* (Washington, DC: Review and Herald Publishing Association, 1980); Rice, *God's Foreknowledge and Man's Free Will* (Minneapolis: Bethany House Publishers, 1985).

Divine Question."[20] The one feature of open theism that even its critics seem to appreciate is its emphasis on the personal qualities embedded in the biblical descriptions of God. And the growing interest in the topic of divine suffering in recent decades indicates that a number of theologians appreciate one of open theism's principal concerns.[21]

The essential thesis of open theism is that this portrait of God has abundant biblical support, is eminently defensible philosophically, and provides a rich resource for personal religion. In other words, it nicely meets all the essential criteria of theological adequacy.

Far from limiting God, then, open theism provides a rich and vivid portrait of God's relation to the creaturely world. The concept that God dynamically interacts with creation attributes to God a range of positive experiences that traditional views of divine power and knowledge exclude. With an open future, God is capable of surprise, delight, the momentary appreciation of the creatures' experiences as they happen in all their concrete detail. In comparison, it is the traditional view of God's relation to the world that is limited. It excludes from the divine reality some of the most important features of personal existence.

There are those who appreciate the emphasis that open theism places on God's momentary sensitivity to the experiences of God's creatures and seek to combine this feature with the traditional view of divine fore-knowledge. The fact that God knows ahead of time that something will take place, they argue, does not prevent God from experiencing it in a more concrete way when it actually happens. "Just because God knows in advance that some event will occur, this does not preclude God from experiencing appropriate emotions and expressing appropriate reactions when it actually occurs."[22]

Unfortunately for those who seek such a rapprochement between the biblical emphasis on momentary divine sensitivity and the traditional

---

[20]See Steven C. Roy, *How Much Does God Foreknow? A Comprehensive Biblical Study* (Downers Grove, IL: InterVarsity Press, 2006), 125n1.

[21]See, for example, Terence E. Fretheim, *The Suffering of God: An Old Testament Perspective* (Fortress Press, 1984), and William C. Placher, *Narratives of a Vulnerable God: Christ, Theology, and Scripture* (Louisville, KY: Westminster John Knox Press, 1994).

[22]Bruce Ware, quoted in Roy, *How Much Does God Foreknow?*, 175.

view of foreknowledge, the latter renders it incoherent. The traditional view of divine foreknowledge collapses any distinction between antici-pation and realization. According to the classical view, God's knowledge of the future is exhaustive: God knows the entire future, the future in all its detail. If so, then God not only knows exactly what will occur, God also knows every aspect of his own response to what will occur, and to know that, in effect, is to have the experience already. If God foreknows all, then God's experience already includes all. Actual occurrences contribute nothing new.

CONCLUSION

In short, there are good reasons for open theists to eliminate limit lan-guage from our descriptions of the open view of God. Such language suggests that the open theism is deficient in comparison to the tradi-tional alternatives; it lacks something that they affirm. And in doing so, it obscures the positive value of the perspective and makes answering critics and solving problems the major agenda that open theism faces. Instead, I propose a different tack. Open theism is attractive not pri-marily because it is defensible but because it so nicely expresses the bib-lical portrait of God, because it is theologically profound and religiously meaningful. To quote Clark Pinnock once again, he values open theism because it "accentuates, not diminishes, how truly glorious God is."[23]

I would like Pinnock's aspiration to set the tone for the following chapters. Our objective in each is not to defend open theism from its critics, nor to answer all the questions it raises, but to explore the rich possibilities it provides for understanding the various facets of Christian faith. A full-fledged theology from the perspective of open theism has yet to be written, and this isn't it, but a cursory exploration of its potential may strengthen the hope that that objective will eventually be realized.

I should also emphasize that these are the reflections of one open theist, not a definitive account of open theism as such. Open theism is a per-spective, not a system, and those who find its central insights helpful have

---

[23]Pinnock, *Most Moved Mover*, 18.

pursued them in different directions, and they will no doubt continue to do so. My hope is that the following reflections will illustrate the potential of open theism to stimulate Christian thought across a wide range of issues and invite further discussion. Theologians are always in search of ways to express Christian faith that are biblically faithful, logically attractive, and personally helpful. For many of us, the open view of God provides a valuable resource in this endeavor.

CHAPTER SEVEN

OPEN THEISM AND THE TRINITY

THE VARIOUS FACETS OF CHRISTIAN FAITH are so closely connected that any attempt to provide an organized account of them faces serious challenges. As John Calvin notes in the opening words of his *Institutes of the Christian Religion*, "Nearly all the wisdom we possess, that is to say, true and sound wisdom, consists of two parts: the knowledge of God and of ourselves. But while joined together by many bonds, which one precedes and brings forth the other is not easy to discern."[1]

THE TRINITY AND RELATIONALITY

And if it is hard to distinguish between the knowledge of God and of ourselves, the same is certainly true when it comes to different aspects of the doctrine of God itself. Every statement we make about God seems to presuppose others. Take, for example, Karl Rahner's famous pronouncement—Rahner's Rule, it is often called—the "economic" Trinity is the "immanent" Trinity, and the "immanent" Trinity is the "economic" Trinity.[2] It indicates that an account of God's activity in the world provides a portrait of God's own identity, and conversely, that an understanding of God's inner nature is the key to understanding God's relation to the world. The two are so closely connected that it is impossible to contemplate either without touching on the other.

---

[1]John Calvin, *Institutes of the Christian Religion*, ed. John T. McNeill, trans. Ford Lewis Battles, 2 vols. (Philadelphia: Westminster Press, 1960), 1.1.1 (p. 35).
[2]Karl Rahner, *The Trinity*, trans. Joseph Donceel (New York: Herder and Herder, 1970), 22.

As we have seen, the central focus of open theism is God's relation to the world.[3] It views creation as God's ongoing project, rather than a finished product, or as God's adventure, rather than his invention. Its emphasis is on God's dynamic interaction with creation. Most of the questions that the open view of God generates concern the inferences its proponents draw from this interaction for God's own experience. Since the world God created is dynamic, open theists reason, God's experience of the world is dynamic as well. And this conclusion, as we have seen repeatedly, is what distinguishes open theism from more traditional views of God.

In this chapter, I would like to take things a step further and explore the implications of open theism for God's own identity. We have explored at some length open theism's view of God's relation to the world. Our concern now is the view of God that lies behind it. Or, to use Rahner's terminology, what view of the immanent trinity corresponds to a dynamic view of the economic trinity?

In response to the question *What kind of world did God create?*, open theists conceive the world as depending entirely on God for its origin and its continued existence. It is a world characterized by relationality and temporality, and because it's a world that matters to God, God's experience includes all that happens in the world, as it happens, moment by moment. Closely connected to this view of God's relation to the world lies open theism's answer to the question, *What kind of God created the world?* Though God is utterly distinct from the world, and though the world owes its existence entirely to God's creative and sustaining power, the relationality and temporality characteristic of the world are reflections of God's own reality. And properly understood, these are among the qualities that find expression in doctrine of the Trinity. While the doctrine of the Trinity has been central to the Christian view of God ever since its development in the fourth and fifth centuries, just what it means and how important it is have always raised questions. Over the centuries, its popularity among theologies has waxed and waned. And even those who

---

[3]Note the subtitle of John Sanders's book, *The God Who Risks: A Theology of Divine Providence*, 2nd ed. (Downers Grove, IL: InterVarsity Academic, 2007).

accept the doctrine are sometimes tepid in their support. In Emil Brunner's judgment, for example, the doctrine "did not form part of the early Christian—New Testament—message, nor has it ever been a central article of faith in the religious life of the Christian church as a whole, at any period in its history." Consequently, "the ecclesiastical doctrine of the trinity is not a biblical kerygma, not the kerygma of the church, but . . . a theological doctrine which defends the central faith of the Bible and of the Church."[4] In other words, the doctrine may serve an apologetic purpose, but it does not belong to the heart and soul of Christian faith.

From the latter part of the twentieth century on, however, there has been a flourishing—some would say an explosion—of interest in the Trinity.[5] Though recent discussions are far too numerous and complex for us to review here, some of them have important implications for an open view of God.

First of all, the Trinity is a portrait of God that arises from salvation history. Nearly all the major problems in the history of trinitarian thought result when people abstract from this history and treat God as an independent object of speculation.[6] At the same time, God's saving actions are a display of God's very being, a manifestation of God's inner reality. According to Karl Barth, for example, God "is amongst us in humility, our God, God for us, as that which He is in Himself, in the most inward depth of His Godhead. . . . In the condescension in which He gives Himself to us in Jesus Christ He exists and speaks and acts as the One He was from all eternity and will be to all eternity."[7] Similarly, the connection Rahner makes between the "economic" and the "immanent" Trinity affirms that the revelation of God in salvation history is a genuine

---

[4]Emil Brunner, *The Christian Doctrine of God*, trans. Olive Wyon (Philadelphia: Westminster Press, 1941), 205, 206.

[5]So many studies have accumulated that there are now books discussing all the books on the topic. See, for example, John Thompson, *Modern Trinitarian Perspectives* (New York: Oxford University Press, 1994).

[6]Catherine Mowry LaCugna emphasizes this point: "the quest for knowledge of God or of God's *ousia* 'in itself' or 'by itself' is doomed to fail"(*God for Us: The Trinity and Christian Life* [New York: HarperCollins, 1991], 193).

[7]Karl Barth, *Church Dogmatics*, trans. Geoffrey Bromily and Thomas Torrance (T. & T. Clark, 1956), IV/1, 193.

self-revelation, a portrayal of what God is really like. We can know who, or what, God is by looking at God's activity in the world. To quote Catherine LaCugna, "The very nature of God who is self-communicating love is expressed in what God does in the events of redemptive history. There is no hidden God . . . behind the God of revelation history, no possibility that God is in God's eternal mystery other than what God reveals Godself to be."[8]

Moreover, God's revelation in the history of salvation is a genuine self-*giving*. God's true self, God's innermost reality, comes to expression in God's dealings with creation. Consequently, God's saving actions are central to our understanding of God's identity. In creating and saving a world, he commits himself to the world in such a way that his own destiny, and his own identity, are forever linked to that of his creatures. Like generals who acquired titles from their battlefield triumphs, God's very name derives from his saving activity. For Christians, the way the Trinity *names* God—as Father, Son and Spirit—identifies God with reference to the definitive moments in salvation history, the mission of the Son and the sending of the Spirit.[9]

Now, if salvation history is a revelation of God's inner reality, we must think of God in a way that is consistent with what we find in this history. And since the qualities of sensitivity, care, commitment, self-giving, and

---

[8]LaCugna, *God for Us*, 322. Cf. the assertion of Robert W. Jenson: "Each of the inner-trinitarian relations is then an affirmation that as God works creatively among us, so he is in himself" (*The Triune Identity: God According to the Gospel* [Philadelphia: Fortress, 1982], 107).

[9]Jenson explores at length the significance of the designation *Father, Son, and Spirit* as a "naming-formula" for God. The expression is "appropriate to name the gospel's God because the phrase immediately summarizes the primal Christian interpretation of God" (*The Triune Identity*, 18). Other theologians are equally insistent that the Trinity is a name, and the reality it names is not merely one among several versions of "theism." Says Stanley Hauerwas, "I do not believe that the trinitarian Father, Son, and Holy Spirit is an image. Rather Trinity is a name. Christians do not believe that we first come to know something called God and only then further learn to identify God as Trinity. Rather, the only God Christians have come to know is Trinity: Father, Son, and Holy Spirit" (*Wilderness Wanderings: Probing Twentieth-Century Theology and Philosophy* [Boulder, CO: Westview, 1997], 29). In a similar vein, L. Gregory Jones asserts, "Christians are not concerned primarily with theism (i.e., the notion that there is a general object of ultimate concern, a divinity); we are concerned, rather, to narrate the doctrine of God's Trinity. The Christian affirmation of the Trinity is not a notion 'added to' a theistic affirmation; it *is* the primary affirmation about the God Christians worship" (*Embodying Forgiveness: A Theological Analysis* [Grand Rapids: Eerdmans, 1995], 84).

self-sacrifice are prominent in salvation history, as the cross supremely testified, these are the qualities that characterize God's essential reality. Accordingly, we attribute complexity to the inner life of God. God is not sheer, undifferentiated unity. God is a dynamic, living reality. Indeed, as process thought insists, God is relational. The expressions *Father, Son,* and *Spirit* point to relations that constitute God's being. We cannot go beyond the relations of Father, Son, and Spirit to a divine essence that precedes them, because there is no such essence. The relations constitute the being of God.[10]

THE TRINITY AND TEMPORALITY

Along with relationality, the doctrine of the Trinity also applies temporality to the inner being of God. In Keith Ward's words, it stresses "the creative, relational, and unitive involvement of God in the temporal structure of the created universe" and "the importance of that temporal structure to the self-expression of the divine being."[11] Robert Jenson is more emphatic: "The three derive from God's reality in time, from time's past/present/future. . . . The relations are either *temporal* relations or empty verbiage."[12]

The doctrine of the Trinity shows that the contingent world has profound significance for God. As Wolfhart Pannenberg argues, God's decision to create is entirely free, but having chosen to create, God commits himself so profoundly to the world that his very existence is bound up

---

[10]As Clark Pinnock says, "God's nature is that of a communion of three Persons who exist in mutual relations with one another. Each is distinct from the others, but each is what it is in relation to the others. God exists in a dynamic of love, an economy of giving and receiving" (*Flame of Love: A Theology of the Holy Spirit* [Downers Grove, IL: InterVarsity Press, 1996], 30). Or, to quote LaCugna once again, "The point of the doctrine of the Trinity is that God's *ousia* exists only in persons who are toward another, with another, through another" (LaCugna, *God for Us,* 193). Elizabeth A. Johnson makes the same point: "Trinitarian communion itself is primordial, not something to be added after the one God is described, for there is no God who is not relational through and through. . . . For God as God, divine nature is fundamentally relational" (*She Who Is: The Mystery of God in Feminist Theological Discourse* [New York: Crossroad, 1994], 227, 228).

[11]Keith Ward, *Religion and Creation* (Oxford: Oxford University Press, 1996), 345.

[12]Jenson, *The Triune Identity,* 125-26. Cf. the title of Ted Peters's study, *God as Trinity: Relationality and Temporality in Divine Life* (Louisville, KY: Westminster John Knox, 1993). This paragraph and a portion of the previous section were previously published by the author as "Process Theism and the Open View of God: The Crucial Difference" in *Searching for an Adequate God,* ed. John B. Cobb Jr. and Clark H. Pinnock, 198-98. (Grand Rapids: Eerdmans, 2000).

with what he has made.[13] The Son brings into existence a creation distinct from God out of his own eternal self-distinction from the Father.[14] And through the Spirit the Son brings the creatures into his own fellowship with the Father.[15] The goal of creation is thus "the participation of creatures in the trinitarian fellowship of the Son with the Father."[16] Thus, God willingly links his own destiny to the destiny of the world, and henceforth the future of the world becomes part of God's own future.

Trinitarian theism attributes the world's existence to the freedom of divine love. God is under no compulsion to create; he chooses to create. And having chosen to create, God commits himself unconditionally and sacrificially to the world he loves. He devotes himself to its welfare, expresses his innermost life in his care for it, and finds joy and fulfillment in bringing it into intimate fellowship with him. On this account, the world has intradivine significance. God brings the world into existence in an act of love and generosity, and he embraces the world within his own life. Everything that happens in the world makes a real difference to God.

Among the many recent reflections on the Trinity, I find those of Robert W. Jenson particularly interesting.[17] As he sees it, the Trinity is not only important to a Christian understanding of God, it is the very essence of that understanding.[18] He develops his position in careful conversation with early trinitarian thought, and it will be helpful for us

---

[13]Pannenberg, *Systematic Theology*, trans. Geoffrey W. Bromiley, 3 vols. (Grand Rapids: Eerdmans, 1991–1998), 1:447.

[14]Pannenberg, *Systematic Theology*, 2:63; cf. 30, 58.

[15]Pannenberg, *Systematic Theology*, 2:32.

[16]Pannenberg, *Systematic Theology*, 2:75.

[17]The doctrine of the Trinity has generated serious discussion among open theists. For an extensive development of the topic from an open theist's perspective, see William Hasker, *Metaphysics and the Tripersonal God*, Oxford Studies in Analytical Theology (Oxford: Oxford University Press, 2013). According to Hasker, an advocate of social trinitarianism, "The Trinity is not a single person, but the closest possible union and communion of the three divine persons. Yet in virtue of the closeness of their union, the Trinity is at times referred to *as if* it were a single person" (258). For the views of an open theist who objects to social trinitarianism, see Dale Tuggy, "Divine Deception, Identity and Social Trinitarianism," *Religious Studies* 40 (2004): 269-287.

[18]Jenson develops his views on the Trinity primarily in two major projects, *The Triune Identity* and the two volumes of his *Systematic Theology* (New York: Oxford, 1997–1999), which are respectively titled *The Triune God* and *The Works of God*.

to follow his thinking for a bit. Jenson accepts the familiar observation that the Christian religion emerged from the encounter between biblical religion and the thought-world of late antiquity. But instead of fusing the gospel with Greek culture, he argues, early Christian thinkers deliberately refused to do so, and the doctrine of the Trinity is the fruit of their efforts. Consequently, the doctrine of the Trinity is not the product of Hellenic influence, it is the product of resisting Hellenic influence.[19]

As Jenson describes it, the critical difference between Christianity and Hellenism involved divergent views of God and time. At its heart, Greek religion was a quest for something that could resist the flow of time, for an aspect of reality impervious to change.[20] The gods' one defining characteristic was therefore immortality, immunity to destruction, and the true object of Greek religion was timelessness as such. (Think of Zeus conquering Chronos.) Biblical thought could not have been more different. The Greeks insisted that divinity wasn't involved in time; the Hebrews insisted that it was. And instead of conceiving of eternity as abstraction from time, they viewed God's eternity as faithfulness through time.[21]

The Greek vision of things had a profound effect on early Christology. Christians who made the Hellenistic assumption that the divine is impervious to time were left with an enormous gap between God and the world, and this space is where they located Christ. As they envisioned it, Christ's role is to mediate between the timeless, immutable God and the temporal, transitory world. Since he stands midway between the two, however, Christ must be subordinate to God and less than fully divine. Eusebius argued that we need descending images "because God's involvement in

---

[19]Cf. *The Triune Identity*, 34. Material in the remainder of this chapter is adapted by permission from Springer Nature Customer Service Centre GmbH: Springer Nature, *Philosophia* 35, no. 3. Richard Rice, "Trinity, Temporality, and Open Theism," January 1, 2007.

[20]According to Thomas Cahill's readable account, for Greeks and Romans "only that which *is* forever is truly intelligible and worthy of contemplation. The idea is what is interesting; the individual is beside the point." In contrast, for Jews and Christians, "There was no eternal cosmos circling round and round. Time is real, not cyclical; it does not repeat itself but proceeds forward inexorably, which makes each moment . . . precious" (*Sailing the Wine-Dark Sea: Why the Greeks Matter* [New York: Doubleday, 203], 259).

[21]Jenson, *The Triune Identity*, 59, 58.

the world of time, including the history of salvation, is contrary to proper deity." Consequently, the Son, the Logos, is inferior to God, an originated being, though nevertheless "God of a sort."[22] Arius, too, was motivated by the late Hellenistic need to escape time. Because he accepted Origen's concept that God is unoriginated and devoid of internal differentiation, Arius concluded that "the Son is not unoriginated, nor is he in any part of the Unoriginated." Accordingly, "there was once when he [the Logos] was not." And because Christ is involved with time he cannot really be God. The Logos may be God for *us*, but it cannot be God in himself.[23]

If trinitarian reflection began with the mistaken view that God is timeless and the Logos must be inferior to God, the mature doctrine developed as a rejection of these ideas. Its objective was to affirm both Christ's full divinity and God's intimate connection with temporal, creaturely reality. As expressed by Athanasius and confirmed by the Council of Nicaea, God is inherently relational. The Father-Son relation is internal to God's being. And since God is God precisely in his relatedness, it is the Trinity as such, not the Father alone, who is God. Later in the fourth century, the Cappadocian fathers solidified God's relationality by eliminating subordinationism. As Jenson describes it, they took the "hypostases" and "distinctions" Origen had used to connect God to time vertically, and they placed them horizontally within the divine reality. In this way Father and Son could be one God without ranking them ontologically.[24]

More of this would take us too deeply into the intricacies of trinitarian reflection than we can afford to go here, but the central point is clear. God is inherently relational. The expression "Father, Son, and Holy Spirit" names the one God and identifies him as having deity in a complex and interactive way.[25] Furthermore, the implications of this concept of God for our salvation are profound. For as God is thus conceived, there is no distance between him and us that needs to be overcome. "Each of the

---

[22]Jenson, *The Triune Identity*, 79.
[23]Jenson, *The Triune Identity*, 81-82.
[24]Jenson, *The Triune Identity*, 89-90.
[25]Jenson, *The Triune Identity*, 112.

Trinitarian relations is an affirmation that as God works creatively among us, so he is in himself."[26]

Furthermore, there is a "tensed" quality to the divine relations. Salvation history comprises the manifestations of a divine reality, all of which is involved in each great act. Unlike the Greek view that God's self-identity is immune to all outside influence, leaving him changeless and impassible, the Trinity imputes change, dynamism to God.[27]

According to Jenson, virtually all of the insights of the Eastern fathers were lost when the Trinity came to the West. Confused by their terminology, Western theologians employed what they thought were Latin equivalents (but weren't) in a way that not only obscured but distorted the Cappadocians' intent. And they set Western thought on a course that renders the Trinity at best incomprehensible and at worst a distortion of the biblical portrait of God.

As Jenson describes it, the central culprit in this story was Augustine, who attributed to God the very characteristics of Greek ontology that the Cappadocians sought to overcome. They wanted to show that God is inherently related to his temporal creation; Augustine wanted to show what God is in himself, apart from creation. For the Cappadocians, God is complex: it is precisely the togetherness of the identities that constitutes God. But for Augustine, God is simple; each identity possesses an abstract divine essence in exactly the same way, so the distinctions among them are lost.[28] According to Jenson, the Nicenes called the Trinity God *because* of the triune relations and differences; Augustine calls the Trinity God *in spite of* them.[29]

With these moves, Augustine severed the Trinity from its anchor in salvation history and cast it adrift on a sea of philosophical speculation. When you think of God, Augustine maintains, you think "a greatest and highest substance that transcends all changeable creatures. . . . And so if I ask, 'Is God changeable or unchangeable?'" you will quickly respond . . . ,

---

[26]Jenson, *The Triune Identity*, 107.
[27]Jenson, *The Triune Identity*, 112.
[28]Jenson, *The Triune Identity*, 119-20.
[29]Jenson, *The Triune Identity*, 118.

'God is changeless.'" Here is the essential distinction between creatures and God: "speak of the changes of things, and you find 'was' and 'will be'; think God, and you find 'is' where 'was' and 'will be' cannot enter." God not only does not change, he cannot; just so, "he is rightly said *to be*." God, in other words, is being itself, "he who is."[30] Thus conceived, God is timeless and impassible, untouched and untouchable by the temporal world.[31]

But let us return to Jenson's central point. Only salvation history gives meaning to the trinitarian language of persons and relations. And if the mighty acts of God are constitutive of divine reality, we must conceive of God as inherently and essentially temporal. With this, the entire sweep of philosophical theism that insists on divine simplicity, impassibility, and timelessness gives way. Because the name *Father, Son, and Holy Spirit* derives its meaning from God's reality in time, the relations that constitute God are "either *temporal* relations or empty verbiage."[32]

As we noted, Jenson is just one in a growing chorus of theologians who make this point. Another is Wolfhart Pannenberg, according to whom God's actions in salvation history reveal that God's inner reality consists of "concrete life relations."[33] And for him, as for Jenson, the Trinity is not derived from God's essence, the Trinity *is* God's essence. Consequently, we never get behind the Trinity to something more basic or original. If

---

[30] Jenson, *The Triune Identity*, 117-18.

[31] Augustine's trinitarian meditations were a magnificent mistake, of course. For in his attempt to describe the inner life of the divine, Augustine discovered the inner life of the person and thus began the long journey of introspection that produced our Western concept of the individual. As far as human consciousness is concerned, we are still benefiting from his insights. The emergence of the self in Western thought, as well as its subsequent demise, has attracted a great deal of scholarly attention. See, for example, Charles Taylor's magisterial account, *Sources of the Self: The Making of the Modern Identity* (Cambridge, MA: Harvard University Press, 1989). A number of works deal with various aspects of the modern and/or postmodern self, including Adam B. Seligman, *Modernity's Wager: Authority, the Self, and Transcendence* (Princeton, NJ: Princeton University Press, 2000) and Calvin O. Schrag, *The Self After Postmodernity* (New Haven, CT: Yale University Press, 1997). An influential sociological study of the self in contemporary America is Robert Bellah et al., *Habits of the Heart: Individualism and Commitment in American Life* (Berkeley: University of California Press, 1985). In *The Social God and the Relational Self: A Trinitarian Theology of the Imago Dei* (Louisville, KY: Westminster John Knox, 2001), Stanley J. Grenz provides an account of the self's long history and proposes a revisionary interpretation of the self that draws on the recent emphases in trinitarian thought on personness and community (55-56).

[32] Jenson, *The Triune Identity*, 125-26 (emphasis his).

[33] Pannenberg, *Systematic Theology*, 1:335, 323.

God is truly love, there are relations in the very depths of God's being. God's fundamental reality is Father, Son and Spirit.[34]

For both Jenson and Pannenberg, then, complexity, relationship, and temporality are intrinsic to the divine life. The acts of God in the history of salvation are more than a record of what God does, they are a portrait of what God is.

In spite of their affirmations that God is deeply related to the temporal world, and that his relations to the world express God's very nature, both theologians also make statements that deny divine temporality. "For God to create," says Jenson, "is for him to *make accommodation* in his triune life for other persons and things. . . . In himself, he *opens room*, and that act is the event of creation. We call this accommodation in the triune life 'time.'"[35] Divine temporality is not essential to God; it is a result of his creative activity. Time, he says, is "the room God makes in his eternity for others than himself."[36] Evidently, then, temporality is a characteristic of creation, but not of God himself.

We find a similar discrepancy in Wolfhart Pannenberg's formulations. Like Jenson, Pannenberg affirms God's relation to history as the key to understanding the divine reality, and, again like Jenson, he affirms the principle that the immanent Trinity is identical to the economic Trinity. But then he proceeds to deny God's temporality. The divine life, he says, is characterized by an "eternal simultaneity."[37] Whereas creatures are "subject to the march of time," "All things are always present to [God]."[38] God exists in "an undivided present."[39]

To be faithful to the biblical portrait of God, we will view the mighty acts of God as revelatory of the divine reality—the basis of the doctrine

---

[34]Although God's identity finds expression in his relation to the world, for Jenson God's identity does not depend on the world. God in himself, he asserts, could have been the same God he is had there been no creation, and no trinitarian history (*The Triune Identity*, 139). Indeed, God could have been triune in some other way, even though we cannot imagine how (141).

[35]"Created time is accommodation in God's eternity for other than God" (Pannenberg, *Systematic Theology*, 2:25).

[36]Pannenberg, *Systematic Theology*, 46.

[37]Pannenberg, *Systematic Theology*, 3:607.

[38]Pannenberg, *Systematic Theology*, 1:410.

[39]Pannenberg, *Systematic Theology*, 3:630.

of the Trinity. But to do this, we must go beyond Jenson and Pannenberg. They affirm that God is related to the temporal sphere, and then go on to speak of God as overcoming time or as incorporating all of time in a single moment. In effect, it denies divine temporality to envision time as a sphere that God includes or surrounds, or draw a sharp line between "created time" and "triune time."[40]

If God's mighty acts are the key to God's identity, then God's temporality must involve something more than connecting to a sphere of reality that is other than God. Indeed, if God is temporal in the way that the doctrine of the Trinity requires, God's own reality must consist of an ongoing series of experiences.[41] In other words, God experiences events as they happen, not all at once.

As we have seen, many object to the idea of divine temporality on the grounds that it reduces God to the level of the creatures. It collapses the difference between God and the world. Instead of isolating God from the world, as the Greeks did, it seems to immerse him in it and turn him into another version of ourselves.

The assumption here, typical of Greek thought, is that temporal passage represents loss and is therefore unworthy of divinity. If God changed with time, then God would lose value, becoming less than he was before. On the other hand, if God grew over time, then God would always be less than he could be. Either account conflicts with the idea of divine perfection—the concept, as Anselm put it, of "a being than which nothing greater can be conceived."[42] Perfection and change seem to be contradictory. What is perfect is complete and fixed. The challenge,

---

[40]Jenson, *Systematic Theology*, 2:345.

[41]This point requires extensive development, which space prevents us from providing here. For a classic discussion of the issues, see Nelson Pike, *God and Timelessness* (London: Routledge, 1970; reprint Eugene, OR: Wipf and Stock, 2002). For a more recent discussion, see Greg Ganssle and David Woodruff, eds., *God and Time* (New York: Oxford, 2001). William Lane Craig argues for the tensed theory of time endorsed here in "Omniscience, Tensed Facts, and Divine Eternity," *Faith and Philosophy* 17, no. 2 (April 2000): 225-41. Richard E. Creel also deals with a wide range of issues connected to the theme of divine eternity in *Divine Impassibility: An Essay in Philosophical Theology* (New York: Cambridge, 1986). Creel argues, confusingly, that God's knowledge of the actual world changes but that God is nevertheless changeless, not only in his nature, but in his will and his feeling as well (204-6).

[42]Anselm, *Proslogium*, chapter 2 (*St. Anselm: Basic Writings*, trans. S. N. Deane, 2nd ed. [LaSalle, IL: Open Court Publishing Company, 1962], 7).

then, is to think of divine temporality in a way that preserves God's generic excellence.

On this point, the views of open theists concur with those of process thinkers. In an essay titled "The Temporality of God,"[43] Schubert M. Ogden develops an understanding of divine temporality by carefully analyzing human temporality.[44] Careful reflection reveals that human existence exhibits a twofold character. Each human individual embodies, or incarnates, certain characteristics that provide identity over time. These include characteristics that are common to all human beings, along with distinctive physical features and unique qualities of personality and character. In addition, each concrete moment of life presents a person with stimuli he or she incorporates into a new synthesis of experience. So human existence consists of a number of features that are relatively enduring, *and* a sequence of momentary experiences that include or embody these features.

By analogy, the being of God exhibits a similar dipolarity. It consists of an ongoing sequence of discrete experiences, each of which includes the various qualities unique to the divine reality. God is "an experiencing self who anticipates the future and remembers the past and whose successive occasions of present experience are themselves temporal occurrences."[45] God's life, like all life, consists in a series of momentary experiences. And the best way to express this is not to say "God is in time," but to say "Time is real for God."

As we have seen, for many the notion of divine temporality compromises God's majesty. Since time and eternity are radically opposed, the only way to safeguard God's status as the object of ultimate human

---

[43]Schubert M. Ogden, "The Temporality of God," in *The Reality of God and Other Essays* (New York: Harper & Row, 1966), 144-63. In this essay Ogden provides a succinct account of the process view of God and time, which receives its definitive expression in the writings of Alfred North Whitehead (particularly *Process and Reality: An Essay in Cosmology* [New York: Macmillan, 1929]) and Charles Hartshorne (*Creative Synthesis and Philosophic Method* [Chicago: Open Court, 1970]; *The Divine Relativity: A Social Conception of God* [New Haven, CT: Yale University Press, 1948]; *Reality as Social Process: Studies in Metaphysics and Religion* [New York: Free Press, 1953]).

[44]Since our own reality is the best entrée we have to reality as such, human existence gives us an answer to "the ultimate philosophical question of the meaning of being itself" (Ogden, *The Reality of God*, 148).

[45]Ogden, *The Reality of God*, 152.

devotion is to think of God as impervious to time. But we don't need to deny God's temporality in order to preserve God's generic excellence. We can preserve God's categorical uniqueness by saying, not that God is atemporal, but that God is supremely temporal.[46] Unlike God, creatures are not only temporal, they are temporary. Their experience begins and ends. But God's experience is "everlasting." The sequence of events that constitute his life is without beginning or end.[47] We might say that God's experience, and God's alone, is "eternally temporal."

God is also distinguished from all creaturely reality by the fact his experience is utterly comprehensive. God responds to everything that exists; each momentary experience encompasses the entire contents of the world. In Ogden's words, "God's distinctiveness [is] not an utter negation of temporality but its supreme exemplification. God's eternity is not sheer timelessness, but an infinite fullness of time."[48] God's experience is thus the perfect and complete register of all that happens in the world. In contrast to the unmoved mover of Aristotelian thought, the Bible presents us with a portrait of God as the "most moved mover,"[49] as one who is more sensitive to what happens in the world than anyone or anything else could be.

Ogden's insistence on the sequential nature of God's experience provides a helpful corrective to Jenson's denial that temporality has inner trinitarian significance. But there is an important respect in which Jenson's trinitarian view of God corrects a deficiency in Ogden's dipolar theism. For Ogden, as for process theism in general, the ultimate metaphysical fact is God-and-world, not just God. Without a world of beings

---

[46]Ogden, *The Reality of God*, 157.

[47]"In the case of God," Ogden argues, "what is distinctive is the complete absence of . . . temporal finitude and limitation. . . . God's temporality is not itself temporally determined, so that there is neither a time when God was not yet nor a time when he shall be no more. . . . God's being has neither begun nor will it end, and the past and future to which he is related in each successive occasion of his present experience can be nothing less than a literally limitless past and future" (Ogden, *The Reality of God*, 154).

[48]"In their truly primal forms, temporality and relations structure are constitutive of being itself, and God's uniqueness is to be construed not simply by denying them, but by conceiving them in their infinite mode through the negation of their limitation as we experience them in ourselves" (Ogden, *The Reality of God*, 154).

[49]Cf. Clark H. Pinnock's *Most Moved Mover: A Theology of God's Openness* (Grand Rapids: Baker, 2001).

other than himself to experience, God would have no reality. In other words, God needs the world as much as the world needs God. But this conflicts with the historic affirmations of faith that God alone is supreme, that his existence alone is necessary, and that God creates out of perfect freedom, not out of some sort of necessity.[50]

With his dramatic portrayal of God's inner life as one of complexity, dynamism, and drama, Jenson shows that God is relational not only by virtue of his connection with the world, God is relational in himself. God is not only capable of relationality, God consists of relationality. For this reason, we need not think of God in or by himself as anomalous, or as "lonely." The trinitarian life is filled with experience, unimaginable to us in its richness, complexity, and love. Consequently, creation does not meet a deficiency in the divine reality. To the contrary, it is the overflow of divine love. It freely expresses God's inherent fullness; it extends the inner vitality of God's own life.[51]

To summarize, the doctrine of the Trinity expresses the fundamental conviction that the mighty acts of God in salvation history reveal God's essential reality. And to be faithful to this portrait we must conceive of God's experience as a sequence that has no beginning and no end. In other words, time is real for a God who acts.

---

[50]Ogden's thought differs from that of open theists in another way as well. According to his "re-presentational" view of divine activity, God is not more directly involved in one event than any other, which implies that virtually any event can be construed as an act of God (see Ogden, *Christ Without Myth: A Study Based on the Theology of Rudolf Bultmann* [New York: Harper & Row, 1961]). This may explain why the doctrine of the Trinity has a negligible role to play in his theology.

[51]For further development of the idea that God expresses his innermost life in creation but does not depend on the world for his existence, see my essay "Process Theism and the Open View of God," in *Searching for an Adequate God: A Dialogue Between Process and Free Will Theists*, ed. John B. Cobb Jr. and Clark H. Pinnock (Grand Rapids: Eerdmans, 2000), 199.

CHAPTER EIGHT

HUMAN FREEDOM AND THE OPENNESS OF GOD

AS MANY OF THE CONTROVERSIES SURROUNDING open theism indicate, particularly with respect to divine foreknowledge, the open view of God is closely connected to a libertarian concept of human freedom.[1] As an expression of the love that defines his very being, open theists maintain, God created human beings with the capacity to respond with love to God's love for them. And since love cannot be coerced, the decision to return or reject God's love was theirs to make and remained indefinite until they did so. Along with the freedom to respond to God, open theism also envisions human beings having the freedom to participate in the creative project that God began. To flesh out these ideas we need to look at several topics, including the different forms freedom takes, and the effects on freedom brought about by sin. But we will start with some of the forceful challenges to the very notion of human freedom.

SCIENCE AND FREEDOM

Today questions of freedom are often framed by the results of scientific investigation, and the more science tells us about the physical basis of

---

[1]Brian Gerrish notes the similarity between process theology and open theism in their respective views of freedom. "Process theologians insist that free will is inconceivable without contingency. The future cannot be ineluctably predetermined: in creating humans, God creates cocreators—self-creating creatures. This conclusion agrees with so-called open theism, which argues on biblical grounds, without the appeal to Whiteheadian metaphysics, that the future is 'open' even to God. Since the future does not exist, it makes no sense to suppose that it is known by anyone, including God" (B. A. Gerrish, *Christian Faith: Dogmatics in Outline* [Louisville, KY: Westminster John Knox Press, 2015], 73).

human behavior, including mental activity, the more pressing these questions become. According to one geneticist, the "specter of genetic determinism" is "probably the source of more public concern than any other question about human nature."[2] It certainly has religious scholars concerned. For church historian Martin Marty, "The most urgent agenda item on the religion-and-science front," is not cosmology or evolution, but "scientific understandings of the brain, consciousness, will. . . . Reduce humans to the chemistry of neuron firings in the brain, and you have crossed a new line. The human is then 'nothing but' this or that."[3]

For some people, the scientific study of human behavior provides a clear answer to the question of freedom, and the answer is no. Paul and Patricia Churchland, for example, are advocates of "eliminative materialism." From what neuroscience has already shown us, they maintain, we can be confident that it will eventually demonstrate that there is no such thing as the conventional notion of self, soul, or person.[4] Along with now-discarded concepts like phlogiston and crystalline spheres, the concept of the self is destined for elimination. The time is coming when no one will believe in such a thing.[5]

Daniel Dennett takes another path to the same conclusion. To be consistent, he argues, those who accept evolution as an explanation for the development of life on this planet should also accept the idea that every aspect of human life has a material explanation. "Darwin's dangerous idea" is a "universal solvent," and there is no "cut off" point where evolutionary accounts end and human qualities and characteristics begin. The factors that account for every other aspect of life's history—descent with modification by means of natural selection—can account for all the features of human life, including thought, decision, and action. Darwinism thus dissolves "the illusion of our own authorship, our own

---

[2]V. Elving Anderson, "A Genetic View of Human Nature," in *Whatever Happened to the Soul*, ed. Warren S. Brown, Nancey Murphy, and H. Newton Malony (Minneapolis: Fortress Press, 1998), 68.
[3]Martin Marty, "Against Reductionism," *Sightings*, April 23, 2007.
[4]Paul M. Churchland, *Matter and Consciousness*, rev. ed. (Cambridge, MA: MIT Press, 1988), 43.
[5]Churchland, *Matter and Consciousness*, 44.

divine spark of creativity and understanding."[6] Consequently, "we [must] turn our backs on compelling ideas that have been central to the philosophical tradition for centuries . . . [including] Descartes's *res cogitans* [thinking substance] as a causer outside the mechanistic world."[7]

Everything about us, including consciousness and free will, is ultimately attributable to the process of physical transformation that Darwin described. There is no feature of human life that cannot be accounted for by the incremental advance of complex *physical* phenomena. Not only are we not significantly free, there is no "we" as we conventionally think of ourselves.

Whatever the evidence that supports determinism, something in us deeply resists it. Eliminate freedom, we cannot help but feel, and something essential to our humanity goes with it. As Gary Watson puts it, "The problem of free will is . . . the problem of finding room in the world for ourselves." It is part of the "general difficulty in bringing together our views of ourselves both as moral beings and as creatures of nature."[8] The challenge that neurophysiological reductionism presents to us, then, is whether we can account for contrasting features both of which seem essential to human experience—the fact that we are physical beings in a physical world *and* the conviction that we are free and self-determined.

Materialistic, reductionistic views of the self not only arouse existential resistance, they also contradict the deep-seated religious conviction that human beings are unique among earth's inhabitants. From the perspective of Christianity, human beings belong to the natural order, but the characteristics that distinguish them from other forms of life are not only differences in degree but differences in kind; they confer special abilities and special dignity. As creatures in the image of God, humans reflect the personal qualities of God's own self; they reflect, decide, and act, and bear responsibility for their decisions and actions.

---

[6]Daniel C. Dennett, *Darwin's Dangerous Idea: Evolution and the Meanings of Life* (New York: Simon & Schuster, 1995), 63.

[7]Dennett, "In Darwin's Wake, Where Am I?" *Proceedings and Addresses of the American Philosophical Association* 75, no. 2 (November 2001): 23.

[8]Gary Watson, "Free Agency," in *Free Will*, ed. Gary Watson (New York: Oxford University Press, 1982), 14.

There are different ways to account for human uniqueness. For centuries, the "default" explanation[9] has been dualism—the idea that the true seat of human identity is something nonphysical, an immaterial "mind" or "soul" that somehow connects with the physical body, but is not dependent on it. There is a long history of philosophical reflection on the soul thus conceived and how it relates to the body. Dualism comes in Platonic, Thomistic, and Cartesian varieties. And the idea has some influential contemporary defenders, including Richard Swinburne and J. P. Moreland.[10] But in recent years, the idea has become less and less acceptable to many Christians.

One reason is the lack of Bible support for the concept of an immaterial soul that supervenes on or exists independently of the body. The biblical words for "soul" apply to the human person as a whole, a totality, not to some immaterial substance that is connected to the body during our lives and departs when we die. In the famous words of H. Wheeler Robinson, "The Hebrew idea of the personality is an animated body, not an incarnated soul."[11] More recent studies corroborate Robinson's view. In *Body, Soul, and Human Life: The Nature of Humanity in the Bible*, Joel B. Green draws his investigation to a close with the observation that "our identity is formed and found in self-conscious *relationality* with its neural correlates and embodied *narrativity* or formative histories. . . . Who we are, our personhood, is inextricably bound up in our physicality." And death is "the cessation of one's body, . . . the conclusion of bodily life, the severance of all relationships, and the fading of personal narrative. . . . This means that, at death, the person *really dies*. . . . There is no part of us, no aspect of our personhood, that survives death."[12]

Green's study of human nature is particularly interesting because it combines a careful analysis of biblical anthropology with a close look at

---

[9]I am indebted to Sigve Tonstad for this expression.

[10]Richard Swinburne, *The Evolution of the Soul* (Oxford: Oxford University Press, 1986), 145-60, and J. P. Moreland and Scott B. Rae, *Body and Soul: Human Nature and the Crisis in Ethics* (Downers Grove, IL: InterVarsity Press, 2000).

[11]Quoted in John A. T. Robinson, *The Body: A Study in Pauline Theology* (Philadelphia: Westminster, 1952), 14.

[12]Joel B. Green, *Body, Soul, and Human Life: The Nature of Humanity in the Bible* (Grand Rapids: Baker Academic, 2008), 179.

contemporary neuroscience. And the more contemporary neuroscience discovers about the mind, the more apparent it is that mind and body—that mind and brain, to be specific—are inextricably connected. Thanks in large measure to their study of brain damage and degeneration victims, scientists have determined that psychological capacities are directly associated with particular locations in the brain. Depending on which area of the brain is involved, "very specific losses in the victim's psychological capacities typically result." They may lose the ability to perceive colors, to recognize faces, comprehend speech, or lay down new memories.[13]

On the more positive side, "specific types of cognition—perceptions, memories, emotions—do correlate with specific state changes in specific brain regions."[14] Studies of the prefrontal cortex through the use of electrodes and PET scanning show that specific areas of the brain are stimulated when certain mental activities occur. And the study of corticospinal excitability by means of focal, single-pulse transcranial magnetic stimulation applied to the scalp indicates that various moods, the presence of sad or happy thoughts, are related to different hemispheres of the brain.[15] The list goes on, but the conclusion is clear. The human mind, with all its capacities, is inextricably connected to the brain.[16]

Those who agree that human life is inextricably physical yet accept the Christian affirmation of human uniqueness must look for an alternative to reductionistic materialism. And in recent years a number of scholars have taken a position they identify as "nonreductive physicalism." They agree that we are *fully* material: there is nothing about us that is not involved in the physical world. But they insist that we are not *merely* material: there is more to human existence than physical processes alone.

---

[13]Churchland, *Matter and Consciousness*, 143.

[14]Philip Clayton, "Neuroscience, the Person, and God: An Emergentist Account" in *Neuroscience and the Person: Scientific Perspectives on Divine Action*, ed. Robert John Russell, Nancey Murphy, Theo C. Meyering, and Michael A. Arbib (Vatican City: Vatican Observatory Publications, 2002), 189.

[15]As Philip Clayton puts it, "There is no point in hiding one's head in the sands of a prescientific age that denied the dependence of the mental on the physical" ("Neuroscience, the Person, and God," 184).

[16]Clayton, "Neuroscience, the Person, and God," 189.

Even though the distinctive features of human cognition are connected to the physical, they are somehow distinguishable from them.

From this perspective, biology and neuroscience, while indispensable to our knowledge of the human, do not explain everything about us. When a brain exhibits the level of neurological complexity found in humans, these scholars argue, it supports a distinctive type of mental behavior. New qualities develop. Through self-awareness and self-transcendence a human being becomes self-directing, or free, in ways that reductionism cannot adequately account for. Among the scholars who have contributed to this perspective, Nancey Murphy and Philip Clayton are especially well-known. Central to their account of human uniqueness are concepts like supervenience, emergence, and downward causation.

As Murphy describes it, reductionism implies that there is only one sort of causation, namely, bottom-up causation. The behavior of wholes can be explained entirely by the behavior of their parts, and every feature of an organism can be attributed to lower level factors. A careful analysis of the distinctive qualities of human mentality, however, does not support this explanation. Although there is nothing in human experience that does not depend on more simple forms of life, complex wholes exhibit qualities that cannot be explained by the laws that govern the behavior of their parts.[17] Consequently, bottom-up causation will not suffice; we need top-down causation too.

In spite of the fact that our cognitive activities have a neural basis, then, the laws of neurobiology do not account for all our activities. Our complex neural mechanism makes it possible for us to objectify ourselves and our behavior in light of certain standards or expectations, and to adjust our behavior in response. But since these higher-level evaluative processes alter neural structure, these abstract goals become "causal factors in their own right."[18] There is thus a dimension of human existence that is inextricably connected to our physical components, but cannot be reduced to them.

---

[17]Nancey Murphy, *Bodies and Souls, or Spirited Bodies?* (Cambridge: Cambridge University Press, 2006), 77.

[18]Murphy, *Bodies and Souls*, 102.

For Philip Clayton, the essential idea of "strong emergence," as he phrases it, is that the brain is basic to all mental life, and neurological complexities make possible complex mental experience. Equally important, however, certain aspects of our experience are "irreducibly mental." They lie "beyond the reach" of neuroscientific accounts.[19] Moreover, there is a two-way interaction between the physical and the mental. Mental phenomena not only depend on physical phenomena, mental experience alters the behavior and structure of the brain. The "causal line" moves from physical inputs to the mental level, then along the line of mental causation, with one thought influencing another, and down again to make new records and synaptic connections within the brain. So there is only one physical system—the mind is not a spiritual substance outside it—but higher-level phenomena exercise a causal influence on the system as a whole.[20]

For nonreductionists like Murphy and Clayton, then, human mental behavior exhibits qualities that neuroscientific explanations alone could never account for.[21] We may share physical, social, and emotional characteristics with other forms of life on this planet. And we may be embodied in physical forms as they are, dependent on the external and internal physical resources that make life on any level possible. But our complex mental activities make us unique among all living things and distinguish our minds from our bodies, inseparable though they are. And these features provide a basis for affirming the person, or the self, as a reality with its own integrity as well as unique responsibilities and dignity. They support the notion that we ourselves, not our bodies, brains, or neurons, are the authors of our actions.[22]

---

[19]Philip Clayton, "Neuroscience, the Person, and God: An Emergentist Account" in *Neuroscience and the Person: Scientific Perspectives on Divine Action*, ed. Robert John Russell, Nancey Murphy, Theo C. Meyering, Michael A. Arbib (Vatican City: Vatican Observatory Publications, 2002), 188.

[20]Clayton, "Neuroscience, the Person, and God," 196.

[21]Despite their general agreement, there are differences between these two nonreductionists. Unlike Murphy, who regards the finite order as "a fundamentally physical order," Clayton maintains that it is "not a purely physical universe." Because it is "the site of the emergence of Spirit," the finite order has "genuinely spiritual properties" ("Shaping the Field of Theology and Science: A Critique of Nancey Murphy" [*Zygon*, vol. 34, no. 4 (December 1999), 615]).

[22]Murphy, *Bodies and Souls*, 109.

PHILOSOPHY AND FREEDOM

Besides the discoveries of neuroscience, evidence of a philosophical nature also supports an affirmation of human uniqueness. Suppose we make a basic philosophical move and think about thinking, or reflect on the activity of reflection. In fact, let's reflect on the work we just reviewed by both reductionists and nonreductionists on human mental life. It seems clear that participants on both sides share the assumption that the human mind has the ability to arrive at knowledge. Otherwise, what point would there be in conducting research, drawing conclusions, and formulating arguments? The very claim to know something affirms one's capacity to know, and this obviously entails the existence of the knowing self. Whenever a person examines evidence and draws conclusions, she implicitly affirms herself as the agent who does so, even if she insists that there is no such thing as agency!

This self-referential argument appears in what is known as "transcendental philosophy."[23] Transcendental philosophers explore the foundations of knowledge as such, and their particular focus is "the thinker's own act of knowing."[24] When we review the operations in which the human mind engages, as Bernard Lonergan argues, from sensing and perceiving, through inquiring and understanding, to reflecting and affirming, we find that all of them involve the "self-affirmation of the knower."[25]

If I ask if I am a knower, "the fact of the asking and the possibility of the answering are themselves the sufficient reason for the affirmative answer."[26] Self-affirmation, then, is not a conclusion from prior premises, but a recognition of what is already at work in the concrete activities of

---

[23]According to a dictionary definition, transcendental philosophy examines "the a priori conditions of knowledge, which precede all experience of objects and which are the primary constituents of all objects of knowledge and hence make knowledge possible (Hans Michael Baumgartner, "Transcendental Philosophy," in *Encyclopedia of Theology: The Concise Sacramentum Mundi*, ed. Karl Rahner [New York: Seabury, 1975)], 1743).

[24]Baumgartner, "Transcendental Philosophy," 1745.

[25]Bernard J. F. Lonergan, *Insight: A Study of Human Understanding* (New York: Philosophical Library Inc., 1970), 319. Lonergan, one of the most influential thinkers of the last century, is often referred to as a "transcendental Thomist."

[26]Lonergan, *Insight*, 319.

knowing.[27] And it has the quality of necessity. Any claim to know something therefore unavoidably affirms the existence of the self as knower. The talking skeptic is mired in contradiction.[28] "If reductionism were true," as Nancey Murphy exclaims, "no rational person could accept it because there would be no rational persons!"[29]

THEOLOGY AND FREEDOM

Finding evidence for personal freedom is important for open theism, but equally important is an understanding of just what it is that makes freedom so important. If open theism is essentially about God, someone may ask, why do open theists attach such significance to a particular perspective of humanity? Doesn't it detract from the glory of God to place such emphasis on human freedom, and to insist that a certain concept of human freedom is indispensable, namely, libertarian freedom? One who thinks so is James K. A. Smith. In a thoughtful article that appeared around the time open theists were facing severe criticism, Smith downplays the importance of human freedom. In fact, he argues that the concept of freedom open theists espouse ultimately fails to recognize the supremacy and centrality of God in the biblical view of things.

As Smith describes it, the basic problem with open theism is its concept of libertarian freedom. Such freedom is, yes, "freedom to do otherwise," the standard definition of libertarian freedom. But he goes on. Libertarian freedom is also freedom "from external constraints," freedom "to be autonomous and self-determining." In other words, freedom to go one's own way rather than follow God's way. On this

---

[27]Cf. David Tracy, *The Achievement of Bernard Lonergan* (New York: Herder and Herder, 1970), 100-101.

[28]Another "transcendental Thomist," Karl Rahner, makes the point this way. "Even when man would want to shift all responsibility for himself away from himself as someone totally determined from without," he is the one who does this. And in so doing, he "shows himself to be something other than the subsequent product of such individual elements" (*Foundations of Christian Faith: An Introduction to the Idea of Christianity*, trans. William V. Dych [New York: Seabury, 1978], 30-31). Lonergan has a high estimate of such self-affirmation. He says it can "provide a secure and personally verifiable guide to all methodical and scientific activity" (Tracy, *Achievement*, 103).

[29]Murphy, *Bodies and Souls*, 109.

account, "sin and evil result from the desire to be autonomous, to secure one's independence from God."

In place of this negative view of freedom, Smith offers a "positive" understanding of freedom as "empowerment," as the ability to achieve the good—"not just the ability to choose, but the ability to choose rightly." What gives freedom value, he says, is the opportunity it provides us to participate in God, the goal of human flourishing. This more adequate view of human freedom, he concludes, could free us "from enslavement to libertarian notions of human autonomy."[30]

From an open theist perspective, Smith is right about freedom, but wrong about open theism. It is certainly true that the value of freedom is the opportunity it provides us for fellowship with God. It is the capacity a loving and generous God gave human beings so they could return God's love for them and participate in fulfilling God's purposes for creation. So instead of viewing freedom as something negative, as a basis asserting our autonomy, separating ourselves from God and departing from God's will, open theists view freedom as something positive. And they see freedom "to do otherwise" as the necessary concomitant of a genuine willingness on the part of human beings to accept God's invitation to join in fulfilling his purposes for them and for the created world around them. True, such freedom involved the possibility of rejecting God, but that was not its purpose. In a word, open theism views the freedom with which God endowed human beings as freedom *for*, not freedom *from*.[31]

Libertarian freedom is important to the open view of God, then, not because it gives humans the opportunity of saying no to God, but because it gives us the opportunity to say yes, to welcome God's invitation to participate in his creative activity and contribute to the world's development. This appears at several points in the creation narratives in Genesis 1–3.

---

[30]James K. A. Smith, "What God Knows: The Debate on 'Open Theism,'" *Christian Century*, July 12, 2005, 31-32.

[31]To put it another way, human beings were "predestined" to life, in the sense that all the conditions for an abundant life were made available to them, and that this was what God intended for them. But from the perspective of open theism, it was a destiny they were invited to accept, it was not a destiny fixed by fate. To make it theirs, they needed to choose it.

According to Genesis 1, God created human beings in his image and gave them dominion over what he had created. This indicates that God placed humans in a position that resembled God's own sovereignty over the world, and suggests that their role was to represent God within the world, indeed, to participate in extending God's activity within the world.[32] They were to be creative in their sphere as God was in his.

Genesis 2 describes God inviting Adam to name the animals, giving him the prerogative of assigning them their places in the created sphere. In the mentality of biblical times, nothing fully existed without a name, and to name something was to exercise authority over it.[33] Moreover, just as creative activity was a form of divine self-expression, the invitation to participate in the creative process gives human beings an opportunity for self-expression, indeed, for self-realization. To a significant extent, what we are depends on the decisions we make.

Thus, as arresting as the question of whether or not we enjoy libertarian freedom may be, a more inspiring thought is the contribution that freedom makes to our existence as persons. It expresses the status that humans enjoy as creatures who bear the image of God. The biblical accounts of creation depict God as exercising great freedom in deciding to create and in choosing what kind of world and what kind of beings he wanted to bring into existence.[34] The descriptions of humans as bearing God's image and exercising dominion are strong indications that human beings were to join God in the ongoing work of creation, to

---

[32]Theologians disagree as to whether the expression *image of God* is better understood as a quality or a relationship, but the literary context favors the latter. Directly after God said, "Let us make humankind in our image, according to our likeness," he said, "And have dominion . . ." (Gen 1:27-28). The image of God involves a specific relationship between human beings and the rest of creation. Human beings enjoy the status of dominion, or sovereignty, over other forms of reality. In this vein, Wolfhart Pannenberg describes the image of God as humanity's "creative mastery of existence" (*What Is Man? Contemporary Anthropology in Theological Perspective*, trans. Duane A. Priebe [Philadelphia: Fortress, 1970], 15).

[33]Names were an integral part of something's identity in the ancient world. Nothing fully existed unless/until it had a name. For a name to be blotted out or forgotten was regarded as horrifying. (Cf. *damnatio memoriae*, the practice in ancient Rome of condemning the memory of someone who had dishonored the state.)

[34]The biblical accounts conflict with other ancient accounts of creation, like the *Enuma Elish*, according to which the world, including human beings, emerges from a conflict between different superhuman powers.

contribute to the fulfillment of God's purposes, to participate in shaping the world's destiny.

Besides what might be called creative freedom, the sort of freedom God endowed humans with when he created them in the divine image, humans were also given moral freedom, freedom to do right or wrong. From God's command not to eat of the tree of knowledge of good and evil (Gen 2:17) two things are clear. Adam had the capacity or the freedom to eat of the tree and thus to disobey God. But it was also God's definite desire that he refrain from doing so. And God did what he could to encourage Adam and Eve's obedience by warning him of dire consequences if he violated God's command.

There is an important distinction, then, between moral freedom and what we have called creative, or aesthetic, freedom. In the case of moral freedom—represented by the command not to eat of the tree of knowledge of good and evil—the options are distinct, the consequences are dramatically different, and God expresses a strong preference for which of them Adam and Eve should choose. Obedience leads to life, disobedience to death. In this case of creative or aesthetic freedom, the options are many and all of them are positive. When God invited Adam to name the animals, it appears that Adam was free to name them whatever he chose and that God would have been pleased with any of his choices.[35]

No facet of the freedom that God granted humans is more significant than the freedom intrinsic to interhuman relationships. Humans were entrusted with the God-given privilege of bringing other human beings into being: "God blessed them, and God said to them, 'Be fruitful and multiply, and fill the earth and subdue it'" (Gen 1:28). We owe our very existence to interpersonal interaction. Procreating is a form of creating. Our genetic composition comes from other human beings. Beyond our sheer existence, we owe our lives to others in other important ways as

---

[35]In *The Lost World of Genesis 1: Ancient Cosmology and the Origins Debate* (Downers Grove, IL: IVP Academic, 2009), John H. Walton describes God's activity during creation week as functional rather than originating in nature. That is to say, it consisted of assigning the various elements, components, of the earth their place, that is, the role they were to play, in the order of creation. Similarly, one might argue, in naming the animals Adam assigned them the roles they were to play in the future of God's created order.

well. And what we are inevitably reflects the multiple influences other people have on us. We are not only physically embodied, we are socially embedded. We are dependent on our parents for years, in contrast to many other forms of life. And we are affected by the decisions and actions of other people throughout our lives.[36]

FREEDOM'S CONSEQUENCES

One of the things that makes freedom so important is the fact that its exercise has permanent consequences. We see the significance of the role God envisioned when he created human beings in his image in the fact that God respects their decisions and allows their actions to "play out" over time. This aspect of freedom does not always receive the attention it deserves. When we think of the temporal aspect of freedom we are likely to devote attention to the various things that may influence someone's choice, including factors that even the subject may not be aware of: hidden influences, cultural assumptions, inherited tendencies. After all, no decision is made in a vacuum. But influence runs the other direction as well. The decisions we make often have significant, irreversible effects. Our attitudes and motives as well as our conscious actions have effects that last, perhaps long into the future. The biblical portrayal of the final judgment underscores the enduring impact and the eternal significance of one's life in all its facets.

Respecting freedom involves more than just allowing people to make choices. It involves accepting, or respecting, the consequences of those choices, however long they may last. We see this in the biblical portrayal of God's activity in human lives. Over the course of time, God's ongoing interaction with people on individual, communal, and national levels takes the stage. We see God committed to live with the consequences of human choices and actions, whether they please him or not. And out of respect for us as genuine agents, God sustains the temporal continuum

---

[36]For an illuminating discussion of the interrelation between the physical and social aspects of human life, see Warren S. Brown and Brad D. Strawn, authors of *The Physical Nature of Christian Life: Neuroscience, Psychology, and the Church* (New York: Cambridge University Press, 2012).

on which our actions take place. Having endowed humans with freedom, God always takes into account their decisions and actions. God may respond in a variety of ways, but the human contributions to the ongoing course of events are never canceled.

An example of this is God's reaction to the Israelites' desire to have a king, so they could be like other nations (1 Sam 8:4). In reality, they were rejecting God as their king and setting themselves on a path of oppression. Samuel warned them of all the things a king would do, from forcing their sons and daughters to serve him, to taking a share of their crops and their flocks, and in effect turning them into his slaves. In time, the prophet warned, the people would cry out against the oppression their king would bring.

The people insisted and God relented. He granted their wish, and Saul became the first king of Israel. It didn't go well, so God replaced him with David, a man after God's own heart. But David succumbed to the temptations of concentrated power, slept with another man's wife, took the man's life, and his monarchy took a turn for the worse. Eventually, four of his sons were killed, including Absalom, who posed a serious threat to his father's throne. Nevertheless, the figure of the king became a prototype of the Messiah to come, who would fulfill God's promise to establish a kingdom where his will would be perfectly fulfilled.[37]

In summary, Christianity attributes great complexity to human beings. As creatures, we are part of nature. We share many characteristics with other forms of life on this planet. We too are physical, finite and mortal. But we are "more than nature" in certain important respects. Superior intelligence is the feature that most obviously distinguishes us from other living creatures. But more important than intelligence, it is the quality of freedom that gives us the capacity for self-determination, elevates us to the realm of the personal, helps us to master our environment, and enables us to touch the divine. We are creatures, then, and we never lose our creatureliness, but we are unique creatures. As persons, we bear the image of God.

---

[37]Note the second petition in what is typically referred to as the Lord's Prayer: "Your kingdom come" (Mt 6:10).

FREEDOM AND SIN

If nothing is more important to a Christian understanding of humanity than freedom, nothing is more important to a Christian understanding of freedom than the concept of sin. "Man has always been his own most vexing problem," announces Reinhold Niebuhr in the opening sentence of his classic, *The Nature and Destiny of Man*.[38] And the most perplexing of our complexities is the one that sin creates. The concept of sin points to a tragic discrepancy between the ideal and the actual in human life, between what we are and what we are meant to be. It expresses the recognition that things not only could be different, they should be different, and the fact that they aren't is our own fault.

As described by the great Protestant Reformers of the sixteenth century, sin points to the fact that our predicament is not only tragic, it is total. It affects everything about us. Since human existence involves a number of different dimensions, and all of them are intimately connected, a problem anywhere in human life is a problem everywhere. Consequently, a fundamental flaw in the human situation affects everything we do and everything we are, and its consequences take many different forms.

Some of the classic ideas used to interpret sin underscore its holistic character. This is the import of the Reformation concept of "total depravity." Contrary to the impression it sometimes gives, this expression does not mean that everything about human beings is as bad as it could possibly be. Instead, it means that sin affects the entire human being. As John Calvin put it, "The whole man is overwhelmed—as by a deluge— from head to foot, so that no part is immune from sin and all that proceeds from him is to be imputed to sin."[39] Sin touches us all, and it touches all there is of us—physically, mentally, socially, and spiritually. There is nothing about us that sin does not damage.

The concept of original sin is often misunderstood as well. It signifies that sin is primarily a condition, not just an action. We are not sinners because we sin; we sin because we are sinners. Thomas Aquinas explained

---

[38]Reinhold Niebuhr, *The Nature and Destiny of Man*, 2 vols. (New York: Scribner's, 1941, 1943), 1:1.
[39]John Calvin, *Institutes of the Christian Religion*, ed. John T. McNeill, trans. Ford Lewis Battles, 2 vols. (Philadelphia: Westminster Press, 1960), 2.1.9 (p. 253).

original sin by comparing it to original righteousness. As he described it, original righteousness is the harmonious arrangement of all the faculties with which God created us. It is the perfect organization of will, desire, and what he calls "irascible power" (determination, perhaps)—all under the sovereign control of reason.[40] In contrast, original sin is the disruption of the powers that make us what we are. It refers to the fact that our lives are in disarray. The various elements of our being conflict with each other; they take on a life of their own and run out of control.[41]

If Aquinas is right, nothing essential to our humanity is lost as a result of sin—otherwise we would no longer be human—but everything about us is less than it should be. Sinful human beings are a little like a broken-down automobile. All the parts may be there, but none of them works like it is supposed to. We still have our faculties, but they no longer function as they were meant to—either individually or together. Instead of complementing one another, our various powers work against each other. We are mired in disruption and conflict.[42]

And in one of the Bible's most famous descriptions of sin, chapter seven of Paul's letter to the Romans, the apostle describes the tragic conflict that sin precipitates within the sinner's own life. "I do not understand my own actions. For I do not do what I want, but I do the very thing I hate. . . . I can will what is right, but I cannot do it. For I do not do the good I want, but the evil I do not want is what I do. Now if I do what I do not want, it is no longer I that do it, but sin that dwells within me" (Rom 7:15, 18-20).[43]

---

[40]"There was a time when original justice enabled reason to have complete control over the powers of the soul and when reason itself was subject to God and made perfect by him. But original justice was lost through the sin of our first parent. . . . In consequence, all powers of the soul have been left to some extent destitute of their proper order" (*Summa Theologica*, 12ae, q. 85, art. 3 [*Nature and Grace: Selections from the Summa Theologica of Thomas Aquinas*, trans. and ed. A. M. Fairweather, volume 11 in the Library of Christian Classics (Philadelphia: Westminster, 1954), 130]).

[41]Perhaps the expression "lose your temper," supports this conception of sin.

[42]It is natural to think of sin as conflict, but the symbolism of evil includes a host of metaphors, among them isolation and defilement. Sin interrupts all the essential relationships that constitute human existence, and it leaves us feeling guilty and stained. For an influential portrayal of sin as defilement, see Paul Ricoeur, *The Symbolism of Evil*, trans. Emerson Buchanan (Boston: Beacon Press, 1967).

[43]Scholars differ widely in the interpretation of Paul's words. There is disagreement as to whether this conflict is one of which the sinner is conscious or not and as to whether the conflict occurs

A more obvious manifestation of this basic conflict involves our relations with other people. Human beings are essentially, in fact constitutionally, social.[44] We owe our very existence to two other human beings and the fact we are physically embodied and socially embedded to a great extent determines what we are. One of our fundamental human needs is companionship. We know that life alone is not worth living. Yet it is equally obvious that life together is extremely difficult.

The most vivid example of this is the perpetual unrest and discord that engulf peoples and nations. In the twentieth century human beings arguably made more technological progress than in all previous history, yet we killed one another at a rate that defies comprehension—by the tens of millions, in two global wars and dozens of other conflicts. In fact, mass destruction may be the most conspicuous legacy of our time.

The conflicts and rivalries that take such tragic and vivid form in war are universally at work in human experience. Sin prevents us from seeing the true worth of human beings, our own or anyone else's. And because sin distorts our perspective, it is virtually impossible for us to see our own needs and the needs of others with equal clarity, so we instinctively act to protect our own interests whenever we feel our security threatened. And the way we typically do this reveals just how pervasive and insidious sin is. Instead of forcibly asserting myself to your disadvantage if we both want the same thing, I will try to find reasons to show that I need it or deserve it more than you do. To get what they want, people typically invent arguments to justify behavior that has no other source than unwarranted self-interest.

This tendency reveals two things about us. We are naturally self-centered, *and* our self-centeredness makes us uncomfortable. I want to think, and I want you to think, that I am not selfish—that my actions are motivated by concerns loftier than self-interest, even when they aren't.

---

in the life of a person before or after conversion. For a discussion of these issues, see Krister Stendahl's article, "The Apostle Paul and the Introspective Conscience of the West" (*Harvard Theological Review* 56 [1963]: 199-215).

[44]One could find a resemblance between human relationality and the relationality which, on a Trinitarian view of God, is characteristic of God's own being. And this may be another way in which humanity bears the image of God.

The fragmenting effect of sin thus emerges both in our alienation from one another, in the way we exploit one another to our own ends, *and* in our denials that this is what we actually do.

What is true of individuals is even more the case when groups and communities are involved.[45] Like individuals, groups typically pursue their own interests, but the selfishness of groups has different qualities. It is less obvious, since large numbers of people are involved, so it is easier for its members to rationalize and more difficult for them to counteract. As Reinhold Niebuhr argues, some institutions are so large that they can make extravagant claims seem plausible in ways that mere individuals never could. In addition, human institutions lack some of the moral resources available to individuals. Occasionally an individual will manage to look beyond his or her own interests and affirm the full significance of other people, but for groups this is virtually impossible. Human collectives—whether families, races, classes, nations, or even churches—are notoriously incapable of self-criticism. When a group senses a threat to its security, it consistently places its own interests first.

FREEDOM AND SALVATION

At the root of all the conflicts and contradictions that result from sin is our fundamental conflict with God. Our natural inclinations set us on a collision course with God's priorities. While virtually all Christians would agree that sin seriously affects our capacity to respond to God with love and gratitude, there are differences among them as to whether sin diminishes this capacity or utterly destroys it. As we noticed, the great Reformers insisted that sin affects the entire person, and they interpreted this to mean that sinful human beings have no capacity to respond to God's love. Salvation is entirely a matter of divine grace. Indeed, salvation is entirely a matter of divine decision.

In his exchange with Erasmus on the matter of free will, Martin Luther asserts, "With regard to God, and in all that bears on salvation or damnation, [man] has no 'free will' but is a captive, prisoner, and bondslave,

---

[45]Reinhold Niebuhr examines the differences between individual and group morality, and the lack of it, in another illuminating study, *Moral Man and Immoral Society* (New York: Scribner's, 1932).

either to the will of God or to the will of Satan."[46] We do not have the freedom to say yes to God. And neither, as John Calvin is famous for insisting, do we say no because we are free. Whether or not we accept or reject God's offer of salvation is not something left up to us. It is something God decides. Calvin attributes the eternal destiny of both saved and lost to the unilateral will of God. Wherever God's decision "holds sway," he says, there is no consideration of good works.[47]

The question of sin's effect on freedom has generated a significant theological divide among Protestants. From a Calvinist perspective, fallen human beings have no capacity to respond to God, and their salvation is therefore entirely dependent on divine grace. And since God's grace cannot fail to be efficacious, their salvation is assured; in other words, it is unconditional. For Arminians, including open theists, God graciously makes salvation available to us, but whether or not someone receives salvation depends on his or her response to God's offer. God ardently hopes that we will accept his invitation, but the decision is up to us; in other words, salvation is conditional.

Calvinists and Arminians both face challenges in their attempts to account for the effects of sin on our freedom to respond to God's offer of salvation. If, as Calvinists maintain, God is entirely responsible for our salvation—human achievement has nothing to do with it—and this necessarily implies that God's will is all-determining, how can one avoid the conclusion that God is responsible for all that happens in the world, including evil and suffering? But if, as Arminians grant, the effects of sin are devastating, where do we get the ability to accept God's offer of salvation? What accounts for that?

Both sides resort to careful maneuvering in response. Calvinists solve their dilemma by distinguishing between what God ultimately wants to happen and what he allows to happen.[48] Many Arminians account for

---

[46]Quotations from *The Bondage of the Will* in Jennifer L. Bayne and Sarah E. Hinlicky, "Free to Be Creatures Again," *Christianity Today*, October 23, 2000, 41, 42.

[47]Calvin, *Institutes of the Christian Religion*, ed. John T. McNeill, trans. Ford Lewis Battles, 2 vols. (Philadelphia: The Westminster Press, 1960), 3.22.2-3 (pp. 934-35).

[48]As a contemporary Calvinist puts it, God's "wish" is different from God's "will." The former refers to "God's general intention, the values with which he is pleased. The latter is God's specific

the ability of sinful humans to accept the gift of salvation by distinguishing between saving grace and enabling, or "prevenient," grace. A distinctive emphasis of Methodism, for example, is the belief that the offer of salvation is universal, and all human beings can be saved, because our fallen state is "offset by preliminary or prevenient grace which operates to some extent in all men and leads them towards conversion."[49] So, in spite of the effects of sin, human beings are given the ability to say yes to God, though this does not by itself produce a positive response.[50]

Another possibility is that the effects of sin are "total" in the sense mentioned earlier with reference to total depravity. That is to say, they are comprehensive in that they affect everything about our humanity, but not in the sense that they destroy anything essential to us. If we viewed a positive orientation toward the divine as an essential aspect of human existence, then we could conclude that even in a fallen state, human beings have a natural desire for fellowship with God that persists in spite of sin, truncated or distorted though it may be.

The spiritual journey of a well-known open theist illustrates the contrast. Converted as a teenager, Clark Pinnock began his theological life as a Calvinist. But he developed doubts about Calvinism as he read the book of Hebrews, with its urgent calls to persevere and warnings about falling away. These statements seemed to conflict with one of Calvinism's famous five points, "the perseverance of the saints," and once the thread was pulled, Pinnock recounts, the whole garment of Calvinism began to unravel. Drawing on the Bible, then, and his own religious experience as well, he began to see that "reciprocity and conditionality had to be brought into the picture of God's relations with us in creation and redemption," and with this the deterministic model of God gave way. The

---

intention in a given situation, what he decides shall actually occur." And there are many times when God wills to permit "what he really does not wish." Consequently, we should say that the will of God "permits rather than causes sin," even though by not preventing it "God in effect wills the sin." Millard Erickson, *Christian Theology* (Grand Rapids: Baker, 1983), 361. Erickson describes himself as a "soft Calvinist."

[49]A. Raymond Gorge, "Methodism," in *A Dictionary of Christian Theology*, ed. Alan Richardson (Philadelphia: Westminster Press, 1969), 214.

[50]From a Calvinist perspective, divine grace is effective in bringing its recipient salvation and is not, in any sense, a halfway, or preparatory, measure. Simply put, divine grace is saving grace.

"insight of reciprocity" led him to accept the "universal salvific will of God" and dispense with the "morally loathsome" doctrine of double pre-destination. Eventually it led him to free will theism, with its open view of the future and its revisionary concept of divine foreknowledge.[51]

Whether they see it as a vestige of our natural inclination to respond to God or a special manifestation of divine grace that counteracts the effects of sin, open theists affirm that because God "desires everyone to be saved and to come to the knowledge of the truth" (1 Tim 2:4), he provides us the personal freedom to accept his offer of salvation. Though salvation is due entirely to divine grace, God respects the decisions we make in response. The numerous invitations we find in the Bible to choose God's way or accept God's gifts are indications that personal sal-vation is a gift to be received voluntarily, not a divine assignment.

---

[51]Clark Pinnock, "From Augustine to Arminius: A Pilgrimage in Theology," in *The Grace of God, the Will of Man: A Case for Arminianism*, ed. Clark H. Pinnock (Grand Rapids: Zondervan Aca-demic, 1989), 15-29.

CHAPTER NINE

▸▸▸▸▸▸ CHRISTOLOGY AND ▸▸▸▸▸▸
▸▸▸▸▸▸ THE OPENNESS OF GOD ▸▸▸▸▸▸

IN AN ARTICLE THAT APPEARED IN 2009, Michael Zbarschuk challenges open and relational thinkers to explore the christological implications of their position more fully. True, he says, they find in biblical accounts of Jesus' life and teachings support for a dynamic, interactive view of God's relation to human beings and for the elevation of love as the most fundamental attribute of God. But apart from the "illustrative" value that Christ's life provides, there is little exploration of the larger significance of Christ's work.[1] So what open and relational thinkers need to do is "revisit their theological reflection, making Christ the center, rather than the periphery, of their ongoing thinking on these and other important theological issues."[2]

This relative lack of attention to christology among openness theologians, he notes, stands in marked contrast to the work of a number of process theologians who devoted extensive attention to the implications of christology.[3] For Marjorie Suchocki, in particular, love and justice occupy a prominent place in Jesus' ministry, and the cross provides a conspicuous demonstration of the "constancy and strength" of God's

---

[1] "There are no specific treatments of Christ from any of the leading open and relational theologians" (Michael Zbarschuk, "Process Theology Resources for an Open and Relational Christology," *Wesleyan Theological Journal* 44 [Fall 2009]: 155).

[2] Zbarschuk, "Process Theology Resources," 167.

[3] Zbarschuk specifically mentions Henry Nelson Weiman, Bernard Loomer, Bernard Meland, John Cobb Jr., and David Griffin.

love, as well as God's pain.[4] She also interprets the resurrected Christ with reference to his continuing influence in the church and God's ongoing care for the world.

Zbarschuk then suggests three ways in which the relational and incarnational strands drawn from process thinkers could be woven into open and relational theology. The most promising, he says, is the incarnational theme that God's power is "limited, cooperative, partial, dependent, and open to failure and defeat." Accordingly, the divine word of love is crucified and risen "again and again and again." Second, the cross stands as a refutation of divine triumphalism, for the incarnational God revealed in Christ has not and may never decisively, finally defeat evil. And third, God's saving activity within the world comprises an ongoing, incomplete process that manifests itself in all the world's religions, and should not be identified distinctly, let alone exclusively, with any one of them, including Christianity.[5]

As we shall see, open theists can benefit from Zbarschuk's call to develop christological themes across the full range of God's relation to the world, but they are unlikely to accept the specific features of his incarnational view of God. True, God is always and everywhere interacting with creaturely agents and working to redeem creation from self-destructive forces and influences. But for open theists, this does not exclude the belief that the life, death, and resurrection of Jesus represent a distinct manifestation, indeed the decisive manifestation, of God's presence within the world. Christ's universal significance derives from, and depends on, the unique identity of this particular person, who appeared within human history at a specific time and place and who lived, as every human life is lived, in bodily form, subject to the frailty and mortality of all human existence. Open theists also believe that the forces of evil were decisively defeated at the cross and will be eradicated from the universe when God's purposes for creation are fully achieved.

Open theism thus shares the conviction of orthodox Christianity that Christ represents the supreme revelation of God, unsurpassed and

---

[4]Zbarschuk, "Process Theology Resources," 162-63.
[5]Zbarschuk, "Process Theology Resources," 165-66.

unsurpassable. What happened in the life, death, and resurrection of Jesus was not only representative of the way God is always working to achieve his purposes. But in the life of this particular person, as nowhere else, was God present personally. Thus, Christ is uniquely representative of God because he was God, and it is precisely because God is decisively manifested in this historic life that we can affirm God's universal love for the world, his enduring commitment to its welfare, and his intimate involvement with every member of the human family. And this suggests that the person and work of Christ, to invoke a time-honored distinction, are closely connected.

In an earlier chapter, we mentioned the significance of the claim that God was in Christ for our understanding of the divine reality. As we noted, the doctrine of two natures as formulated by the ecumenical councils of Nicaea (325) and Chalcedon (451) preserved distinctive Christian claims for the person of Christ from influences in the ancient Mediterranean world that would have threatened the heart of Christian faith. Instead of placing Christ on a level lower than deity itself, giving him an intermediate position between divinity and the creaturely world, the councils affirmed the Christ was fully equal to God, and therefore that God, indeed, Godself had entered the world in the person of Christ. The effect was to show, as Karl Barth memorably put it, that "For God it is just as natural to be lowly as it is to be high, to be near as it is to be far, to be little as it is to be great."[6]

Discussions of the two natures typically focus on the person of Christ. How are we to understand the union of the human nature with the divine? What role in Jesus' life did his divine nature play? Was he gifted with divine power? Was he possessed of divine knowledge? As for his humanity, we may wonder how his physical and mental experience compared to that of human beings in general. Did Jesus get hungry and tired? Did he need food and sleep? Did he have social needs? Did he reach out for human companionship? Was he sensitive to the way people reacted to him? Was he reassured by their acceptance, disappointed by their

---

[6]Karl Barth, *Church Dogmatics*, trans. Geoffrey Bromily and Thomas Torrance (T. & T. Clark, 1956), IV/1, 192.

rejection, fearful of their hostility? Perhaps most important, what was the nature of Jesus spiritual life? Did he face temptation as other humans do? Did he find it easy or hard to deal with?

For traditional Christianity, Jesus was distinguished from all other men and women not only because he uniquely represented God, but also because he was uniquely representative of humanity. We could also phrase this coincidence with reference to the work of Christ. Christ's mission was to portray God to the world, to teach men and women what God was really like. At the same time, his purpose was to serve God with the same devotion that God wants from every human being. So, there is a "bidirectionality" in the life that Jesus lived, rendering service to God and to humanity at the same time. And by the end of his life, his service was complete. There was nothing more he could have done. In his words, "It is finished."

In order to see what a Christology of open theism might look like, we'll look at the two facets of service we just mentioned—Jesus' service to God and to his fellow human beings.

GLORIFYING GOD THE FATHER

Jesus' willingness to accept God's will, however costly that might be, is nowhere more vividly portrayed than in the great temptations, or tests, that he faced. From the perspective of open theism, it is significant that Jesus' loyalty to God was something he willingly accepted; it presupposes that his obedience was a choice, not a foregone conclusion. On the most natural reading of the biblical accounts, Jesus' temptations were real— that is, he had the freedom to yield to them or resist them.[7] And they appear to have been particularly forceful at two crucial junctures in his life—one in the wilderness at the beginning of his ministry; the other at the end in Gethsemane. There are different vantage points from which to view Jesus' wilderness temptations, but it is illuminating to view each of them as related to the use and abuse of power (Mt 4:1-11). All the temptations involved the exercise of power, although power figures in each temptation in a distinctive way.

---

[7]According to the book of Hebrews, Jesus was "one who in every respect has been tested as we are, yet without sin" (Heb 4:15).

In the first temptation, the devil says to Jesus, "If you are the Son of God, command these stones to become loaves of bread" (Mt 4:3).[8] The temptation presupposes that Jesus had the power to do what the devil suggested, or at least that he had reason to believe that he had such power. Why would this have been a test? Because Jesus was alone in the wilderness, on the verge of starvation, wondering perhaps just what God had in mind for him. Or wondering perhaps if God had forgotten about him entirely. As the Gospel records it, this temptation came within weeks of Jesus' baptism, when a voice from heaven identified Jesus as "my beloved Son" and anointed him with the Holy Spirit. And what does being God's Son mean, if it doesn't involve enjoying divine prerogatives and using divine power to meet your needs? So the temptation here seems to be to lay hold of divine power, to secure your place in the world. God is a reservoir of enormous power. If you are God's Son you have that power. Use it to solve your problems and meet your needs. Use it! That was the gist of the devil's suggestion.

Jesus' reply to the temptation reveals a different understanding of his role as God's Son. Divine sonship does not take the wide road of power. It follows the narrow path of submission, the path of trust and obedience. Jesus doesn't claim God's power for himself, nor does he expect it to work for his personal advantage. Being God's Son does not mean that the course of his life will be more comfortable than that of other people. It will not provide an easy solution to the problems that all humans face. It will not protect him from hunger and thirst, from disappointment and loneliness, from hostility and death. Divine power is not a ready-made solution to the problems of life.

In his reply to the tempter, "One does not live by bread alone, but by every word that comes from the mouth of God" (Mt 4:4), Jesus indicated that the voice from heaven declaring him to be God's Son was all the assurance he needed. He would trust God's word. He would not seek a demonstration of his divine status.

---

[8]Some of the information in this section was previously published in my article, "The Place of the Dramatic in God's Overall Plan," At Issue, SDAnet, accessed November 6, 2019, http://sdanet .org/atissue/discern/dramatic.htm.

The devil assured Jesus that his possession of divine power would provide comfort and security. But Jesus indicated that his relation to divine power would not be to use it, but to submit to it. Divine sonship takes him not to the heights of privilege, but to the depths of obedience. Being God's Son means, not claiming God's prerogatives, but submitting to God's ways, trusting God to use him as he will. It is the path marked out in Philippians 2:5-8, from the realm of glory to the depths of suffering. No, Jesus would not claim divine power. And this set the stage for the second temptation.

The devil took Jesus to the pinnacle of the temple and asked him to cast himself down, trusting God to save his life. He even quoted a Bible promise to justify this dramatic request. "Throw yourself down, for it is written, 'He will command his angels concerning you, and 'On their hands they will bear you up, so that you will not dash your foot against a stone'" (Mt 4:5-6).

Just what was the devil asking Jesus to do and why would this request have been at all enticing to him? In resisting the first temptation, Jesus demonstrated that he would not claim divine power for himself. He would trust God implicitly, whatever the consequences might be. Starving or dying, he would not use his power as God's own Son to save himself.

In reply the devil seems to be saying, "All right, then, you say you are willing to trust God completely. Let's see if you really mean it. You say you will depend on God's words for life itself. Well, here are some of God's words to live by. 'Cast yourself down and his angels will bear you up.' Are you willing to stake your life on God's words? If you are, then put him to the test."

Here again, the central issue is one of power. Only here it is not the belief that Jesus had divine power himself. It was the belief that he could get God's power to work for him. Was he sure of God's care for him? Why not put God in a position where he has no choice but to show it and rescue him? In refusing to "claim the promise" the devil offers him, Jesus says no to all divine manipulation, all promise claiming whose basic objective is to get God to give us what we want.

Jesus' response indicates that the proper attitude of prayer is one of commitment, not demand. The purpose of prayer is not to maneuver God into a position where he has to do what we ask. The purpose of prayer is to put us in a position where we are willing to accept whatever God has for us.[9] Jesus responded to the devil's second temptation by refusing to use God's word as a basis for making demands of God. Again he quoted the Bible. "Again it is written, 'Do not put the Lord your God to the test'" (Mt 4:7). As these words indicate, faith doesn't test, faith trusts. It does not insist on its own way, it follows God's way. It breathes the spirit of Jesus' last great prayer of submission, "Not my will but thine be done."

The last of Jesus' temptations in the wilderness also dealt with power. In this case, the devil showed Jesus all the kingdoms of the world in their splendor and offered to give them to him, if he would but bow down and worship him. This is an intriguing temptation, because it seems so preposterous. How could the devil possibly have thought that Jesus would entertain the slightest thought of bowing down and worshiping him? After all, the first two commandments deal with God's exclusive claim on our devotion. You shall have no other gods. You shall not bow down to them.

Has the devil run out of ideas here? Is he flailing away in desperation, like a boxer who's behind on points and needs a knockout to win the bout? Or does this temptation somehow reach into Jesus' thinking more deeply than either of the earlier two? And how is power involved in this temptation?

The kingdoms of this world, as the Gospel puts it, stand in sharp contrast to the kingdom that is not of this world—the kingdom that Jesus came to establish (cf. Jn 18:36). And a major difference is the role power plays in the way they are established. The kingdoms of this world come into existence through the exercise of force. The strong impose themselves

---

[9]In the great "faith chapter," Hebrews 11, the author lists a number of biblical characters who showed great faith in God's promises. And what is remarkable is that none of the promises came true in the way they originally hoped and expected. In the apostle's words, "All these died in faith without having received the promises, but from a distance they saw and greeted them. . . . *Therefore* [Greek: *dio*] God is not ashamed to be called their God" (Heb 11:13, 16).

on the weak and achieve their will by superior power. The devil was offering Jesus the opportunity to stand at the pinnacle of power, to impose his will on all the earth's inhabitants, to have his desires fulfilled because his subjects were not strong enough to resist.

This offer also included an attractive alternative to the path of suffering that Jesus' mission involved. The kingdom Jesus came to establish could only become a reality through his suffering and death. It was not based on power, but on love, on a love that fully enters the human condition and wins allegiance by demonstrating service and care. A kingdom that rests on power is not the sort of kingdom Jesus came to build. But the building of *his* kingdom comes at a very high price. It requires the king to serve and sacrifice. In fact, it ultimately requires the king to die.

The devil was offering Jesus something of a different nature. All he had to do was acknowledge the devil's power and that power would become his own. If you have great power, you can do great good. And if you have enough power, you can achieve your good goals easily, without having to get people to agree or even cooperate with you. Yet Jesus was emphatic. "Away with you, Satan! For it is written, 'Worship the Lord your God, and serve only him'" (Mt 4:10). What does it mean to worship God? Among other things, it means to value the things that God values, to commit yourself to God's way of doing things, to the sort of kingdom that he wants to build.

Following Peter's confession at Caesarea Philippi, "You are the Messiah, the Son of the living God" (Mt 16:16),

> Jesus began to show his disciples that he must go to Jerusalem and undergo great suffering at the hands of the elders and chief priests and scribes, and be killed, and on the third day be raised. And Peter took him aside and began to rebuke him, saying, "God forbid it, Lord! This must never happen to you." But he turned and said to Peter, "Get behind me, Satan! You are a stumbling block to me; for you are setting your mind not on divine things but on human things." (Mt 16:21-23)

The forcefulness of Jesus' reply to this temptation suggests that it may have been attractive for Jesus to avoid the suffering his mission involved.

The third temptation concerned the goal of his mission, reestablishing God's kingdom or reign in the world. Would Jesus accept the suffering this involved (cf. Mt 16:15-16, 21; Lk 9:20-22), or look for an easier way? The third temptation presented itself to Jesus again, as we see from his plaintive prayer in Gethsemane: "Father, if you are willing, remove this cup from me; yet, not my will but yours be done" (Lk 22:42). By his life, death, and resurrection, Jesus fulfilled God's will for him. In every respect, he remained faithful to his statement of his mission. "I delight to do your will, O my God," could easily have been the motto of his life (Ps 40:8), even when it included suffering. And it certainly did, as the New Testament consistently emphasized. Jesus was tested by what he suffered (Heb 2:18). Indeed, "In the days of his flesh, Jesus offered up prayers and supplications, with loud cries and tears, to the one who was able to save him from death, and he was heard because of his reverent submission. Although he was a Son, he learned obedience through what he suffered" (Heb 5:7-8).

In spite of the severe struggles they involved, Jesus never succumbed to temptation. He remained faithful to God's will, in spite of the tremendous cost it involved. The question open theism raises is whether or not his faithfulness was assured in advance. Was it a certainty from the beginning or a genuine achievement, something that became definite when it actually occurred? The consequences if Jesus had failed are unimaginable to us, and the Bible affirms that Jesus emerged triumphant from all his spiritual trials. And for many, both factors point to the conclusion that there was no way Jesus' mission could have failed. On the other hand, the powerful portrayal of Jesus struggling with temptation, suffering from the tests to his loyalty, strongly suggests that the outcome was not definite until Jesus fully and finally submitted himself to God's will, no matter what it cost him. Open theists maintain that God took a risk in creating a world where there was genuine creaturely freedom and suffered the pain of human disloyalty. Perhaps God took another risk in sending his Son into the world with the possibility that he too could fail the test of loyalty.

For many Christians, this prospect is unthinkable; to some, even offensive. As they see it, there is simply no way the plan of salvation could have failed, no way Christ could have yielded to the tempter's wiles. Open theists themselves are not agreed on this issue. As we have noted, Gregory Boyd is one for whom God saw all the possible directions the future could take, and eliminated those in which his purposes would not be achieved. My own view is that the success of Christ's mission was not finalized until his threefold commitment in Gethsemane, "Thy will be done," set him irreversibly on the path of suffering that ended with his death. For me, this conclusion underscores God's incomprehensible love in the gift of the Son (cf. Jn 3:16).

At the same time, in light of our earlier analysis of risk, it could very well be that the chances of Christ's failure, though real, were minimal, perhaps minuscule, especially considering the tremendous benefits of all that they made possible. According to the letter to the Hebrews, Jesus "the pioneer and perfecter of our faith . . . for the sake of the joy that was set before him endured the cross, disregarding its shame, and has taken his seat at the right hand of the throne of God (Heb 12:2). Perhaps he, like Paul, considered "the sufferings of this present time . . . not worth comparing with the glory about to be revealed to us" (Rom 8:18).

As we suggested above, there is a sense in which Jesus' life of service had a bidirectional quality; it involved serving others as well as serving God. And there are biblical indications that the two coincided—that Jesus fulfilled God's will by caring in various ways for his fellow human beings, and doing so at the cost of his very life. One of these may be a key text in the Gospel of Mark: "For the Son of Man came not to be served but to serve, and to give his life a ransom for many" (Mk 10:45). With this in mind, let us review some of the forms his service to others involved.

CHRIST'S MINISTRY TO OTHERS

As typically interpreted, the christological formula "two natures, one person" applies to Christ's essential identity. But, following Zbarschuk's suggestion, I would like to explore its possible application to the work of Christ as well. A careful look at the ministry of Jesus reveals that his twofold identity as divine and human is reflected in the twofold nature of his work. What Jesus accomplished in his life and death expresses God's love for fallen humanity and at the same time embodies the service that human beings owe to their Lord. He serves as God's representative to humanity, and humanity's representative to God.

In certain respects some of the familiar theories of atonement focus on one or the other of these dimensions. The satisfaction theory construes the death of Christ as fulfilling humanity's obligation to God. Christ's sacrifice as a human being meets the requirements of the divine nature for justice. In contrast, the ransom theory views Christ's death as something God provides on humanity's behalf, especially in the "Christus victor" motif made famous by Gustav Aulen. Without entering into the complex issues of just how Jesus' death solves the problem of sin, we see in the ministry of Jesus a manifestation of the two directions his service comprised—God's service to us and our service to God. God's loving nature finds supreme expression in the gift of the Son. And human destiny finds fulfillment in the service to God of which Jesus' ministry is the supreme example.

The open view of God provides the basis for a profound appreciation for the nature and scope of Christ's ministry. As described in the Gospels, Jesus' ministry was noteworthy for its inclusiveness. Jesus affirmed the significance of all human beings, whatever their stage in life, social status, physical or moral condition. He cared for the young and the old, for the sick and the healthy, for the innocent and the guilty, for men and women, for Jews and Gentiles, and for heathens as well as worshipers of the true God.

He not only affirmed the value of all human beings, his ministry addressed human needs across the entire scope of our existence. There is no aspect of human life that did not concern him. His concern for spiritual well-being comes most readily to mind, especially when we think of his various sermons and discussions. But his concern for physical health is vivid as well in the Gospel accounts of his miraculous healings.

The overarching theme of Jesus' preaching, according to the first three Gospels, was "the kingdom of God" or the "reign of God," as the original expression is more accurately translated (see Mk 1:15). Jesus announced the coming of God's kingdom. He urged people to prepare for its arrival. He told parables to illustrate its principles. And he performed miracles as signs of the kingdom of God. Jesus' miracles have what scholars call a "proleptic" quality. They show what life will be like when God's reign is fully realized. In God's kingdom, suffering is a thing of the past; people are free from all the destructive elements that dominate and intimidate us now. There is no disease, death, or demonic possession. There is nothing natural or supernatural to threaten our welfare.

Jesus' miracles show that God's kingdom is not only a reality yet to come, it is present in significant ways as well. In fact, it is the power that sustains the world now. In an important way, Jesus' miracles are windows on a deeper level of reality. They open our eyes to the ultimate order of things. Though blighted by sin, this is still "our Father's world." Indeed, divine power is no less responsible for the food we eat daily than it was for the loaves and fishes that fed the five thousand in Jesus' Galilean ministry. Divine power is no less responsible for our health and our recovery from illness than it was for the people Jesus healed. They remind us that God is at work in the world in unspectacular, unsensational ways. They show that "the ordinary is extraordinary."[10] Like the sort of lenses that enable people to see things in the dark, Jesus' miracles open our eyes to the incessant workings of divine power that surround and sustain us. Miracles provide vivid demonstrations of the fact that God is constantly at work to bless and benefit us.[11]

Jesus' miracles also reveal God's commitment to life in this world. The kingdom of God is not "otherwordly." People who enter the kingdom are not transported from this realm to another. Instead, the kingdom enters

---

[10]One writer on the life of Christ puts it this way: "The Saviour in his miracles revealed the power that is continually at work in man's behalf, to sustain and to heal him. Through the agencies of nature, God is working, day by day, hour by hour, moment by moment, to keep us alive, to build up and restore us" (Ellen G. White, *The Ministry of Healing* [Mountain View, CA: Pacific Press Publishing Association, 1905], 112-13).

[11]We are concerned here with the theology of healing that Jesus' miracles suggest. The philosophical literature dealing with miracles is vast, of course, and tends to focus on the question of whether extraordinary or "supernatural" events are metaphysically possible. The issue is important, but it has limited relevance to our interests here.

this world and transforms it. In the apocalyptic vision of the new earth, God dwells with humans, not by taking them away from this world to be with him, but by coming into the world to be with them.

We see the comprehensive nature of God's work in the world in the fact that Jesus' ministry embraced all aspects of human existence, including its physical, spiritual, emotional, and social dimensions. Two-thirds of the miracles specifically described in the Gospels are miracles of healing—more if you count the three people Jesus raised from the dead and the demon-possessed who were ill as well. He cured blindness, deafness, leprosy, and paralysis. More accurately, he cured the blind, the deaf, the leprous, and the paralyzed, for his concern was directed primarily toward the victim, not the disease. So it is apparent that physical restoration was an essential part of Jesus' ministry.

We also see Jesus' concern for physical well-being in several of his so-called nature miracles. He stilled a life-threatening storm on the Sea of Galilee, and on at least two occasions he fed the hungry crowds that followed him into the wilderness. The feeding of the five thousand, one of the few miracles mentioned in all four Gospels, illustrates the interrelation of the physical and the spiritual in Jesus' thinking. It temporarily satisfied the hunger of a great many people, but the sermon Jesus preached shortly after, "the Bread of Life Discourse," connects this miraculous provision of physical food to the spiritual food that Jesus brings to human beings as "the bread from heaven": "I am the living bread that came down from heaven. Whoever eats of this bread will live forever; and the bread that I will give for the life of the world is my flesh" (Jn 6:51). Thus, our need for physical nourishment symbolizes our need for spiritual food, and Jesus Christ is the ultimate source of both.

While Jesus' miracles affirm the importance of the physical, they also affirm the importance of what lies beyond the physical, and they show that the two are intimately related. Humans live by bread, to be sure, but not by bread alone, but by every word that proceeds from the mouth of God (Mt 4:4). The Greek word for "heal," *sōzō*, also means "save," so it nicely expresses the view that spiritual and physical restoration are aspects of one comprehensive experience. When Jesus described his work as salvation, he no doubt saw it as including both physical and spiritual dimensions. In fact, on one occasion Jesus compared his work to that of a physician, suggesting that he envisioned his ministry as a whole as a ministry of healing: "Those who are well have no need of a physician, but those who are sick" (Mt 9:12).

Jesus' entire ministry was directed toward spiritual ends, of course. Its primary objective was to restore human beings to a proper relationship with God. He announced that God's kingdom was imminent, and he saw himself as its personal representative. He invited people to enter the kingdom and described the various principles of "kingdom life" in numerous sermons and parables.

Jesus also showed great concern for the marginalized, and he met people in great need, and healed their diseases, but he took account of much more than their physical condition. A good example is his response to the woman who touched his garment in a desperate attempt to find relief from a hemorrhage. She was healed of her disease, but that wasn't enough for Jesus. He wanted to hear her story too. So he listened while she poured out "the whole truth," as the Gospel puts it. He also called the woman "daughter" and commended her for her faith (Mk 5:24-34).[12]

In the thinking of some scholars, Jesus was unique in offering the invitation to salvation to individual human beings, especially to individuals who lay outside the circle of religious respectability. His open acceptance of sinners, women, and foreigners mystified his followers and scandalized his critics. He offered them places in the kingdom of God alongside Israelites of good and regular standing. In fact, he asserted they would enter the kingdom *before* these respectable people (Mt 21:31).

According to David Bentley Hart, "The Christian account of reality introduced into our world an understanding of the divine, the cosmic, and the human that had no . . . equivalent elsewhere and [it] made

---

[12]He also commended the centurion who asked him to heal his servant (Mt 8:10, Lk 7:9) and the Syrophoenician woman who begged him to heal her daughter (Mt 15:28).

possible a moral vision of the human person that has haunted us ever since, century upon century."[13] The doctrine of the incarnation shows that

> a person is not merely a fragment of some larger cosmic or spiritual category . . . but an irreducible mystery. . . . This immense dignity—this infinite capacity—inheres in every person, no matter what circumstances might for now seem to limit him or her to one destiny or another. . . . The rise of Christianity produced consequences so immense that it can almost be said to have begun the world anew: to have "invented" the human . . . to have determined our vision of the [universe] and our place in it, and to have shaped all of us . . . in the deepest reaches of consciousness.[14]

As Jesus described it, the kingdom of God reaches across every imaginable human barrier. It transcends all the differences that divide and separate people from one another—national, social, racial, cultural, political, economic, sexual, linguistic, and even moral. It ultimately bridges the widest of all chasms, the one that separates sinners and the sinned against, wrongdoers and their victims. Forgiveness obviously has a vertical dimension—it restores us to fellowship with God. But it has a horizontal dimension too. It brings wrongdoers and their victims together and unites them in a fellowship of love. This is clearly the import of Jesus' comments on forgiveness, particularly his parable of the unforgiving servant (Mt 18:23-35). And its importance in the Christian scheme of things is clear from this request in Jesus' model prayer, "forgive us our debts, as we also have forgiven our debtors" (Mt 6:12).

We see the healing of relationships, the restoration of community, in a number of Jesus' miracles, as well as his teachings on forgiveness. Each of the individuals he raised from the dead was restored to a bereaved family—Jairus's daughter, the son of the widow of Nain, and Lazarus of Bethany. Their physical restoration was a means of achieving social restoration. The same is true of other miracles. Jesus healed people of diseases that carried a strong social stigma, diseases that forced their victims

---

[13]David Bentley Hart, *Atheist Delusions: The Christian Revolution and Its Fashionable Enemies* (New Haven, CT: Yale University Press, 2009), 203.
[14]Hart, *Atheist Delusions*, 211, 213.

to leave society, to live apart from family and friends, and to avoid participating in worship.

When Jesus healed these people of their various ailments, he restored them to their communities. He sent lepers to the priest to be examined (Mk 1:40-45 [and parallels]; Lk 17:14). Once officially declared clean, they could return to their families. He pronounced a woman whose back he straightened a "daughter of Abraham," to remind those in the synagogue of her true identity (Lk 13:10-17). And he sent the Gerasene demoniac back to his friends and his home (Mk 5:29; Lk 8:39).

When we look at Jesus' ministry, then, we see that it clearly involved the entire spectrum of personal needs—physical, spiritual, emotional, and social. In fact, there is no essential aspect of human life that his ministry did not touch. And it is significant that Jesus not only cared *for* the whole person, he also cared *with* his whole person. His concern for people defined his existence, and it affected every dimension of his life. As recorded in what some take to be the "key text" of the earliest Gospel, Jesus described the purpose of his mission this way: "For the Son of Man came not to be served but to serve, and to give his life a ransom for many" (Mk 10:45).

Jesus' care for others was the central burden of his spiritual or devotional life. The Gospels describe him spending a good deal of time in prayer (Mk 1:35; Lk 11:1). In the great intercessory prayer of John 17, Jesus poured out his concern for his inner circle of followers. He prayed for their spiritual security and the success of their future mission in the world. There are indications that he prayed for people individually too. When Simon Peter boasted of his loyalty, Jesus replied, "I have prayed for you that your own faith may not fail" (Lk 22:32).

Jesus placed the welfare and security of his disciples before his own interests. When he was arrested, he asked his captors to let his companions go (Jn 18:8). And during his crucifixion, in the throes of his final agony, he made provision for his mother's care (Jn 19:26-27). In the so-called farewell discourses, the extent of Jesus' concern for his others become vividly apparent. Jesus offered his followers his own fellowship with the Father. His highest joy was to bring them into the intimate circle of love that defined his own relationship with God. He wanted them to enjoy the same privileges that he did as God's own Son (Jn 14–17).

On several occasions, according to the Gospels, Jesus was "moved with compassion" or "pity" when faced with human need—when he met a leper (Mk 1:41), when he witnessed the sorrow of a mother whose only son had died (Lk 7:13), and when he saw the crowds following him, "like sheep without a shepherd" (Mk 6:34). (The same expression appears in Jesus' parables, where it describes the feelings of the father for his wayward son and the response of the Good Samaritan to the wounded traveler on the Jericho road [Lk 15:10; 10:33].) The Greek behind this expression is a blunt and forceful term, referring to the inner parts or organs of the body. It connotes deep-felt, spontaneous emotions that affect us viscerally, so to speak, as opposed to the "nobler affections like love and hate, courage and fear, joy and sorrow."[15] The essential idea is that these scenes of human suffering hit Jesus in the pit of the stomach. In a similar way, Jesus was deeply moved by the mourners as he neared the grave of his friend Lazarus, and burst into tears himself (Jn 11:35).

Love is no doubt the quality we most readily associate with Jesus. And his love for people is nowhere more evident than in his relation to his disciples, his closest followers and his innermost circle of friends. As the introductory verse to the passion story of the fourth Gospel puts it, "Jesus knew that the hour had come to depart from this world and go to the Father. Having loved his own who were in the world, he loved them to the end" (Jn 13:1). The expression "love to the end" may refer to the fact that Jesus loved his disciples to the end of his life, which is certainly true. It may also indicate that Jesus showed the full extent of his love for them by taking the path that led to Calvary, making the ultimate sacrifice. If so, his actions bear witness to his words, "No one has greater love than this, to lay down one's life for one's friends" (Jn 15:13).

Jesus was generous with his company. He spent a great deal of time in public. He mingled with people freely. He shared his provisions with them, and he accepted their hospitality in return. He ate with the

---

[15]Helmut Koester, *"Splanchnon,* etc.," in *Theological Dictionary of the New Testament,* ed. Gerhard Friedrich, trans. Geoffrey W. Bromiley, 10 vols. (Grand Rapids: Eerdmans, 1964-1976), 7:549.

in-crowd, with Pharisees, and he ate with social outcasts as well (Lk 7:36; 15:1-2). In fact, Jesus was so social that his critics accused him of being "a glutton and a drunkard, a friend of tax collectors and sinners" (Mt 11:19; Lk 7:34). The Gospels show that Jesus could engage people from completely different social strata. John 3 records his conversation with Nicodemus, a Pharisee and a member of the Sanhedrin, the highest Jewish council. John 4 records his conversation with a Samaritan woman who had a checkered personal history. We cannot imagine a social situation that would have brought these two individuals together—Nicodemus and the woman. Yet Jesus was perfectly at ease with each of them.

Jesus was so committed to offering others his companionship that he had no place to call his own. As he exclaimed on one occasion, "Foxes have holes, and the birds of the air have nests; but the Son of Man has nowhere to lay his head" (Mt 8:20; Lk 9:58). He sacrificed personal comfort and security so others could benefit from his ministry. Jesus also affirmed human happiness. He attended feasts and celebrations, and he performed his first "sign" at a wedding in Galilee (Jn 2:1-11).

When we look at the various dimensions of Jesus' own life, it is clear that he poured himself out in service and ministry. All his personal resources were involved in his devotion to others. Physically, spiritually, emotionally, and socially—Jesus drew on every facet of his life to bless and benefit humanity. It is no wonder that Christians have viewed his ministry as a costly sacrifice and find a precedent for his life and work in the servant songs of Isaiah. He identified with the objects of his care so completely that he became one with them. He suffered in their suffering, and his suffering became the means of their salvation.[16]

Jesus' ministry is noteworthy for both its scope and intensity. There was no aspect of human existence that did not concern him, there was no one who lay outside the circle of his compassion, and there was no resource available to him that he did not invest in his attempt to meet their complex and varied needs. This is true not only in the sense that he drew on the full range of his personal powers to serve others, but in the

---

[16]Note the parallels between 1 Pet 2:21-25 and Is 53:3-12.

sense that "emptied" himself of these resources (cf. Phil 2:7). When his ministry came to an end, there was nothing more he could have done to achieve the goals of his mission. There was no avenue of service he had not explored, no physical, mental, emotional, or spiritual resource yet available to him. His sacrifice was complete. When Jesus reached the end of his life, he had revealed "the full extent of his love" (Jn 13:1 NIV 1984).

Jesus' concern for people extended beyond individual human beings. As we shall see in the next chapter, his mission included the creation of a new community, a fellowship whose members would exhibit the same love and support for each other that he displayed in his own life, and who would reach out to embrace people from every nation and every station in life. In other words, Jesus envisioned the most inclusive community possible—a community that recognized no boundaries, a community open to everyone, to the entire world.

To this end he gathered an inner circle of followers around him and devoted a great deal of time to them. His disciples were the beneficiaries of his most extensive teaching, so they in turn could minister to others (see Mt 5:1). But Jesus reached beyond them as well. To illustrate the nature of this community, he developed conspicuous associations with those least likely to be candidates for God's kingdom in the conventional thinking of the day, such as tax collectors and "sinners" (Lk 15:1-2).[17] He also identified with those in need. In the climactic parable of the Olivet Discourse, the parable of sheep and goats, the king identifies himself with the hungry and thirsty, with the stranger, the naked, the sick and the imprisoned (Mt 25:37-40).

CONCLUSION

A Christology consistent with the open view of God affirms with traditional Christianity that the revelation of God in the figure of Jesus was unprecedented, unsurpassed, and unsurpassable, and can only be described as a

---

[17]The citizens of the kingdom Jesus describes in the Beatitudes include a surprising group of people—the poor, the meek, those who mourn, the merciful, the persecuted, the hungry and thirsty, etc.—not the sort most people would expect to build up a kingdom of any significance (Mt 5:3-13).

manifestation of God's personal presence within the conditions of finite, human existence. As the apostle Paul put it, "God was in Christ" (2 Cor 5:19). And open theists accept the conviction affirmed by the councils of Nicaea and Chalcedon that the historical figure of Jesus is appropriately characterized as a union of two natures in one person. As the definitive representative of God, Jesus provides a revelation of God that is clearer than any other and makes it possible for us to connect with God more closely than through any other avenue. As recounted in the Gospel of John, Jesus' farewell discourses underscore the uniqueness of Jesus' own relation to "the Father" and the connection to God that he makes available to others:

> Thomas said to him, "Lord, we do not know where you are going. How can we know the way?" Jesus said to him, "I am the way, and the truth, and the life. No one comes to the Father except through me. If you know me, you will know my Father also. From now on you do know him and have seen him." Philip said to him, "Lord, show us the Father, and we will be satisfied." Jesus said to him, "Have I been with you all this time, Philip, and you still do not know me? Whoever has seen me has seen the Father." (Jn 14:5-9)

But along with their embrace of Christian tradition, open theists share the view articulated by process theologians that the biblical descriptions of Jesus provide a vivid portrayal of God's constant and comprehensive care for and involvement in human life. As we have seen, the life, ministry, and death of Jesus portrays God as always, everywhere, and intimately present to human beings, tenderly surrounding them with love, fully sharing in their joys and sorrows, constantly affirming their value and continuously drawing them toward the fulfillment of his ideals for them. So even as they affirm the orthodox view of his person and his work, open theists embrace the expansive vision of God's work in the world that Christ's life and death vividly symbolize.

A variety of biblical statements affirm the comprehensiveness of God's love and the universality of Christ's significance. The Prologue to the Gospel of John describes the Word as the source of life—"all things came into being through him," and "the true light, which enlightens everyone, was coming into the world" (Jn 1:3, 9). As described in Acts, Paul assured his listeners on the Areopagus of Athens that God gives "to all mortals life and breath and all things," and "is not far from each one of us" (Acts 17:25, 27). The deutero-Pauline letter of 1 Timothy affirms what is sometimes called "the universal salvific will of God": "God our Savior . . . desires everyone to be saved and to come to the knowledge of the truth" (1 Tim 2:3-4).

There is good reason to explore the wide-ranging implications of Christ's significance. For open theists, the distinctive claims that Christian orthodoxy makes for Jesus are not at all incompatible with a vision of the "cosmic Christ." Indeed, they provide a solid foundation for it.

CHAPTER TEN

OPEN THEISM AND THE CHALLENGE OF CHURCH

WITH ITS EMPHASIS ON HUMAN FREEDOM, especially libertarian freedom, open theism seems open to the criticism that it leaves little room for a robust doctrine of the church. After all, if we are free to make individual choices and the most important decision we could ever make determines our eternal destiny, some may wonder what need there is for close connections with others. It may appear that open theism bolsters the individualism that pervades contemporary Western culture and poses an obstacle to anything like a close community. In this chapter we'll look at the central role that community plays in the Christian understanding of salvation and look for evidence that it is perfectly compatible with an open perspective on human freedom.

THE CHURCH AS A UNIQUE SOCIAL REALITY

The church is unlike anything else in human experience. We may find analogies for the church in other human groups, we may find precedents for it in other communities, and we may find metaphors to illustrate it here and there throughout our experience. But there are things about the Christian church that distinguish it from every other social arrangement. What is it that makes the church so special?

The Bible's most important descriptions of the church come from the chronological bookends of the New Testament—the letters of Paul and the Gospel of John. According to these sources, the church is the creation of the Holy Spirit, who extends Christ's saving work in the world, and the central dynamic of the church is the love that Jesus' life perfectly exemplified.

The "farewell discourses" that culminate in Jesus' "high priestly" prayer (Jn 14-17) reveal that the purpose of Jesus' ministry was to create a community whose inner dynamic reflects God's inner reality. These important chapters show that Jesus sought to bring his disciples into the love that radiates between the Father and the Son—the endless circle of affection that is central to God's life, the affection that *is* God's life. Thus Jesus says, "As the Father has loved me, so I have loved you; abide in my love. If you keep my commandments, you will abide in my love, just as I have kept my Father's commandments and abide in his love" (Jn 15:9-10; cf. Jn 14:16-17, 23; 15:12; 16:27; 17:20-23). In the fellowship of the church, God embraces human beings within God's own life.

The goal of Jesus' mission to the world is thus to incorporate his followers within the fellowship that defined his own relation with God.[1] And the Spirit is involved in every phase of the process. First, the Spirit unites the Father and the Son. This is the essence of God's own life. Second, the Spirit unites Christ with his followers. Following his earthly life, Jesus continues to be present with his disciples through the Spirit he promised to send them. And third, the Spirit unites Christ's followers with one another. So, by virtue of its connection to God, in Christ, through the Holy Spirit, the church is a unique social reality, a community unlike any other. In their togetherness-in-Christ, people experience new and unprecedented forms of fellowship.

Central to the New Testament concept of church, then, is the conviction that Christ creates a new "communal consciousness," a new way of thinking, feeling, and relating to others. The cultivation of this sense of community was the overriding concern of Paul's letters. The purpose

---

[1]Wolfhart Pannenberg describes it this way: the Spirit connects believers with the Son, and in so doing incorporates them into God's own life. Consequently, believers' relation to God reflects Christ's own relation to God. The same mutual love that unites Father and Son in eternity appears in them. They receive the gift of the Spirit from the Father and the Son, and when they are linked to the Son by faith and baptism, they become members of his body. As a result, they share in Jesus' own sonship and participate in God's own life. Like Jesus, they receive the Spirit from the Father, and return it by offering prayer and praise. See *Systematic Theology*, trans. Geoffrey W. Bromiley (3 vols; Grand Rapids, MI: Eerdmans, 1991-1998), 3:11.

of his missives was to help early Christian congregations understand their identity in Christ and fulfill that identity in the way they lived, specifically in their relations with one another.

Accordingly, Paul's letters typically divide into two parts—theological and "paranetic," or practical. The apostle first tells his readers about the glorious blessings that salvation brings, the new reality that God makes available in Christ. Then he tells them how to live lives that are consistent with their spiritual identity. His letter to the Ephesians provides a good example of this format. After a glorious description of the church, Paul transitions to a discussion of various practical matters with this statement:

> I therefore, the prisoner in the Lord, beg you to lead a life worthy of the calling to which you have been called, with all humility and gentleness, with patience, bearing with one another in love, making every effort to maintain the unity of the Spirit in the bond of peace. (Eph. 4:1-3)

In his most famous statement on the topic, Paul identifies the central elements of Christian existence as faith, hope, and love. All of them apply to Christian corporate life, but it is particularly love that imparts to the Christian community its unprecedented, unparalleled quality of life (1 Cor 13:13). The love its members have for each other is what sets the church apart from all other human societies.

Because they belong to a loving community, members of the church share one another's experiences, both positive and negative. "Bear one another's burdens," Paul wrote to the Galatian Christians, "and in this way you will fulfill the law of Christ" (Gal 6:2). Members of the Christian community reach out and share each other's sorrows and difficulties. In the church as in the body—Paul's famous metaphor—"If one member suffers, all suffer together with it" (1 Cor 12:26).

In the life together that Christ makes possible, mutual suffering leads to mutual comfort. "For just as the sufferings of Christ are abundant for us, so also our consolation is abundant through Christ. . . . We know that as you share in our sufferings, so also you share in our consolation" (2 Cor 1:3-7). Deep channels of sympathy and support connect members to one another in the Christian community.

Because the church is a loving community, its members also tend to each other's needs. "Whenever we have an opportunity," says Paul, "let us work for the good of all, and especially for those of the family of faith" (Gal 6:10). The New Testament devotes considerable attention to this theme, and it was a prominent feature in the way the earliest Christians lived. Members of the Jerusalem community cared for their own. They ate together daily (Acts 2:46). They shared everything they had. In fact, "no one claimed private ownership of any of his possessions" (Acts 4:32). As a result, "there was not a needy person among them, for as many as owned lands or houses sold them and brought the proceeds of what was sold. They laid it at the apostles' feet, and it was distributed to each as any had need" (Acts 4:34-35). There was apparently a "daily distribution of food" to provide for those like widows who needed assistance (Acts 6:1).

According to the letter of James, professions of religious devotion are worthless unless people care for others within the community of faith. "What good is it, my brothers and sisters," James demands, "if you say you have faith but do not have works? Can faith save you? If a brother or sister is naked and lacks daily food, and one of you says to them, 'Go in peace; keep warm and eat your fill,' and yet you do not supply their bodily needs, what is the good of that? So faith by itself, if it has no works, is dead" (Jas 2:14-17). Thus, true faith comes to expression in the way we care for fellow Christians.[2]

As a serving community, the church reenacts and extends the ministry of Jesus, who "came not to be served but to serve" (Mk 10:45). In a vivid demonstration of his willingness to serve, Jesus washed his disciples' feet, and told them to follow his example (Jn 13:12-15). And of course, the ultimate act of service was his death on the cross (Mk 10:45). As he told his disciples, "No one has greater love than this, to lay down one's life for one's friends" (Jn 15:13).

---

[2]There is evidence that Christians cared for those outside the community too. Galatians 6:10 encourages believers to do good to all people. Bruce Winter argues that the early church taught a civic consciousness among its members (*Seek the Welfare of the City: Christians as Benefactors and Citizens* [Grand Rapids: Eerdmans, 1994], 3).

And because the church is a loving community, it is also a forgiving community.[3] Paul's letters underline the importance of forgiveness in a number of places. "Be kind to one another, tenderhearted, forgiving one another, as God in Christ has forgiven you" (Eph 4:32). "Bear with one another and, if anyone has a complaint against another, forgive each other; just as the Lord has forgiven you, so you also must forgive" (Col 3:13).

Christ's saving work thus comes to vivid expression in the unique quality of life that Christians share. "By this everyone will know that you are my disciples," Jesus said, "if you have love for one another" (Jn 13:35).[4] Christ makes available to people a quality of life together, or a specific type of community, that is radically different from all other human groups or societies. In the quality of their relationships and the nature of their fellowship, in the content of their shared experiences, the members of the church enjoy a glimpse of our original life together and a foretaste of the life to come. Indeed, the remarkable relationships that characterize the members of the Christian community represent the clearest demonstration of God's power in the world. In the love they show each other, they provide a vivid display of Christ's enduring presence.

A conspicuous feature of Christianity from its beginning was an emphasis on charity as the paramount Christian virtue and the corresponding affirmation that every human being has unique dignity and unqualified value, whatever his or her social status or physical condition. Following the example of Jesus' life of self-sacrificing service, early Christians too were open to people of all classes and cultures. And there were members of the community who devoted themselves to the welfare of others, including the diseased and the destitute. As some see it, this contribution to human values was revolutionary. Nothing in the world of late antiquity, nothing in classical

---

[3]For Reinhold Niebuhr, forgiveness is "the final form of love" (*The Irony of American History* [New York: Scribner's, 1952], 63).

[4]Compare these words from 1 John: "Since God loved us so much, we also ought to love one another. . . . If we love one another, God lives in us, and his love is perfected in us. . . . God is love, and those who abide in love abide in God, and God abides in them. . . . Those who love God must love their brothers and sisters also" (1 Jn 4:11-21).

culture, compared to the willingness of Christians to jeopardize their own well-being in serving others. Greek and Roman paganism had acknowledged no such duties.[5]

Christians not only cared for people individually, they eventually established institutions to provide for care—hospitals for the sick and welfare centers for the needy. In the words of one historian of medicine,

> Christianity planted the hospital. . . . By 250 the Church in Rome had developed an elaborate charitable outreach, with wealthy converts providing food and shelter for the poor. After Constantine officially recognized Christianity, Christians established hospitals throughout the empire. . . . By the mid sixth century Jerusalem had one with 200 beds, and another in Constantinople was bigger still. . . . By 650, Constantinople had a hierarchy of physicians and even teaching facilities, a home for the elderly and, beyond the walls, a leper house. [They all] shared a common . . . ethos of charity.[6]

The revolution in values that Christianity brought about was profound because it eventually, dramatically, and permanently transformed the prevailing perspective on the human in Western civilization: *eventually*, because it took a long time for its ramifications to develop in the form of laws and institutions—the abolition of slavery was not achieved until the nineteenth century, the establishment of equal rights in the United States only in the mid-twentieth century; *dramatically*, because it involved such a novel perspective of the human; and *permanently*, because even those who reject everything else in religion, at least many of them, affirm the values that stem from the revolution. Instead of following Nietzsche, who bemoaned Christianity's cultivation of charity and compassion, they accept the idea that all human beings deserve respect.

---

[5]St. Fabiola was an affluent fourth-century convert to Christianity. She founded a hospital and dedicated her life to charity among Rome's sick poor. "She assembled all the sick from the streets and highways and personally tended the unhappy and impoverished victims of hunger and disease." She often washed wounds "which others—even men—could hardly bear to look at. . . . She founded a hospital and gathered there the sufferers from the streets, and gave them all the attention of a nurse. . . . How often she carried home, on her own shoulders, the first and poor who were plagued by epilepsy! How she washed the pus from sores which others could not even behold!" (Roy Porter, *The Greatest Benefit to Mankind: A Medical History of Humanity* [W. W. Norton, 1997]), 87-88.

[6]Roy Porter, *The Greatest Benefit to Mankind*, 87.

There is another characteristic of Paul's letters that underscores the importance of community to his thinking. While he was obviously interested in Christianity as a "global" phenomenon—for example, he praised Christians in one area for caring for and assisting those in another[7]—the principal object of the apostle's concern was the way Christians interacted with each other within their small local communities. He wanted his fellow believers to develop an intimate connection with each other within the specific locales where they lived.[8]

No model from their contemporary society perfectly fits these early Christian congregations, but the closest social correlate was "the intimacy of the local household assembly." Within these communities, as Wayne A. Meeks describes them, "a high level of commitment is demanded, the degree of direct interpersonal engagement is strong, the authority structure is fluid and charismatic . . . , and internal boundaries are weak."[9] Moreover, each congregation brought into fellowship "persons of a wide mix of social levels."[10] And each congregation "enjoyed an unusual degree of intimacy, high levels of interaction among members, and a very strong sense of internal cohesion and of distinction both from outsiders and from 'the world.'"[11] In fact, in his earlier letters, Paul only uses the word "church," or *ekklēsia*, to refer to specific groups of people, probably never more than thirty or so, who met together on a regular basis.[12]

---

[7]In 1 Cor 16:3, Paul speaks of "collections" that would provide a gift to believers in Jerusalem.

[8]According to Wayne Meeks, even though Paul wanted "the intimate, close-knit life of the local groups [to be] seen . . . simultaneously [as] part of a much larger, indeed ultimately worldwide, movement or entity," it was "concern about the internal life of the Christian groups in each city that prompted most of the correspondence" (*The First Urban Christians: The Social World of the Apostle Paul* [New Haven and London: Yale University Press, 1983], 74). Material in this paragraph and the remainder of this section was published previously in Richard Rice, "From Adventist Anthropology to Adventist Ecclesiology," *Spectrum: Journal of the Association of Adventist Forums* 43, no. 2 (Spring 2015) 60-64, 80, republished with permission of *Spectrum* as above.

[9]Meeks, *The First Urban Christians*, 190.

[10]Meeks, *The First Urban Christians*, 191.

[11]Meeks, *The First Urban Christians*, 74.

[12]According to Robert Banks, "In these early letters of Paul [1–2 Thess, 1 Cor, Gal, Rom], the term *ekklēsia* consistently refers to actual gatherings of Christians as such, or to Christians in a local area conceived or defined as a regularly assembling community. . . . The word does not describe all the Christians who live in a particular locality if they do not gather. Nor does it refer to the sum total of Christians in a region or scattered throughout the world at any a particular time"

Because the Christian life as Paul envisioned it involved close relations among Christians, it is no surprise that he was greatly distressed when he received reports that there was disharmony among them, or that some members were slighting those who had less wealth or worldly status. He was dismayed, for example, when he learned that there was jealousy and quarreling among the Christians in Corinth (1 Cor 3:3), along with divisions and factions (1 Cor 11:18-19), and that some even disregarded the needs of others when they had their communal meals. Indeed, his beautiful description of love appears within an extended appeal to the Christians in that city to care for, rather than elevate themselves above, one another (1 Cor 12–14).

We find even more striking evidence of the importance Paul attached to the internal life of the community in the fact that his letters say little about the relationships of Christians to those outside the community and next to nothing about sharing their faith with non-Christians. According to Robert Banks, "Nothing in Paul's writings suggests that the gathering of believers has a *direct* function vis-à-vis the world." The "body" metaphor "basically refers to the interaction of the members with one another, not with outsiders."[13] For Terence Donaldson as well, there is a striking absence from Paul's letters of any attempt to mobilize his congregations for ongoing evangelistic activity.[14] "Nowhere," he exclaims, "do we find [in Paul's letters] a single injunction to evangelize!"[15] So it was not the relation between the church and the world, not the way Christians treated people outside the community, that occupied Paul, but relations within the community, the way Christians treated each other.

(*Paul's Idea of Community: The Early House Churches in their Cultural Setting*, rev. ed. [Peabody, MA: Hendrickson, 1994], 35).

[13] Banks, *Paul's Idea of Community*, 64.

[14] Terence L. Donaldson, "The Field God Has Assigned: Geography and Mission in Paul," in *Religious Rivalries in the Early Roman Empire and the Rise of Christianity*, ed. Leif Vaage (Waterloo, ON: Wilfrid Laurier University Press, 2006), 112. Donaldson takes exception to some of the prevalent views of Paul's ministry and its intended results. He argues that it was not the apostle's conscious strategy to plant churches around the Roman Empire with the intention that they would extend a program of evangelization. Nor was the eventual success of Christianity the result of a deliberate and organized program of mission (109). See also Donaldson's paper "The Absence from Paul's Letters of Any Injunction to Evangelize" (Society of Biblical Literature, Annual Meeting, Nashville, November 19, 2000).

[15] Donaldson, "Field God Has Assigned," 118.

The central object of concern that comes to expression in Paul's letters was the life Christians shared within small, concrete communities of faith. As he describes it, the life Christ makes available takes its primary form in the fellowship of local Christian congregations. And when he gave practical spiritual advice, he was typically thinking of the way people interacted with the fellow believers whom they knew well and frequently associated with.

SALVATION AND COMMUNITY

We see Paul's concern for community not only in the abundant practical advice he gives to believers. It even takes priority over what, for many people, is the most important concept of all in Paul's theology, namely, salvation through faith. As Gunther Bornkamm describes it, for example, the gospel of justification by faith alone was a "specifically Pauline creation," and it was this doctrine that "gave the unity of the church composed of Jews and Gentiles its first real theological basis."[16]

True, a central concept in Paul's account of salvation is righteousness by faith, the idea that we are saved entirely by God's grace, not by success in keeping the law. And this idea was certainly revolutionary for Paul, since he grew up regarding the law as a means of salvation.[17] But as the most dramatic exclamation in his writings indicates, there was something that amazed him even more—the unique community that righteousness by faith makes possible: "O the depth of the riches and wisdom and knowledge of God! How unsearchable are his judgments and how inscrutable his ways!" (Rom 11:33).

What amazed Paul was the remarkable inclusivity of this community. It overcomes all the barriers that naturally separate people—not only the division between Jews and Gentiles, but also divisions between male and female, slave and free, moral and immoral, even sinners and sinned-against. So, the reason righteousness by faith is so important to Paul is the fact that it makes this community possible. No matter how different members of the church may be in other respects, they are identical in

---

[16]Gunther Bornkamm, *Paul*, trans. D. M. G. Stalker (New York: Harper & Row, 1969), 115.
[17]Paul describes the dramatic shift in his perspective on legal righteousness in Phil 3:4-9.

one respect that matters more—they are all saved by grace through faith. And because this great fact is true of each of them, they all belong to the same community. The plan of salvation provides for a community so inclusive that it brings together people from every conceivable background and overcomes all the obstacles that divide them. Righteousness by faith is the means, Christian community is the end.

We see this trajectory in familiar passages like Ephesians 2. Paul begins by assuring his readers that they are saved from sin by trusting in God's gracious gift, not by relying on their good works (Eph 2:8-9). Then he comes to the main point. He reminds his readers, "Gentiles by birth," as he calls them, that they were once without Christ, far off, aliens from the commonwealth of Israel, strangers to the covenants of promise, without hope and without God in the world. But now they are one with God's people. Christ Jesus, he emphasizes, "has made both groups into one and has broken down the dividing wall" between them. He abolished the law "that he might create in himself one new humanity" and "reconcile both groups to God in one body" (Eph 2:12-16). The ultimate effect of Christ's work is thus to bring diverse people together to form one radically inclusive community. Salvation by faith is important: it provides the basis for this community. It is the one and only way by which anyone is saved, Jew and Gentile alike.

We find the same strategy in Galatians 3. Paul asserts that faith, not the law, is the basis of salvation (Gal 3:10-14). "In Christ Jesus you are all children of God through faith," he summarizes (Gal 3:26). Then he draws this momentous conclusion: "There is no longer Jew or Greek, there is no longer slave or free, there is no longer male and female; for all of you are one in Christ Jesus" (Gal 3:28). Because all are saved on the same basis, all belong to the same community. Christ levels all the factors that typically divide people.[18]

All this leads to a rather dramatic conclusion. As the New Testament describes it, the church is not incidental to the experience of salvation, it

---

[18]Paul's most famous letter follows the same pattern. In Rom 1–8 he presents a detailed explanation of righteousness by faith. And in Rom 9–11 he shows what this means for human community: people of all backgrounds, Jews and Gentiles alike, are incorporated within the fellowship of God's love.

is integral, indeed central, to it. The culmination of Christ's saving work is the creation of a community that bears his name and embodies his love. Consequently, no one can be a Christian, not in the full and fundamental sense of the word, and *not* be part of the Christian community.

THE ROAD TO INDIVIDUALISM

The idea that the church is important faces stiff resistance in the thinking of many people.[19] In fact, during many years of teaching religion, I have found no aspect of Christian faith that generates more opposition among college-age young people than the doctrine of the church. And it is a well-established fact that interest in organized religion has declined precipitously in recent times, as the number of "nones," for "no religious affiliation," has risen.[20] This is not necessarily to say that people are no longer interested in religion. To the contrary, there is a considerable interest, but to a greater degree than ever before, people today are more interested in *religion* than in *religions*. They are not aligning themselves with established communities. They are not looking for a tradition to follow or an organization to join. They are looking for something that will help them in their personal spiritual quest. They are looking for a satisfying religious experience wherever they can find it. And many of them have serious questions, not just about specific beliefs and practices, but about the whole idea of corporate religion. As they see it, religion is deeply personal, and that means it is essentially private. Whether or not your religion involves a community is up to you. It's entirely discretionary.

To distill this challenge to a single expression, let us describe it as the challenge of *spiritual individualism*. One of the things that makes individualism such a formidable challenge is that fact that it is hard for

---

[19]Some of the concepts in this section and the next are adapted from a previously published article. Richard Rice, "The Challenge of Spiritual Individualism (And How to Meet It)," *Andrews University Seminary Studies* 43, no. 1 (Spring 2005): 113-31.

[20]For an informed and thoughtful discussion of this phenomenon, see Elizabeth Drescher, *Choosing Our Religion: The Spiritual Lives of America's Nones* (Oxford: Oxford University Press, 2016). According to the statistics she provides, fully thirty-five percent of Americans under age thirty have no religious affiliation (6). Another of the growing number of books on the topic is James Emery White, *The Rise of the Nones: Understanding and Reaching the Religiously Unaffiliated* (Grand Rapids, MI: Baker Books, 2014).

people to see it as a challenge. In fact, it's hard for them to see it at all. The fundamental assumptions of any age or culture are so deeply woven into the fabric of people's thinking that it seems unnatural to question them. We typically think *with* them, not *about* them.

Individualism is one such concept. It is one of the most influential and pervasive elements of Western consciousness, so ingrained in our thinking that it is integral to the way most of us think. Like many of our cultural assumptions, however, it has a history, and its roots reach deep into the soil of Western tradition.[21]

By many accounts, "the inaugurator of the modern concept of the self" was Augustine, the great Latin father, who sought God by journeying into the soul. Several centuries later, Boethius defined a person as "the individual substance of a rational nature." Coupled with Augustine's introspection, Boethius' elevation of the individual eventually led to the familiar concept of the self as "the stable, abiding reality that constitutes the individual human being."[22]

Once this notion of the self was established, the big question was how to understand it. What is this inner reality? The answer of the Enlightenment was *reason*. For Rene Descartes and his successors, the self-conscious, rational self, certain of its own existence, was the final arbiter of truth.[23] Immanuel Kant's careful analyses of reason completed the long progression to

---

[21]The emergence of the self in Western thought, as well as its subsequent demise, has attracted a great deal of scholarly attention. The most comprehensive discussion to date is no doubt Charles Taylor's magisterial account, *Sources of the Self: The Making of the Modern Identity* (Cambridge, MA: Harvard University Press, 1989). A number of works deal with various aspects of the modern and/or postmodern self, including Adam B. Seligman, *Modernity's Wager: Authority, the Self, and Transcendence* (Princeton, NJ: Princeton University Press, 2000) and Calvin O. Schrag, *The Self After Postmodernity* (New Haven, CT: Yale University Press, 1997). An influential sociological study of the self in contemporary America is Robert Bellah et al., *Habits of the Heart: Individualism and Commitment in American Life* (Berkeley: University of California Press, 1985). Stanley J. Grenz provides a readable and reliable account of the self's long history in *The Social God and the Relational Self* (Louisville, KY: Westminster John Knox, 2001). The affective domain of our experience has received considerable attention recently. See, for example, A. R. Damasio, *Descartes' Error: Emotion, Reason, and the Human Brain* (New York: Putnam, 1994), and Martha Nussbaum, *Upheavals of Thought: The Intelligence of Emotions* (New York: Cambridge University Press, 2001).

[22]Grenz, *The Social God*, 63-67.

[23]"While I thus wished to think everything false, it was necessarily true that I who thought so was something. Since this truth, *I think therefore I am, (or exist)*, was so firm and assured that all the most extravagant suppositions of the skeptics were unable to shake it, I judged that I could safely

radical individualism, the view that essential humanity is the thinking individual, self-conscious and detached, the master of an objective world. In contrast, the self as Romanticism viewed it is particular rather than universal, and it consists of feelings, rather than reason.[24] The key to happiness was to embrace oneself, to celebrate one's own nature. The Romantic self is the self-absorbed self, devoted to itself, affirming of itself.[25]

Certain religious developments are closely tied to this narrative. Martin Luther found assurance in the soul's trust in God, the personal experience of faith. And we see inwardness and individuality in the understanding of religion that followed the Reformation. For Puritans, Pietists, and their heirs, true religion is essentially internal. We experience it individually and we feel it so deeply that it transforms our behavior.[26]

Ever since Augustine, then, Western thought has been preoccupied with the discovery and the fulfillment of the individual—discovery by introspection, by turning within ourselves, and fulfillment either through rational self-mastery, or through a celebration of personal uniqueness. Throughout its variations, however, the idea persists that the real person, the true self, is something that lies within us, and the essential unit of human reality is the individual by him- or herself. In other words, the modern self is the solitary self, detached and disconnected from others.

On this atomistic concept of humanity, society is nothing more than "a collection of autonomous, independent selves, each of whom pursues his own ends."[27] People may still form relationships, but they do so only to meet their individual needs. If they don't need the group in order to reach their private goals, they feel free to leave. The object of their commitment is the self, not the community.

---

accept it as the first principle of the philosophy I was seeking" (*Discourse on Method and Meditations*, 24 [Quoted in Grenz, *The Social God*, 69]).

[24]Grenz, *The Social God*, 105.

[25]Eventually the Romantic quest for self-expression "opened the door for the loss, dissipation, or deconstruction of the self that developed in the twentieth century." For radical postmoderns, the self is not an object in the natural world, but a cultural artifact. All that's left is a decentered, fleeting self, constructed at each moment of its existence, splintered into multiple subjectivities (Grenz, *The Social God*, 118, 134, 136).

[26]Grenz, *The Social God*, 82-85.

[27]Grenz, *The Social God*, 99.

It is not hard to see why individualism poses a formidable obstacle to genuine community. If the individual is the center of religious life, and the essential function of religion is to help people face their individual personal challenges and enhance their private experience, then the value of corporate religion—communities, organizations, institutions, traditions—is problematic. For some, religious communities are unnecessary. When people say, "I'm spiritual, but I'm not religious," they usually mean that they value a private connection with the divine, but they have no interest in religious organizations. Others believe that religious organizations have value, but only because they can help people to meet private spiritual needs. But they are not necessary for everyone, and not required for anyone.

RESPONDING TO SPIRITUAL INDIVIDUALISM

Religious individualism poses a tremendous challenge to Christianity in the Western world today, not just because it leads people to discount the importance of the church, but because it makes it difficult for them to comprehend the meaning of the church. From Augustine onward, the broad sweep of Western thought, secular and religious alike, elevates the individual as the fundamental unit of humanity. And since religion is essentially inward, it is intensely private.[28] It belongs to the sphere of inner life that we can access only by ourselves. Others may advise and encourage us as we take our journey, but we must ultimately take it alone.

In spite of the widespread appeal of individualism today and the corollary resistance to community, there are ways to counter its influence. One is to differentiate individuality from individualism. In contrast to the way individualism undermines community, individuality and community are not only compatible, they enhance rather than conflict with each other. In fact, that is arguably the thesis of Paul's well-known discussion of spiritual gifts in 1 Corinthians 12:12-14. As he explains it, the various qualities and abilities that make us different from each other are

---

[28]According to Richard Sloan of Columbia-Presbyterian Medical Center, for example, health care givers have no business getting involved in the spiritual life of their patients, because religion is essentially a private matter (Claudia Kalb, "Faith and Healing," *Newsweek*, November 10, 2003, 50).

not an obstacle for unity, but a reason for it. Like a human body, which exists through the coherence of its various organs—all of which have essential contributions to make—the Christian community assumes a distinct form of life by virtue of the complementary differences that characterize its members. So, it's not unity *in spite of* diversity, it's unity *because* of diversity. It is the presence of significant differences among its members that makes the church's rich complex unity what it is.

Another way of countering the individualism of our culture is to point out that the value we instinctively place on the individual person actually has its roots in religion, specifically, in Judaism and Christianity. As recounted by Wolfhart Pannenberg, individuals enjoyed no independence in archaic societies. The lived in a "wide-branched kinship system," where their rights and duties were exactly determined.[29] Things began to change for Israel around the time of the exile, when the prophets Jeremiah and Ezekiel held that it was no longer the case that children and grandchildren should atone for the sins of their parents. Instead each individual was responsible for him/herself. "The righteousness of the righteous shall be his own, and the wickedness of the wicked shall be his own" (Ezek 18:20). And in postexilic Judaism the hope of the resurrection arose in response to the conviction that the meaning of life must be realized in the lives of individual human beings. And since this doesn't always happen before someone dies, there must be a life to come where it does. The preaching of Jesus further emphasized the importance of the individual with his assurance that God cares for each lost person with infinite love and individuals determine their eternal destiny in a personal decision of faith. The infinite value of the individual is thus a central idea in Christianity.[30] This suggests that opposing individualism does not mean a loss of individuality. And since eternal destiny depends on the exercise of personal choice, personal freedom has an indispensable role to play. At the same time, as we shall note in the next chapter, communal life too plays an important role in the life to come.

---

[29] Wolfhart Pannenberg, *Anthropology in Theological Perspective*, trans. Matthew J. O'Connell (Philadelphia: Westminster Press, 1985), 165.

[30] Pannenberg, *Anthropology*, 166-67.

Yet another reason for us to reconsider our views of the individual—and to refocus our attention on the concrete dynamics of Christian community—is growing evidence for the physical basis of human existence. In fact, recent developments in neuroscience support the biblical emphasis on community. In *The Physical Nature of Christian Life: Neuroscience, Psychology, and the Church*,[31] Warren S. Brown and Brad D. Strawn argue that the formative factors in our personal development are almost exclusively interpersonal. Human beings are not only embodied in physical forms but embedded in a physical world surrounded by other embodied human beings. In terms of the rather technical language of complex dynamical systems, characteristics like minds and personalities can emerge from ongoing interactions involving millions of parts. A collection forms a "system" when the individual parts function as a unity. And a system is "dynamical" in the technical sense when it has the capacity to reorganize in response to changes in the environment. Physically embodied, socially embedded in the world, and participating in various dynamical systems, the human self or person is subject to continual growth and transformation.[32]

From this perspective on human nature, spiritual individualism is a contradiction in terms. According to Brown and Strawn, the familiar notion that authentic spirituality is intensely private is the consequence of the anthropological dualism that dominated Christian thought through much of its history. For those who conceive the soul as a reality distinct from the body, it is natural to regard one's spiritual life as basically private and inward and to view the relationships Christians have with one another as incidental to their spiritual identity. Connecting with other church members has no vital role to play in one's spiritual life, and participating with others in worship and service is reduced to a matter of personal preference. Such an outlook makes genuine Christian community impossible.

---

[31]Warren S. Brown and Brad D. Strawn, *The Physical Nature of Christian Life: Neuroscience, Psychology, and the Church* (New York: Cambridge University Press, 2012).

[32]Material in this paragraph and the three that follow was published previously in Richard Rice, "From Adventist Anthropology to Adventist Ecclesiology," *Spectrum: Journal of the Association of Adventist Forums* 43, no. 2 (Spring 2015) 60-64, 80, republished with permission of *Spectrum* as above.

A mere collection of people who "swarm" at the same time and place could never become more than a loose association of the independently spiritual. It could never become a body in any significant sense, let alone "the body of Christ."[33]

On the view that human beings are both physically embodied and socially embedded, however, spirituality is not only closely connected to community, personal growth is actually a product of congregational growth. Because the processes of human formation in general are primarily social, spiritual growth as well is social and interpersonal. It can only occur within community, indeed, within close-knit communities whose members spend significant time together and learn to trust one another. It cannot happen when groups are too large or when members meet together only sporadically.[34]

Furthermore, in a system where significant growth can take place, there is reciprocal interaction between the individuals and the group. In a church as in family, influence flows from the individual to the group, and from the group back to the individual. As a result of these interactions, the roles members play will be flexible, and the group as a whole proves to be more than the sum of its individual parts. "Families and churches develop capacities that go well beyond the singular capacities of any of the individuals in the family or church."[35] So the church is not a vague collective, the sum total of the members' individual experiences. Rather, it is the corporate experience of the community that gives its individual members their identity.[36]

To participate in a community, then, does not compromise individual fulfillment, it cultivates and shapes it. We achieve true individuality—we come to understand the reality, the scope, and the proper exercise of personal freedom—through the influence of the important communities to which we belong. While freedom is essential to our identity as creatures in God's image, it is not undefined or unlimited.

---

[33]Brown and Strawn, *Physical Nature of Christian Life*, 120.

[34]Brown and Strawn, *Physical Nature of Christian Life*, 101.

[35]Brown and Strawn, *Physical Nature of Christian Life*, 129.

[36]In fact, our modern appreciation for the individual, and our insistence that each human being has unalienable rights, is arguably the fruit of biblical principles.

It will ever remain, as philosopher Paul Ricoeur puts it, "an only human freedom."[37]

In his familiar account of the "ontological elements," Paul Tillich includes two polarities that relate to our concerns here. They are individualization and participation, and freedom and destiny.[38] While the first element in each polarity is essential to our existence, its counterpart is equally important, and it acquires significance only in the relationship to which it belongs. Consequently, the concept of freedom that is central to open theism is not something that isolates individuals from others. Instead, it draws us together. And instead of setting us on a course of arbitrary choosing, it calls us to accept the destiny for which we have been created. To affirm freedom is not to suggest that our destiny is a matter of arbitrary choice. It is to recognize that our destiny is something that we are invited to affirm and embrace.

If individuality and community are integrally connected, and interdependent, we should think of the two as forming a polarity, in contrast to a contradiction or an antithesis.[39] The elements in a polar contrast do not compete with each other, they complement each other. In fact, each enhances the other. The nemesis of community is not individuality, but individualism, the elevation of one's own importance above that of others, the pursuit of one's own interests at the expense of others. Although there is a great deal in Christian faith that opposes individualism, there is nothing that denies the significance of the individual.

The Bible affirms the value of the individual in various ways. One is by emphasizing personal responsibility. Certain passages insist that God will not condemn people for the sins their parents committed.[40] Each

---

[37] Paul Ricoeur, *Freedom and Nature: The Voluntary and the Involuntary*, trans. Erazim V. Kohak (Evanston, IL: Northwestern University Press), 486.

[38] Paul Tillich, *Systematic Theology*, 3 vols. (Chicago: University of Chicago Press, 1951-1963), 1:174-86).

[39] According to Tillich, freedom and destiny form one of the three "polarities" that constitute the "basic ontological structure." The "first element expresses the self-relatedness of being, its power of being something for itself, while the second element expresses the belongingness of being, its character of being a part of a universe of being." *Systematic Theology*, 1:165.

[40] A notable passage is Ezek 18, where the word of the Lord asserts, "It is only the person who sins that shall die" (Ezek 18:4; cf. Ezek 18:20).

one is responsible for his or her own status before God. The biblical idea of the resurrection also affirms the value of the human individual. Citizenship in God's kingdom is not just for the generation that happens to be alive when it finally arrives, Paul indicates in 1 Thessalonians. Every human being is important enough to participate in the ultimate fulfillment of human existence. The Bible's most important affirmation of individual value may be Jesus' invitation to everyone to enter the kingdom of God. He assured people that God's kingdom was open to them no matter what their background or social connections were.[41]

From a Christian perspective, then, there is nothing wrong with individuality. To the contrary, every person is the repository of great value. The problem is individualism. Individuality affirms the value of the person; individualism exaggerates and ultimately undermines it. To do justice to the biblical view, we need to replace individualism with individuality. More accurately, we need to replace individualism with individual-in-community. Only if we do this can we become, individually and communally, everything that God wants us to be.

To conclude, Paul's description of spiritual gifts provides a helpful basis for affirming the interconnection between individual and community from a Christian perspective. It is important to appreciate the contrasting qualities and abilities that characterize individuals in a community, but it is even more important to appreciate the value of these distinguishing features. As Paul's reflections on spiritual gifts emphasizes, it's not the fact that people are different from each other that matters; what matters is what they are together. Possessing different gifts, they complement each other. It is contributing their individual abilities to one another that gives each of them his or her true significance, just as the different members of the human body depend on the body as a whole for their existence and derive their significance from their contribution to what the body is. In fact, only within community will we find our fulfillment as individuals.

---

[41]As noted in the previous chapter, we see this in the remarkable juxtaposition of Jesus' dialogues with Nicodemus and the Samaritan woman recorded in Jn 3 and Jn 4. Nicodemus was a Pharisee of high standing, no doubt a meticulous observer of extensive religious requirements. The woman was of another, sharply contrasting, ethnic and social group and checkered personal life.

From this perspective, the more striking the variations, the richer the corporate unity of the various members can be. Therefore, if we think of freedom as the capacity to willingly, voluntarily contribute whatever distinctive gifts and qualities we have to the corporate life of the Christian community, it is clear that freedom is an important aspect of God's hopes for humanity.

While open theism affirms the importance of individual freedom, when connected with the doctrine of the church, it gives the individual Christian greater significance than individualism could ever provide.

 OPEN THEISM AND THE LAST THINGS

THE HOPE THAT GOD'S PURPOSES for creation and for humanity in particular will ultimately reach fulfillment is important for any version of Christianity. Yet no aspect of Christian faith generates a greater diversity of opinion and leaves more questions open than the doctrine of last things. Biblical accounts of the eschaton, the transition from this age to the age to come, contain dramatic descriptions of events such as the return of Christ, the resurrection of the dead, the final judgment, and the restoration of the earth, and a variety of interpretations surrounds each one. While open theists may differ as to how these descriptions should be interpreted, there are certain themes characteristic of open theism that have great significance for human destiny. They include the primacy of divine love, libertarian freedom, and the temporal nature of reality.

Though eschatology has not been one of its more distinctive concerns, open theism is compatible with the concept that there is "one far-off divine event, to which the whole creation moves."[1] And open theists share the expectation that God's purposes will reach fulfillment when history as we know it comes to an end. With believers through the ages they embrace the hope that God's kingdom will come and it will bring into fellowship with God a community of human beings who have responded

---

[1] From the concluding lines of "In Memoriam: A.H.H.A.," by Alfred Lord Tennyson. In one of his memorable statements, process philosopher Alfred North Whitehead asserted the opposite—there is "no far off divine event to which the whole creation moves" (quoted in Dorothy Emmet, *Whitehead's Philosophy of Organism*, 2nd ed. [New York: Springer, 1966], xxxii).

to God's offer of salvation and receive the transformation prefigured by Christ's resurrection. Restored to God's image, they continue their role as God's representatives in the world God has recreated. Free from the consequences of sin, they joyfully enter into fellowship with God, offering him praise and thanksgiving throughout eternity. With this general eschatological vision in mind, we will focus on one theme in particular— the perspective open theism provides with respect to the meaning, value, and certainty of eternal life.

DOES HISTORY NEED AN END?

As we have seen, the concept that time is real for God is basic to open theism. In other words, temporal duration characterizes reality as such, including God's relation to creation. God experiences the events of the finite world as they happen, and the future God brings about consists of an ongoing series of events that never ends. As open theists conceive it, eternal life is everlasting life. It continues into the future without interruption and without end. To etch more sharply the contours of the openness view of the future it may be helpful to compare it to the views of several theologians who are well known for their perspectives on Christian eschatology.

In the Gifford Lectures of 1955, Rudolf Bultmann (1884–1976) presents an existentialist account of Christian eschatology. As he describes it, the idea of history as a process has its roots in the Bible, and early Christians believed that this process would reach its climax in the imminent return of Christ. But when Christ failed to return as expected, Christians, in particular the apostle Paul, had to look for a new understanding of history's meaning. And they found it, not in the future, but in the past—not in the past exactly, but in the present significance of the past. According to the gospel, history's decisive event has already happened.[2] Jesus Christ is the key to history's meaning; he is *the* eschatological event.

Christ becomes available to us—more accurately, Christ confronts us—in the preaching of the gospel. And when we respond in faith to the

---

[2]Rudolf Bultmann, *History and Eschatology: The Presence of Eternity*, The Gifford Lectures 1955 (New York: Harper & Brothers, 1957), 43.

preaching of the gospel, we realize the meaning of history. God's word comes to us, says Bultmann, not as a universal truth, but in the form of address, which demands personal decision.[3] This response involves much more than intellectual assent, of course. Belief in this word "is readiness to submit one's whole life to its judgment and its grace," and "readiness always to hear it anew."[4] The meaning of history, then, is fully realized in acts of momentary responsible decision. And as a result, traditional questions about the meaning of history are irrelevant, as are the traditional concerns of Christian eschatology.

Since the totality of history is not accessible to us, we cannot answer the question of what history means as a whole. Nor can we determine what the future holds or how the world will end or what significance the overall span of human life in the universe may have. But such questions have no bearing on the meaning of Christian faith. From the perspective of faith, "the meaning of history lies always in the present, and when the present is conceived as the eschatological present by Christian faith the meaning in history is realized." To quote the last words of the lectures, "In every moment slumbers the possibility of being the eschatological moment. You must awaken it."[5]

Bultmann's emphasis on the importance of exercising faith here and now, ever and again, is undeniably moving. Yet, important as it is for us to respond to God personally, decisively, and repeatedly, open theists believe, along with many in the Christian world, that the overall course of history does have theological significance and will reach a culmination sometime in the future. As they see it, the Bible portrays a series of historical events as God's progressive revelation to human beings. And while this sequence came to a climax in the life, death, and resurrection of Jesus Christ, it will reach its fulfillment with the future establishment

---

[3]Human freedom is "always realized in the freedom of historical decisions" (Bultmann, *History and Eschatology*, 152).

[4]Rudolf Bultmann, "How Does God Speak Through the Bible?," in *Existence and Faith: Shorter Writings of Rudolf Bultmann*, selected, translated, and introduced by Schubert M. Ogden (Cleveland: Meridian Books, 1960), 169.

[5]Bultmann, *History and Eschatology*, 155. "Every instant has the possibility of being an eschatological instant and in Christian faith this possibility is realized" (154).

of his kingdom. Consequently, God's saving activity is not complete as yet. There is more to come. Even though the decisive events in human history have already taken place, the full effects of what Christ accomplished are yet to be realized.[6]

Another New Testament scholar, Oscar Cullmann (1902–1999), rejects Bultmann's view that the message of the New Testament can be equated with a call to respond to the proclamation of the gospel. It is wrong, he argues, to "contrast Christian existence and salvation history as opposites."[7] This ignores the important role that salvation history— *Heilsgeschichte*—plays in the New Testament. True, he grants, for the writers of the New Testament the "decisive turn of events has already occurred" in Christ, but the death and resurrection of Christ are better understood, not as the end of history, but as the "mid-point" of time, history's decisive turning point. "It is not 'a new time' which is created after Christ," says Cullmann, "but a new division of time."[8]

To illustrate this concept, Cullmann appeals to a distinction between D-day and V-day. "The decisive battle in a war may already have occurred in a relatively early stage of the war, and yet the war still continues . . . until 'Victory Day.'" "Precisely this," says Cullmann, "is the situation of which the New Testament is conscious," namely, that "that event on the cross, together with the resurrection which followed, was the already concluded decisive battle."[9] The decisive midpoint of history has arrived, but the end of history is yet to come. So even though the "already" of Christ's death and resurrection outweighs the "not yet" of the parousia, the "intermediate" period of time between the two is indeed part of salvation history.[10] And "the temporality of this salvation history must not be given up to make way," as Bultmann does, "for an existential *kerygma*."[11]

---

[6]Oscar Cullmann's interpretation of early Christian eschatology stands in sharp contrast to that of Bultmann (see *Salvation in History*, trans. Sidney G. Sowers [New York: Harper & Row, 1967], 183, 185).

[7]Cullmann, *Salvation in History*, 11.

[8]Cullmann, *Christ and Time: The Primitive Christian Conception of Time and History*, trans. Floyd V. Filson, rev. ed. (London: SCM Press, 1962), 92.

[9]Cullmann, *Christ and Time*, 84.

[10]Cullmann, *Salvation in History*, 183, 185.

[11]Cullmann, *Salvation in History*, 186.

In the latter decades of the twentieth century a number of theologians began to emphasize the importance, indeed the centrality, of eschatology to Christian thought. One was Jürgen Moltmann, whose book, *Theology of Hope*, attracted considerable attention. "From first to last," Moltmann asserts, "and not merely in the epilogue, Christianity is eschatology, is hope, forward looking and forward moving, and therefore also revolutionizing and transforming the present."[12]

No theologian gives the future a more prominent role in his interpretation of Christian faith than Wolfhart Pannenberg (1928–2014). In contrast to Bultmann, for whom the meaning of history can be realized in each moment of authentic decision, and in contrast to Cullmann, for whom the decisive event in history has already happened, Pannenberg insists that nothing is more important than the way history ends. Events, like words, he argues, acquire meaning from context, and the ultimate context of historical events is the whole of reality. But history becomes a totality only when it ends, so the final future is essential to the meaning of all that comes before.

For Pannenberg then, everything depends on the way history ends— every historical event, the world as a whole,[13] human existence,[14] and God's reconciling activity.[15] In fact, until history reaches its conclusion, not only God's love and wisdom, but God's very existence, will always be open to question. Nothing achieves its final significance until history comes to an end.

This explains why Pannenberg places such emphasis on the ultimate destiny of human beings. He defends the concept of bodily resurrection against rival notions of life after death, particularly the immortality of the soul. And he argues that resurrection has a corporate, social dimension

---

[12]Jürgen Moltmann, *Theology of Hope: On the Ground and the Implications of a Christian Eschatology*, trans. James W. Leitch (New York: Harper & Row, 1967), 16.

[13]"The eschatological future of God in the coming of his kingdom is the standpoint from which to understand the world as a whole" (Wolfhart Pannenberg, *Systematic Theology*, trans. Geoffrey W. Bromiley, 3 vols. (Grand Rapids: Eerdmans, 1991–1997], 2:146).

[14]"On the path of their history in time objects and people exist only in anticipation of that which they will be in the light of their final future, the advent of God" (Pannenberg, *Systematic Theology*, 3:531). Human destiny "will come only as the goal and consummation of this history" (*Systematic Theology*, 2:227).

[15]"Only in the eschaton does the reconciliation of the world come to completion with the new life of the resurrection of the dead in the kingdom of God" (Pannenberg, *Systematic Theology*, 3:631).

that is lacking from traditional views of immortality.[16] "The new life of the resurrection," he says, is "a removal of the individual autonomy and separation that are part of the corporeality of earthly life, though with no simple erasure of individual particularity."[17] Individuality will evidently be preserved in the final future, but without any of the tensions of rights or rivalry that characterize human relations now.

And just what does this final future consist of? An event Pannenberg variously identifies as "the coming of eternity into time," and "the dissolving of time in eternity."[18] The final future not only renders history a totality, it does so by making all its moments simultaneous. The endpoint is a timeless moment that encompasses the realm of temporal passage and subsumes the entire course of history that precedes it.

Instead of a continuation of experiences, human existence too will consist of a single all-encompassing experience. Just as the divine life is characterized by an "eternal simultaneity," the ultimate destiny of creaturely existence is thus to be "taken up" into "the eternal simultaneity of the divine life." When God's creatures share the eternity of God's own life, they will experience in one timeless moment all the events of their historical existence. "The differences of moments of time and the tenses" will be preserved, but they are "no longer seen apart." Our destiny as individuals will be fulfilled when we belong to the whole of human society across all the separate epochs of history.[19]

From the standpoint of open theism, Pannenberg's eschatology is both promising and disappointing. His view that the end of history brings to light the meaning of history suggests a helpful way to understand the final judgment. When history comes to an end, the essential narrative, or the central plot, of all that has taken place before finally becomes clear. Underlying the ebb and flow of events, the bewildering, apparently meaningless, accumulation of experiences from one day to the next, year in and year out, is God's ongoing effort to bless human life and counteract

---

[16]Pannenberg, *Systematic Theology*, 3:563-73.
[17]Pannenberg, *Systematic Theology*, 3:628-29.
[18]Pannenberg, *Systematic Theology*, 3:595, 607.
[19]Pannenberg, *Systematic Theology*, 3:607.

the effects of sin. For the most part God's workings are imperceptible. Looking back and looking around, all we see is the counterplay between good and evil, both progress and decline, advances in scientific knowledge that improve the quality of life and others that pose new threats to our well-being, social changes that ease tensions in some areas and create new ones in others. Pannenberg suggests that the end of history will bring clarity to the process that precedes it and reveal the true significance of what has gone before.

According to the parable of the talents in Jesus' apocalyptic discourse (Mt 25:14-30), the master's return is a time of reckoning. It reveals which servants have done the master's will, and which haven't. And in his account of the judgment of the nations in the same discourse (Mt 25:31-46), the true significance of people's actions also becomes clear—whether they have lived in harmony with the principles of God's kingdom and whether their lives have been a benefit to others.

Along with the course of history as a whole, then, human beings are confronted with the ultimate destinies they have, in effect, chosen for themselves—either by faithfully serving God or not, attending to the needs of others, or ignoring them. The destiny of human beings is thus determined by the path their commitments have followed over the course of time. In the work of judgment, Pannenberg says, God is not arbitrary; he does not inflict punishment capriciously, but leaves people to the consequences of their own choices.[20]

WHAT DOES ETERNAL LIFE LOOK LIKE?

"The relation between time and eternity is the crucial problem in eschatology," says Pannenberg, "and its solution has implications for all parts of Christian doctrine."[21] Open theists couldn't agree more, which is why they will find Pannenberg's account of the future disappointing. From the important role he assigns to the final future as the key to all that comes before, one might think that the process whose full meaning is finally apparent would continue. But no. For him, the

---

[20]Pannenberg, *Systematic Theology*, 3:611.
[21]Pannenberg, *Systematic Theology*, 3:595.

culmination of history terminates history. Historical process ends in a moment in which time dissolves. According to Pannenberg, God's mode of existence is an eternal present, and history reaches its final consummation when finite beings are incorporated and united into this single momentary experience.

It is hard to imagine what timeless finite existence would consist of. Temporality is inherent to existence as we know it. Indeed, it seems inherent to existence as we could possibly conceive it. So, Pannenberg's designation of the final future as timeless seems incoherent. It seems tantamount to putting the universe on an indefinite "pause."

Perhaps most importantly, the idea of a timeless eternity contradicts the essential insight of the Trinity, namely, that God's dealings with creation express God's innermost life. If God's dealings with the creatures are temporal through and through, and God's own life is not temporal, then these dealings do not portray God's reality after all. But if we think of God's experience, not as the absence of temporality, but as the supreme instance of temporality, we avoid this problem. Pannenberg's eschatology seems to reflect the familiar notion that time and eternity—that change and changelessness—constitute an invidious contrast, in which one element is inferior to the other. If so, we can understand why he views the final future, ultimate human destiny, as a timeless mode of existence. For that brings it closer to the kind of existence that characterizes God himself.

For open theism, however, time and eternity are not opposed to each other, they are perfectly compatible. God is both eternal and temporal, utterly changeless in certain respects, and supremely changeable in others; eternally changeless in his essential nature and everlastingly temporal in his concrete experience. Accordingly, if our "final future" reflects God's own life, there is good reason to view it as an ongoing series of experiences that never comes to an end.

In contrast to Bultmann, then, open theism affirms the importance of historical process. Temporality is essential to our experience, not just moment by moment, but through the accumulation of momentary experiences. And the end of history, that is, the climax of historical process, is important to the meaning of history, as Pannenberg insists. But in contrast to Pannenberg, open theists envision the future that supersedes the present order as a continuation of temporal passage. The life to come consists of an unending series of experiences in a world from which the ravaging effects of sin have been removed.

For traditional Christianity, death is a consequence of sin, and the prospect of a future life untainted by the effects of sin is one of the essential features of the faith. In one of the Bible's most extended discussions of life after death, 1 Corinthians 15, the apostle Paul identifies the claim that Jesus rose from the dead as a central element in the gospel as he originally received and taught it (1 Cor 15:1-4). He proceeds to argue that this provides a basis for Christians' confidence in their own resurrection from the dead and goes on to describe the resurrection life in terms of physical, or bodily, transformation. Other New Testament passages describe the transformation of the world humans will inhabit in the life to come. The canon closes with lyrical portrayals of new heavens and a new earth, where suffering, sorrow, death, and disease are no more, and the redeemed rejoice in the presence of God (Rev 21).

IS ETERNAL LIFE WORTH LIVING?

The notion of a future life raises a host of questions—both religious and philosophical.[22] One longstanding issue is whether or not the human soul is inherently immortal, and if so, how it relates to the body. Does individual human life continue beyond death in a nonphysical form? Does it come to an end with death, and resume when the body is resurrected? Or does it continue in a nonphysical intermediate state and resume a physical form in the resurrection? Each of these positions has the support of certain Christian theologians, but to my knowledge none of them is connected with open theism per se. Thus, instead of pursuing

---

[22]Immortality is one of the topics traditionally covered in textbooks on philosophy of religion, along with miracles, the problem of evil, and various arguments for the existence of God. One of the major questions philosophers deal with is whether personal continuity between our present existence and some sort of postmortem existence is even conceivable.

the complex questions surrounding this issue, let us assume a conservative Christian conviction that there is indeed a life to come, and focus on some questions related to the basic concept of eternal life.

A number of people find the idea of endless life problematic. For some, it's basically unnecessary. We don't need the prospect of unending existence in order to feel that our lives are meaningful. Instead, we find meaning within the framework of a finite timespan. Indeed, for those who share Bultmann's existentialism, the meaning of life can be fully realized in each moment of authentic existence; how long it lasts is comparatively inconsequential.

For others, the concept of human immortality raises moral issues. For one thing, the expectation of unending existence seems presumptuous; it arrogates to humanity an attribute of divinity. From the biblical statement that God alone has immortality (1 Tim 6:16), it appears that God is meant to live forever, but not finite human beings. For another, the idea that eternal life represents a reward for moral behavior seems particularly objectionable. A truly ethical person does what's right because it's right, not because she hopes to be rewarded for it. Then too the reward seems way out of proportion to the accomplishment. Why should people live in bliss forever just because they have lived responsibly for a few years now? Finally, there are people who find the prospect of unending existence downright unappealing. Surely, they surmise, if life went on and on and on, the time would eventually come when we would have done everything worth doing, and from that point on there would be nothing left but endless, mind-numbing repetition. And under those conditions, no one would really want to live forever.

The open view of God turns the edge of these criticisms. First of all, from the openness perspective, everlasting life represents a gift, not a reward. Its only basis is God's generosity; human achievement has nothing to do with it. So the disproportion between what we deserve and what God provides is a source of wonder and thanks, but not a cause for moral reservation. The fact is, we don't deserve what God offers and never could. Our accomplishments have nothing to do with it. The God of open theism is a God whose love accounts for all his dealings with his creatures. He creates and redeems them entirely on the basis of outgoing, overflowing generosity, not because he needs them for anything or owes them anything.[23] The vision of God's inexplicable love and care lays to rest the idea that there is something morally objectionable about the prospect of everlasting life. All of life, future and present, is a gift from God.

As for the idea that unending life would eventually reach a point of diminishing returns and leave us wishing we could be relieved of its tedium, it seems to reflect a lack of imagination. For some reason, we typically find the dark side of human existence more intriguing than its counterpart. The opening lines of Leo Tolstoy's *Anna Karenina* are sometimes cited as a reference to the boredom of happiness. "Happy families are all alike; every unhappy family is unhappy in its own way." Writers sometimes describe how difficult it is to make upright characters interesting. There are so many ways people can do wrong—just think of all the novels, films and television shows depicting dishonesty, betrayal, and crime, for example—that goodness seems bland by comparison. For many readers, the most interesting character in Milton's *Paradise Lost* is Lucifer, the fallen archangel, the paragon of evil. Mark Twain's quip, "Heaven for climate, hell for society," implies the same thing. Sinners are more interesting than saints. Goodness is boring. So, it would seem, a landscape populated by the pure in heart would be stifling in its monotony. And a life of perpetual tranquility would eventually leave us longing for release.

From another perspective, this has it all backward. In the long run, goodness is infinite in exciting possibilities and evil is a descent into the black hole of monotonous futility. In a famous response to the trial of Adolf Eichmann, Hannah Arendt spoke of the "banality of evil." Though

---

[23]As many see it, that was Martin Luther's great discovery five hundred years ago—salvation is due entirely to God's grace—a concept that Augustine before him, and the apostle Paul before him, espoused. As is well known, it was Luther's study of the book of Romans, in particular his discovery that the expression "the righteousness of God" (cf. Rom 3:22) can be interpreted as "the righteousness that comes from God," rather than "the righteousness by which God himself is righteous," that proved to be revolutionary in his understanding of salvation.

not necessarily what she meant by the expression, it captures the insight that evil is tedious, monotonous, and ultimately dull. No matter what form it takes, it eventually comes to the same self-destructive end.

Now imagine growing manifestations of goodness and sources of joy. Visual art and music are human endeavors that come to mind when we think of examples of continuous development, increasing complexity, and the realization of more and more possibilities. Look over the centuries of Western art, for example, and you can see how the creative achievements of one era contribute to those of another. Great artists often study the works of those that came before, find inspiration in their creations, and respond with creative products of their own. They may incorporate the insights of previous masters or deliberately depart from them in expressing their own aesthetic visions.

The same is true in music. In the symphonies of Brahms we hear echoes of Beethoven, for example, and Beethoven's compositions built on the work of composers who preceded him. According to one biographer, "Beethoven founded everything he did on models from the past," and he "was pushing his models in directions innate to them," such as sharper contrasts, a broader variety of keys, longer and more varied developments, "and so on through every dimensions of music."[24] "So a trajectory in Beethoven's work . . . came to rest in the Ninth Symphony," which represented "a continued deepening and expansion of trends that had been in his music all along: bigger pieces, more intense contrasts, more complexity and more simplicity," and which "resonated with the accumulated political and ethical ideas and energies of the previous decades."[25]

We can think of these and other areas of human activity, including the obvious development of scientific knowledge, as ongoing conversations, with people learning from, responding to, the accomplishments of others and adding their own as new insights and ideas accumulate. The idea that unending life would eventually descend into the gloom of unbearable

---

[24]Jan Swafford, *Beethoven: Anguish and Triumph: A Biography* (New York: Houghton Mifflin Harcourt, 2014), 232.
[25]Swafford, *Beethoven*, 832, 837.

monotony is a serious slight to human creativity. The Bible suggests that, if anything, the trajectory goes the other way. In comparison with the fascinating and glorious future God has in store for his creatures, the present is drab and dreary. "For now we see in a mirror, dimly," says the apostle Paul in his famous description of love, "but then we will see face to face. Now I know only in part; then I will know fully" (1 Cor 13:12).

We may find intriguing clues regarding the life to come in the parable of the talents, which appears in the last of Jesus' five great sermons recorded in Matthew. To the servants who faithfully multiplied their talents, the master said, "Well done, good and trustworthy slave; you have been trustworthy in a few things, I will put you in charge of many things; enter into the joy of your master" (Mt 25:21, 23). The reward for faithful service does not bring service to an end. To the contrary, it provides an opportunity for continued service, with greater responsibilities, and above all a deepening relationship with the master. And just as the master finds joy in the service of his faithful servants and welcomes their fellowship, the passage suggests, God enjoys the accomplishments of his people and values their fellowship—important elements in the openness view of the relationship between God and his creatures.

Of course, the question that hovers over all such reflections is whether or not a future life is possible, and this raises a host of challenging questions. The biblical portrayals of bodily resurrection and a new heavens and earth differ dramatically from our experience of death as the end of our individual lives and scientific accounts of the eventual demise of our planet, our solar system, indeed the universe as a whole, as an environment hospitable to human life as we know it. Biblical portrayals of the world to come include transformations of the sort that only transcendent power, divine power, could account for. Open theism affirms the expectation that the fulfillment of God's purposes will include these transformations. Only the power that brought the world into existence and brought Jesus back to life from the dead could bring about the dramatic changes in ourselves and in the world that the fulfillment of God's purposes requires.

ARE GOD'S PURPOSES GUARANTEED?

When it comes to eschatology, one of the pressing questions facing open theists is whether God's purposes for creation will indeed be fulfilled. If human beings are genuinely free in the libertarian sense, God's hopes for them can be realized only if they choose to cooperate. God may earnestly desire their loyalty, he may do everything he can to win it, but in the final analysis the choice is theirs and God is committed to respect their decision. If God's purposes involve the voluntary participation of God's people, then they cannot be achieved by divine fiat.

For many Christian thinkers, the failure of God's purposes is utterly inconceivable, and they find ways to explain why their fulfillment is a certainty. For divine determinists, of course, everything happens by divine decree, so there is no possibility that his purposes will fail. God being God, it's logically impossible.

There are also those who take a less extensive view of divine power—they don't attribute everything that happens to the will of God—but they maintain that God's purposes for each individual will eventually be fulfilled . . . not necessarily in this life, but in the life to come. Prominent among those who respond to the problem of suffering in this way are John Hick and Marilyn McCord Adams. For both, God is not the author of evil and suffering, but his love for each human being is so persistent that everyone will eventually yield to his embrace. John Hick presents his theodicy in two noteworthy books, *Evil and the God of Love* and *Death and Eternal Life*.[26] For Hick the concept of a future life, or lives, is indispensable to an adequate solution to the problem of evil, and he maintains that every human being will achieve ultimate spiritual fulfillment.

For Adams, it is not enough that the sufferings of this life may be overwhelmed by the goodness of God in the future. It is essential that they be *defeated*. And for this to take place, their sufferings must be incorporated

---

[26]John Hick, *Evil and the God of Love*, rev. ed. (San Francisco: Harper & Row, 1978); *Death and Eternal Life* (New York: Harper & Row, 1976).

within one's intimate relationship with God in such a way that the person would not wish that these experiences had never occurred.[27]

Eleonore Stump takes a similar position in *Wandering in Darkness: Narrative and the Problem of Suffering*. Sufferers who are originally denied their heart's desires may ultimately achieve these desires within a personal relationship with God. And "when a person weaves her heart's desires into a deepest desire for God," Stump says, "it is possible for those desires to be transformed . . . so that even the worst external circumstances are not sufficient to prevent their being satisfied somehow in the union of love with God."[28] Moreover, within this intimate relationship with God, the sufferer not only achieves a new form of what was lost, what she ultimately achieves seems to the sufferer "more worth having than what she originally hoped for."[29]

Open theists can appreciate the creative view of divine providence these three thinkers provide. Because time is real for God, God experiences all that happens, it remains in his memory forever, and he responds to events in ways that promote his loving purposes. So, even though the past is permanent in the sense that there is no "cancellation" of what has happened, the consequences of the past are susceptible to creative transformation. They can be incorporated within a new creative synthesis, no matter how negative and tragic they are in themselves.[30]

Another thinker who deals extensively with the fulfillment of God's purposes is Jonathan Kvanvig. In a series of essays titled *Destiny and Deliberation*, Kvanvig develops what he calls "Philosophical Arminianism," a position that "affirms the central importance of libertarian freedom in our understanding of human persons, but refuses to do so in a way that compromises a high concept of God."[31] According to his "exalted" concept

[27]Marilyn McCord Adams, *Horrendous Evils and the Goodness of God* (Ithaca, NY: Cornell University Press, 1999).

[28]Eleonore Stump, *Wandering in Darkness: Narrative and the Problem of Suffering* (New York: Oxford University Press, 2010), 473.

[29]Stump, *Wandering in Darkness*, 473.

[30]Open theists would differ, however, with Hick and Adams in their view that God's purposes will eventually reach fulfillment in the life of every human being.

[31]Jonathan Kvanvig, *Destiny and Deliberation: Essays in Philosophical Theology* (New York: Oxford University Press, 2011), xiv.

of deity, God needs "no cooperation from anything outside himself to accomplish his purposes in creation." So, even though he grants creatures libertarian freedom, God exercises "full and complete providential control" over creation.[32] In contrast, he argues, open theists "openly embrace a loss of full providential control," and this leaves them with a diminished view of God. In fact, given the way they understand libertarian freedom, God is ignorant of significant parts of the future, and this makes the problem of evil even worse than the standard theodical responses do.[33]

Kvanvig evidently wants to hold onto the central claims of both Calvinism and Arminianism. He agrees with Arminians that God grants creatures freedom, but maintains with Calvinists that God's control over creation is all-inclusive. In the final analysis, Kvanvig's "high doctrine of providence" appears to be close to divine determinism. The achievement of God's purposes is assured, because God's power guarantees it.

From the perspective of open theism, Kvanvig's proposal won't work, because we cannot have it both ways. We can't insist that the fulfillment of God's purposes is inevitable and uphold the reality of creaturely freedom. Since the achievement of God's purposes is conditional on creaturely choice, their free response to God's love is essential.

This raises the question of just what constitutes a "high doctrine of providence," and that depends on which picture of God evokes greater admiration—one in which the fulfillment of God's purposes is a foregone conclusion or one in which it represents a genuine achievement. For open theists, a God who is willing to take risks out of love for the creatures, respect and respond to their decisions and actions, whether they please or disappoint him, and pursue his goals for creation no matter what, demonstrates a "higher" view of providence than a God who guarantees their cooperation by exercising complete control. If love is the defining quality of God's nature, and if true love takes risks, makes sacrifices, and suffers the consequences of creaturely rejection, then a God who runs the risk that he may not achieve all he hopes for is supremely admirable.

---

[32]Kvanvig, *Destiny and Deliberation*, xiii.

[33]Kvanvig, *Destiny and Deliberation*, xiii, xii, xv.

It is important to underscore the nature of this risk, of course. The idea that God takes risks does not mean that God is careless. It does not mean that God is dispassionate, casually noting the possibility that people will reject him and coolly accepting it when it happens. Nor does it mean that God has no influence on their choices. To the contrary, God does everything he can, while respecting their freedom, to persuade his people to follow him, as we see in the Bible's many warnings and promises. And God grieves deeply when they go astray. We sense the depth of God's disappointment in the plaintive cry of the prophet Hosea:

> How can I give you up, Ephraim?
>   How can I hand you over, O Israel? . . .
> My heart recoils within me;
>   my compassion grows warm and tender. (Hos 11:8)[34]

For open theists, the crucial question is just what it is that God wills. If God's essential character is one of love and this love comes to expression in the kind of world God created, then the goal that was uppermost in God's mind was that the creatures freely return his love. Was the achievement of this objective inevitable when God decided to create? Could God unilaterally bring about a loving response from his creatures? Not if creaturely choice is a necessary condition of a loving response. For in that case, the fulfillment of God's intention requires that the creatures' response to God is genuinely theirs—something they decide, not something God decided for them.

Where open theism differs from Calvinism, and from attempts of Arminians like Jonathan Kvanvig to demonstrate that the fulfillment of God's purposes is guaranteed, is in its insistence that love involves freedom and that freedom excludes control. For open theists, the exercise of divine power is determined by the choices God makes. And God has the personal freedom to choose how he exercises his power. If God decided to create a world where the creatures could return God's love freely, then God's objective for the world required their loving response to

---

[34]For many, the scene of Jesus weeping over Jerusalem during his "triumphal entry" is a portrayal of the pain God feels when his hopes are disappointed. See Lk 19:28-42.

God's initiative. And their response would not be free, it would not be genuinely loving, if it were predetermined by God.

The crucial question then is what kind of world God wants. And that ultimately depends on which attribute is central to our vision of God. If it's power, then God could bring about any state of affairs that depends solely on divine decision. But if it's love, then God can achieve his objectives only if the creatures' love for him is voluntary. Everything depends on which attribute is more fundamental to our vision of God. Is it power, or is it love?

Given its emphasis on libertarian freedom, people sometimes wonder if open theism raises the prospect that God's purposes could utterly fail to reach fulfillment. If libertarian freedom is an essential human attribute, can we be sure that *anyone* will say yes to God? Is it conceivable that *no one* would accept God's offer of salvation? On the other hand, is it conceivable that *everyone* could eventually say yes to God?

In view of God's relentless love on the one hand and the reality of creaturely freedom on the other, the likelihood of either extreme is practically remote. Theoretically, it is possible that everyone could say yes to God, accept salvation and spend eternity in God's fellowship. Surely, that is what God would want. According to one New Testament passage, God "desires everyone to be saved and to come to the knowledge of the truth" (1 Tim 2:4).[35] At the same time, it is theoretically possible that no one might say yes to God, and reap the eternal consequences of their rejection. But just as God did everything to minimize the likelihood of rejection, God does everything he can to persuade sinners to accept forgiveness and receive the gift of salvation. How many will eventually say yes to God? I don't know that anyone knows. But in light of the biblical portraits of God's persistence in seeking the lost and his willingness, indeed eagerness to forgive, particularly as depicted in the parable of the prodigal son (Lk 15:11-24), it seems highly likely, perhaps practically certain, that God's efforts will not end until a significant number have done so.

---

[35]Cf. the expression, "the universal salvific will of God."

A final question open theism raises concerns the ultimate security of the universe. Once the future God has in store for humanity becomes a reality and the redeemed enjoy God's fellowship in the earth made new, is there a chance that sin could rise again? Is there any guarantee that this won't happen? Is it even theoretically possible that one of the redeemed might choose to reject God? In a famous discussion of human freedom centuries ago, Augustine answered no. As he saw it, human freedom was a temporary endowment. Before the fall, humans had the freedom to sin—*posse peccare* (able to sin). After the fall, they lost that freedom; they were not free not to sin—*non posse non peccare* (not able not to sin). With the gift of salvation came the freedom not to sin—*posse non peccare*. But in the hereafter, the possibility of sin is gone—*non posse peccare*. On this view, personal freedom was a temporary endowment. It lasts until it is clear what people have decided. And then, after a probationary period, it is no longer needed. It has served its purpose. Given the importance open theism attaches to human freedom, this hardly sounds like an ideal state. For if God values a loving response to his own love, and love requires freedom, how can love exist where freedom has been removed? Is eternal security compatible with genuine freedom?

As we have seen, Gregory A. Boyd offers an interesting answer to this. According to Boyd, God sees all possibilities as clearly as if they were actualities and eliminates those in which his ultimate purposes are not fulfilled. Consequently, we can be confident that God's will will ultimately prevail. Genuine as it is, the freedom God grants the creatures is both limited in scope and duration. Because the range of our choices is limited, God knows just what those limitations are. He knows "all past and present variables that come to pass." And because our choices have consequences, including their effect on our future choices, our lives are characterized by "an ever-closing window of opportunity." We either draw closer and closer to God or more and more resistant to him. "We begin by making our choices, but in the end, our choices make us. We are gradually but inevitably becoming the decisions we make."[36]

---

[36]Gregory A. Boyd, "God Limits His Control," in *Four Views on Divine Providence*, ed. Dennis W. Jowers (Grand Rapids: Zondervan, 2011), 193.

This line of reasoning leads Boyd to the conclusion that those who exercise their freedom to accept God's love will eventually reach the point where they have no desire to turn away from him, a point where, we might say, their libertarian freedom dissolves into freedom of spontaneity. From people who freely choose to love, they become "people whose very beings are love."[37]

Boyd provides a helpful account of the course that our decisions often take. We can probably all think of instances when we found it challenging to make a decision because the options were relatively clear and both somewhat attractive. But once we made our selection, and found the consequences rewarding, we followed the course we had begun until we reached the point where we reaffirmed our decision spontaneously. On reflection, we may have realized that we were indeed free to abandon the course we had chosen, but that option no longer held any attraction.[38] In a sense, it was no longer viable. Does this mean we had lost our freedom? Practically perhaps, but certainly not theoretically.

This sort of pathway may account for the twofold description of ultimate human destiny, or destinies, referred to in the Bible—one of inclusion in God's embrace, the other of exclusion from the presence of God. To quote Pannenberg, God executes "what is in the nature of the case."[39]

CONCLUSION

Since love is fundamental to God's character, God seeks the fellowship of his creatures and respects their response(s) to his invitation. Consequently, whatever the specific features of the future life may be, it will

---

[37]Boyd, "God Limits His Control," 194.

[38]The clearest example of this trajectory in my own experience started with a decision I made as a college student, when someone in the swimming class we were taking invited me to go with her to a social the women's club was putting on. I hesitated for a few moments, because I'd been seeing someone else the previous summer. But I realized I couldn't put Gail off, so I said yes. That momentary decision had momentous consequences. Gail and I got married three years later, and not long ago celebrated our fiftieth anniversary. I suppose we are free to leave each other, at least theoretically. But being together is the most natural thing in the world . . . for both of us.

[39]Pannenberg, *Systematic Theology*, 3:611.

involve a renewed and transformed relationship between God and human beings. God so loves and values the ones he created in his image and rescued from sin that he invites them to enter his kingdom forever. Relieved of the inhibiting and debilitating effects of sin, the redeemed will experience uninterrupted fellowship with God. Their insights into God's wisdom will deepen, their appreciation for God's character will grow, their sense of God's majesty will expand, their joy in God's presence will increase, and their praise will more and more fully reflect God's glory.

▸▸▸▸▸▸▸▸▸▸▸ CONCLUSION ▸▸▸▸▸▸▸▸▸▸

IN AN ACCOUNT OF OPEN THEISM'S DEVELOPMENT, Larry Witham asserts, "*The Openness of God* not only spawned a new theological term, soon to show up in popular articles, polemics, and even textbooks, but also reconfigured the landscape of theism."[1] That's generous, but probably not an overstatement. As we have seen, though initial reactions were sometimes dismissive, and it generated vigorous controversy within conservative American Christianity, the ideas central to the open view of God have endured. They have stimulated extensive theological and philosophical discussion, and they have attracted serious attention on an international scale as well.[2] Informed discussions of open theism have appeared in German and Italian, for example.[3] And the symposium volume of 1994 has also been translated into Arabic.[4]

At the same time, open theists have more work to do. At the conclusion of another informed review of open theism, James Rissler offers this observation: "The debate over whether Open Theism correctly portrays God's relationship to His creation involves a complicated web of Biblical data, philosophical arguments, and reflection on the practical theological

---

[1]Larry Witham, *The God Biographers: Our Changing Image of God from Job to the Present* (Lanham, MD: Lexington Books, 2010), 150. According to Witham's account, process philosophy and open theism are noteworthy for the similarities in their views of God as alternatives to the traditional concepts of divine power and control.

[2]There are a number of influential thinkers who either endorse open theism or whose views closely resemble those of open theists, including John Polkinghorne, Keith Ward, and Nicholas Wolterstorff.

[3]Cf. Manuel Schmid, "*Der offene Theismus als bibeltheologische Reformbewegung*" ["Open Theism as a Biblical Theological Reform Movement"], PhD diss., University of Basel, Switzerland, 2008; and a recent article by Italian philosopher Damiano Migliorini, "Il Dio che rischia e che "cambia": introduzione *all'Open Theism*," in *Nuovo Giornale di Filosofia della Religione*, no. 8, Settembre – Decembre, 2018.

[4]*Infetah Allah: El-tahady al-ketaby le alfehem al-takledie an allah* [*The Openness of God: A Biblical Response to the Traditional View of God*], trans. Dr. Girguis Milad (Maktabat El-Kalema Publishing House, 2016).

implications of the view." Consequently, even if one affirms the central tenets of open theism, "there remains the hard work of slowly working through a detailed examination of Scripture and reflection on the Christian life. This is the case for any theology, and it is perhaps especially so for a relatively young theology such as Open Theism."[5]

My attempt to sketch the course open theism has taken so far and offer some suggestions for its further development no doubt exhibits the incompleteness that Rissler has in mind. Open theism arose from the concerns various scholars expressed about a number of venerable and widely accepted ideas about God. And to a number of observers it bore similarities to views that lay outside the boundaries of Christian orthodoxy. But it survived the initial criticisms, garnered measured appreciation, and eventually achieved recognition as a distinct theological position.

Over time, open theists elaborated their basic vision of divine love, highlighting certain elements in the biblical portrait of God and constructing careful arguments for its central convictions: a genuine God-world interaction, the complex exercise(s) of divine power, and the logical content of perfect knowledge. Still, even if one affirms the central tenets of open theism, hard work, as Rissler notes, remains to be done. No Christian belief stands alone; it is inevitably connected to others, and when it comes to the idea of God, it has ramifications for all that Christians believe. "In constructing a ship or a philosophy," Bernard Lonergan remarks, "one has to go the whole way."[6] The same is true of theology.

Though open theism may not have assumed the form of a full-fledged theological system yet, those of us attracted to it find its promise inspiring and definitely worth the effort. And that's why, in addition to a selective account of open theism's history, I have tried to draw a few connections between some of its characteristic concerns and the basic themes of systematic theology.

---

[5]James Rissler, "Open Theism," *The Internet Encyclopedia of Philosophy*, September 1, 2019. www .iep.utm.edu/o-theism/.

[6]Bernard Lonergan, *Insight: A Study of Human Understanding*, 3rd ed. (New York: Philosophical Library, 1970), xiii.

To a certain extent, I suspect, one's theology will always reflect a personal journey. I found the ideas that came to expression in open theism helpful in expressing some convictions that developed over a long time. I recently came across a paper on the doctrine of God I wrote for a college class years ago, and in it I found the straightforward assertion that God is absolute and utterly changeless. For me, obviously, the familiar view of God as timeless and immutable gave way to the picture of God whose love involves infinite sensitivity to all that happens in the world and in our lives.

What Richard Rorty observes of philosophy may well hold true of theology: "It is pictures rather than propositions, metaphors rather than statements, which determine most of our philosophical convictions."[7] There is no question, for example, that the view that God controls the world absolutely and that his purposes cannot fail has remarkable appeal. When combined with the conviction that one is a member of God's elect people, it provides a powerful source of personal confidence.

On the other hand, the picture of God as a waiting father, hoping, indeed longing for the return of his wandering children, pained by their mistakes and thrilled when they accept his love, speaks to profound personal needs as well. This conviction that what happens in the world has a genuine effect on God—that our experiences contribute to God's experience—lies behind such titles as *Most Moved Mover, The God Who Risks,* and *The God Who Trusts.* The God who moves, risks, and trusts is our companion through all of life's experiences, fully aware of and deeply affected by all that we undergo, providing us constant encouragement and help. This, I believe, is the enduring appeal of the openness of God.

A theology worth considering must do more than express personal preference, of course. Besides the inevitable connection between personal experience and theological convictions, there are other qualities that need mentioning too. The value of any explanation, or theory, is measured by its clarity and the adequacy of its explanatory power. Proponents of open theism are convinced that it makes more sense of more

---

[7]Richard Rorty, *Philosophy and the Mirror of Nature* (Princeton University Press, 1979), 12-13.

evidence about God than the alternatives and that it stands up to serious philosophical scrutiny.

When all is said and done, however, the quest for a perfect doctrine of God will always fall short. So those of us who hope that open theism will achieve more generous theological proportions are encouraged by the growing interest around it, but humbled by the knowledge that our work will always be incomplete. No attempt to grasp the grandeur and beauty of God's revelation in Jesus Christ—no matter how expansive its scope, elaborate its expression, or intricate its logic—will ever be more than a faint approximation of its object. Our efforts to do justice to the biblical portrait of God will never succeed because our objective lies beyond the reach of human ability.

The reason for the failure of theology, as Heinz Zahrnt describes it, is the greatness of its object. Yet, as he also notes, it is a task we may not cease to carry out. "We must always dare once again to speak in human words about God," knowing that God must "forgive us our theology, our theology perhaps most of all."[8]

---

[8]Heinz Zahrnt, *The Question of God: Protestant Theology in the Twentieth Century*, trans. R. A. Wilson (New York: Harcourt Brace Jovanovich, 1966), 359.

▸▸▸▸▸▸▸▸▸▸ BIBLIOGRAPHY ▸▸▸▸▸▸▸▸▸▸

Adams, Marilyn McCord. *Horrendous Evils and the Goodness of God.* Ithaca, NY: Cornell University Press, 1999.

Anderson, V. Elving. "A Genetic View of Human Nature." In *Whatever Happened to the Soul?* Edited by Warren S. Brown, Nancey Murphy, and H. Newton Malony. Minneapolis: Fortress Press, 1998.

Anselm, Saint. *St. Anselm: Basic Writings,* 2nd ed. Translated by S. N. Deane. *Proslogium,* Chapter II. LaSalle, IL: Open Court Publishing Company, 1962.

Aquinas, Thomas, Saint. *Summa Theologica,* 12ae, Q. 85, Art. 3. *Nature and Grace: Selections from the Summa Theologica of Thomas Aquinas.* Translated and edited by A. M. Fairweather. The Library of Christian Classics, vol. 11. Santa Ana, CA: Westminster, 1954.

Arminius, Jacobus (James). "A Discussion on the Subject of Predestination, Between James Arminius, D.D., Minister at Amsterdam, and Francis Junius, D.D., Professor of Divinity at Leyden." In *The Writings of James Arminius,* translated by James Nichols and W. R. Bagnall. Grand Rapids: Baker, 1956.

Arminius, James. *The Works of James Arminius.* Translated by James Nichols and William Nichols. 3 vols. Grand Rapids: Baker Book House, 1986.

Banks, Robert. *Paul's Idea of Community: The Early House Churches in their Cultural Setting,* rev. ed. Peabody, MA: Hendrickson, 1994.

Barth, Karl. *Church Dogmatics.* Translated by Geoffrey Bromily and Thomas Torrance. New York: T&T Clark, 1956.

Basinger, David. "Introduction to Open Theism." In *Models of God and Alternative Ultimate Realities,* edited by Jeanine Diller and Asa Kasher. Dortrecht: Springer, 2013.

Bauder, Kevin T., R. Albert Mohler Jr., John G. Stackhouse Jr., and Roger E. Olson. *Four Views on the Spectrum of Evangelicalism.* Grand Rapids: Zondervan, 2011.

Baumgartner, Hans Michael. "Transcendental Philosophy." In *Encyclopedia of Theology: The Concise Sacramentum Mundi,* edited by Karl Rahner. New York: Seabury, 1975.

Bayne, Jennifer L. and Sarah E. Hinlicky. *The Bondage of the Will.* In "Free to Be Creatures Again," *Christianity Today,* October 23, 2000.

Beilby, James K. and Paul R. Eddy, eds. *Divine Foreknowledge: Four Views.* Downers Grove, IL: IVP Academic, 2001.

Bellah, Robert, Richard Madsen, William M. Sullivan, Ann Swidler, and Steven M. Tipton. *Habits of the Heart: Individualism and Commitment in American Life.* Berkeley, CA: University of California Press, 1985.

Bornkamm, Gunther. *Paul.* Translated by D. M. G. Stalker. New York: Harper & Row, 1969.

Boyd, Gregory A. "Evolution as Cosmic Warfare: A Biblical Perspective on Satan and 'Natural' Evil." In Thomas J. Oord, ed. *Creation Made Free: Open Theology Engaging Science.* Eugene, OR: Wipf and Stock, 2009.

———. "God Limits His Control." In *Four Views of Divine Providence,* edited by Dennis W. Jowers. Grand Rapids: Zondervan, 2011.

———. *God of the Possible: A Biblical Introduction to the Open View of God.* Grand Rapids: Baker, 2000.

———. *God at War: The Bible and Spiritual Conflict.* Downers Grove, IL: InterVarsity Press, 1997.

———. *Is God to Blame? Beyond Pat Answers to the Problem of Suffering.* Downers Grove, IL: InterVarsity Press, 2003.

———. *Satan and the Problem of Evil: Constructing a Trinitarian Warfare Theodicy.* Downers Grove, IL: InterVarsity Press, 2001.

Brown, Warren S., and Brad D. Strawn. *The Physical Nature of Christian Life: Neuroscience, Psychology, and the Church.* New York: Cambridge University Press, 2012.

Brunner, Emil. *The Christian Doctrine of God.* Translated by Olive Wyon. Santa Ana, CA: Westminster, 1941.

Bultmann, Rudolf. *History and Eschatology: The Presence of Eternity.* The Gifford Lectures 1955. New York: Harper & Brothers, 1957.

———. "How Does God Speak Through the Bible?" In *Existence and Faith: Shorter Writings of Rudolf Bultmann,* selected, translated, and introduced by Schubert M. Ogden. Cleveland: Meridian Books, 1960.

Cahill, Thomas. *Sailing the Wine-Dark Sea: Why the Greeks Matter.* New York: Doubleday, 2004.

Calvin, John. *Institutes of the Christian Religion.* Translated by Ford Lewis Battles. Philadelphia: Westminster Press, 1960.

———. *Institutes of the Christian Religion.* Translated by Henry Beveridge. Grand Rapids: Eerdmans, 1966.

Canale, Fernando. *Handbook of Seventh-Day Adventist Theology.* Washington, D. C.: Review and Herald Publishing Association, 2000.

Churchland, Paul M. *Matter and Consciousness,* rev. ed. Cambridge, MA: MIT Press, 1988.

Clayton, Philip. *Adventures in the Spirit: God, World, Divine Action.* Minneapolis: Fortress Press, 2008.

———. "Neuroscience, the Person, and God: An Emergentist Account." In *Neuroscience and the Person: Scientific Perspectives on Divine Action,* edited by Robert John Russell, Nancey Murphy, Theo C. Meyering, and Michael A. Arbib. Vatican Observatory Publications, 2002.

Cobb, John B., Jr. and Clark H. Pinnock, eds. *Searching for an Adequate God: A Dialogue Between Process and Free Will Theists.* Grand Rapids: Eerdmans, 2000.

Cooper, John. *Panentheism: The Other God of the Philosophers.* Grand Rapids: Baker Academic, 2006.

Cragg, Gerald R. *Freedom and Authority.* Santa Ana, CA: Westminster Press, 1975. Quoted in *The Struggle for the Soul of the SBC: Moderate Responses to the Fundamentalist Movement,* edited by Walter B. Shurden. Macon, GA: Mercer University Press, 1993.

Craig, William Lane. "Omniscience, Tensed Facts, and Divine Eternity." *Faith and Philosophy* 17, no. 2 (April 2000).

Craig, William Lane and David P. Hunt. "Perils of the Open Road." *Faith and Philosophy* 30, no. 1 (January 2013).

Creel, Richard. *Divine Impassibility: An Essay in Philosophical Theology.* Cambridge: Cambridge University Press, 1986.

Cullmann, Oscar. *Christ and Time: The Primitive Christian Conception of Time and History,* rev ed. Translated by Floyd V. Filson. London: SCM Press, 1962.

Damasio, Antonio R. *Descartes' Error: Emotion, Reason, and the Human Brain.* New York: Putnam, 1994.

Dennett, Daniel C. *Darwin's Dangerous Idea: Evolution and the Meanings of Life.* New York: Simon & Schuster, 1995.

———. "In Darwin's Wake, Where Am I?" *Proceedings and Addresses of the American Philosophical Association* 75 (November 2001).

Donaldson, Terence L. "The Field God Has Assigned: Geography and Mission in Paul." In *Religious Rivalries in the Early Roman Empire and the Rise of Christianity,* edited by Leif Vaage. Waterloo, ON: Wilfrid Laurier University Press, 2006.

Dorrien, Gary. *The Remaking of Evangelical Theology.* Louisville, KY: Westminster John Knox Press, 1998.

Ellis, George F. R. and Nancey Murphy. *On the Moral Nature of the Universe: Cosmology, Theology, and Ethics.* Minneapolis: Fortress Press, 1996.

Elseth, H. Roy. *Did God Know? A Study of the Nature of God.* St. Paul, MN: Calvary United Church Inc., 1977.

Emmet, Dorothy M. *Whitehead's Philosophy of Organism,* 2nd ed. New York: Springer, 1966.

Erickson, Millard J. *Christian Theology.* Grand Rapids: Baker, 1983.

———. *What Does God Know and When Does He Know It? The Current Controversy Over Divine Foreknowledge.* Grand Rapids: Zondervan, 2003.

Fretheim, Terence E. *God and World in the Old Testament: A Relational Theology of Creation.* Nashville: Abingdon Press, 2005.

———. *The Suffering of God: An Old Testament Perspective.* Minneapolis: Fortress Press, 1984.

Friedrich, Gerhard. "Splanchnon," in *Theological Dictionary of the New Testament.* Translated by Geoffrey W. Bromiley and Helmut Koester. 10 vols. Grand Rapids: Eerdmans, 1964–1976.

Ganssle, Gregory E. and David M. Woodruff, eds. *God and Time: Essays on the Divine Nature.* New York: Oxford University Press, 2001.

Geisler, Norman L. *Creating God in the Image of Man?* Minneapolis: Bethany House Publishers, 1997.

Geisler, Norman L. and H. Wayne House. *The Battle for God: Responding to the Challenge of Neotheism.* Grand Rapids: Kregel Publications, 2001.

Gerrish, B. A. *Christian Faith: Dogmatics in Outline.* Louisville, KY: Westminster John Knox Press, 2015.

Gorge, A. Raymond. "Methodism." In *A Dictionary of Christian Theology.* Edited by Alan Richardson and John Bowden. Louisville, KY: Westminster Press, 1969.

Green, Joel B. *Body, Soul, and Human Life: The Nature of Humanity in the Bible.* Grand Rapids: Baker Academic, 2008.

Grenz, Stanley J. *The Social God and the Relational Self: A Trinitarian Theology of the Imago Dei.* Louisville, KY: Westminster John Knox, 2001.

Grossol, Johannes and Leigh Vicens. "Closing the Door on Limited-Risk Open Theism." *Faith and Philosophy* 31, no. 4 (October 2014).

Gruenler, Royce. "God at Risk," *Christianity Today.* March 5, 2001. Responses to the Gruenler interview in "Truth at Risk," in the Reader's Forum of *Christianity Today*, April 23, 2001.

Gulley, Norman R. *Christ Is Coming! A Christ-Centered Approach to Last-Day Events.* Washington, DC: Review and Herald, 1998.

Guthrie, Stan. "Open or Closed?" *Christianity Today*, December 1, 2004.

Hart, David Bentley. *Atheist Delusions: The Christian Revolution and Its Fashionable Enemies.* New Haven, CT: Yale University Press, 2009.

Hartshorne, Charles. *Creative Synthesis and Philosophic Method.* Chicago: Open Court Publishing, 1970.

———. *The Divine Relativity: A Social Conception of God.* New Haven, CT: Yale University Press, 1948.

———. *Omnipotence and Other Theological Mistakes.* Albany, NY: State University of New York Press, 1984.

———. *Reality as Social Process: Studies in Metaphysics and Religion.* Glencoe, IL: Free Press, 1953.

———. *Whitehead's Philosophy: Selected Essays, 1935–1970.* Lincoln: University of Nebraska Press, 1972.

Hasker, William. *Metaphysics and the Tri-Personal God.* Oxford Studies in Analytic Theology. Oxford: Oxford University Press, 2013.

———. *The Triumph of God Over Evil: Theodicy for a World of Suffering.* Downers Grove, IL: IVP Academic, 2008.

Hasker, William, Thomas Jay Oord, and Dean Zimmerman, eds. *God in an Open Universe: Science, Metaphysics, and Open Theism.* Eugene, OR: Pickwick Publications, 2011.

Haught, John F. *God After Darwin: A Theology of Evolution.* Boulder, CO: Westview Press, 2000.

Helm, Paul. *The Providence of God.* Downers Grove, IL: InterVarsity Press, 1993.

Hick, John. *Death and Eternal Life.* New York: Harper & Row, 1976.

———. *Evil and the God of Love,* rev. ed. San Francisco: Harper & Row, 1978.

Huffman, Douglas S. and Eric L. Johnson, eds. *God Under Fire: Modern Scholarship Reinvents God.* Grand Rapids: Zondervan, 2002.

Jenson, Robert W. *The Triune Identity: God According to the Gospel.* Minneapolis: Fortress Press, 1982.

———. *Systematic Theology.* 2 vols. New York: Oxford University Press, 1999.

Johnson, Elizabeth A. *She Who Is: The Mystery of God in Feminist Theological Discourse.* New York: Crossroad, 1994.

Jones, L. Gregory. *Embodying Forgiveness: A Theological Analysis.* Grand Rapids, MI: Eerdmans, 1995.

Jowers, Dennis, and Stanley N. Gundry, eds. *Four Views of Divine Providence.* Grand Rapids: Zondervan, 2011.

Kalb, Claudia. "Faith and Healing." *Newsweek,* November 10, 2003.

King, William McGuire. "God's Nescience of Future Contingents: A Nineteenth-Century Theory." *Process Studies* 9, nos. 3-4, Fall 1979.

Kittel, Gerhard and Gerhard Friedrich. *Theological Dictionary of the New Testament.* Translated by Geoffrey W. Bromiley. Grand Rapids: Eerdmans, 1977.

Kuhn, Thomas. *The Structure of Scientific Revolutions,* 2nd ed. Chicago: University of Chicago Press, 1970.

Kvanvig, Jonathan L. *Destiny and Deliberation: Essays in Philosophical Theology.* New York: Oxford University Press, 2011.

LaCugna, Catherine Mowry. *God for Us: The Trinity and Christian Life.* New York: HarperCollins, 1991.

Lonergan, Bernard J. F. *Insight: A Study of Human Understanding.* New York: Philosophical Library Inc., 1970.

Luther, Martin. Quotations from *The Bondage of the Will.* In Jennifer L. Bayne and Sarah E. Hinlicky, "Free to Be Creatures Again." *Christianity Today,* October 23, 2000.

McCabe, Lorenzo Dow. *Divine Nescience of Future Contingencies a Necessity.* New York: Phillips and Hunt, 1882.

———. *The Foreknowledge of God and Cognate Themes in Theology and Philosophy.* Cincinnati: Cranston and Stow, 1878.

Marty, Martin. "Against Reductionism." *Sightings,* April 23, 2007. www.bobcornwall.com/2007/04/against-reductionism-sightings.html.

McCormack, Bruce L. "The Actuality of God: Karl Barth in Conversation with Open Theism." In *Engaging the Doctrine of God: Contemporary Protestant Perspectives,* edited by Bruce L. McCormack. Grand Rapids: Baker Academic, 2008.

Meeks, Wayne A. *The First Urban Christians: The Social World of the Apostle Paul.* New Haven, CT: Yale University Press, 1983.

Meister, Chad V. *Introducing Philosophy of Religion.* New York: Routledge, 2009.

Meister, Chad V. and James K. Dew, eds. *Perspectives on the Problem of Evil: Five Views.* Downers Grove, IL: IVP Academic, 2017.

Migliorini, Damiano. "Il Dio che rischia e che "cambia": introduzione all'Open Theism," in Nuovo Giornale di Filosofia della Religione, no. 8, Settembre – Decembre, 2018.

Moltmann, Jürgen. *Theology of Hope: On the Ground and the Implications of a Christian Eschatology*. Translated by James W. Leitch. New York: Harper & Row, Publishers, 1967.

Moreland, J. P. and Scott B. Rae. *Body and Soul: Human Nature and the Crisis in Ethics*. Downers Grove, IL: InterVarsity Press, 2000.

Morris, Thomas V. *Our Idea of God: An Introduction to Philosophical Theology*. Downers Grove, IL: InterVarsity Press, 1991.

Murphy, Nancey. *Bodies and Souls, or Spirited Bodies?* Cambridge: Cambridge University Press, 2006.

Niebuhr, Reinhold. *The Irony of American History*. New York: Scribner's, 1952.

———. *Moral Man and Immoral Society*. New York: Scribner's, 1932.

———. *The Nature and Destiny of Man*, 2 vols. New York: Scribner's, 1941.

Nussbaum, Martha. *Upheavals of Thought: The Intelligence of Emotions*. Cambridge: Cambridge University Press, 2001.

Ogden, Schubert M. *Christ Without Myth: A Study Based on the Theology of Rudolf Bultmann*. New York: Harper & Row, 1961.

———. *The Reality of God and Other Essays*. New York: Harper & Row, 1966.

Oord, Thomas Jay, ed. *Creation Made Free: Open Theology Engaging Science*. Eugene, OR: Pickwick Publications, 2009.

———. *God Can't: How to Believe in God and Love After Tragedy, Abuse, and Other Evils*. SacraSage Press, 2019.

———. *The Uncontrolling Love of God: An Open and Relational Account of Providence*. Downers Grove, IL: InterVarsity Press, 2015.

Pannenberg, Wolfhart. *Anthropology in Theological Perspective*. Translated by Matthew J. O'Connell. Philadelphia: Westminster Press, 1985.

———. *Systematic Theology*, 3 vols. Translated by Geoffrey W. Bromiley. Grand Rapids: Eerdmans, 1991–1998.

———. *What Is Man? Contemporary Anthropology in Theological Perspective*. Translated by Duane A. Priebe. Minneapolis: Fortress Press, 1970.

Pears, Iain. *An Instance at the Fingerpost*. New York: Riverhead Books, 1988.

Peckham, John C. *The Love of God: A Canonical Model*. Downers Grove, IL: IVP Academic, 2015.

Peters, Ted. *God as Trinity: Relationality and Temporality in Divine Life*. Louisville, KY: Westminster John Knox, 1993.

Peterson, Michael, William Hasker, Bruce Reichenbach, and David Basinger. *Reason and Religious Belief: An Introduction to the Philosophy of Religion*, 3rd ed. Oxford: Oxford University Press, 2003.

Pike, Nelson. *God and Timelessness*. Reprint, Eugene, OR: Wipf and Stock, 2002.

Pinnock, Clark H. *Flame of Love: A Theology of the Holy Spirit*. Downers Grove, IL: InterVarsity Press, 1996.

——, ed. *The Grace of God, The Will of Man: A Case for Arminianism.* Grand Rapids: Zondervan Academic, 1989.

——. *Most Moved Mover: A Theology of God's Openness.* Grand Rapids: Baker Academic, 2001.

——. "Reconstructing Evangelical Theology: Is the Open View of God a Good Idea?" *Andrews University Seminary Studies* 41, no. 2 (2003), 215-227.

Pinnock, Clark H., Richard Rice, John Sanders, William Hasker, and David Basinger. *The Openness of God: A Biblical Challenge to the Traditional Understanding of God.* Downers Grove, IL: InterVarsity Press, 1994.

Pojman, Louis P. and Michael Rae, eds. *Philosophy of Religion: An Anthology,* 6th ed. Boston: Wadsworth, 2012.

Porter, Roy. *The Greatest Benefit to Mankind: A Medical History of Humanity.* New York: W. W. Norton, 1997.

Pruss, A. R. "Probability and the Open Future View." *Faith and Philosophy: Journal of the Society of Christian Philosophers* 27, no. 2. (April, 2010): 190-96.

Rahner, Karl. *Foundations of Christian Faith: An Introduction to the Idea of Christianity.* Translated by William V. Dych. New York: Seabury, 1978.

——. *The Trinity.* Translated by Joseph Donceel. New York: Herder and Herder, 1970.

Rhoda, Alan R. "Generic Open Theism and Some Varieties Thereof." *Religious Studies* 44 (2008): 225-34.

——. "Probability, Truth, and the Openness of the Future: A Reply to Pruss." *Faith and Philosophy: Journal of the Society of Christian Philosophers* 27, no. 2 (April, 2010): 197-204.

Rice, Richard. "Are We Really Free? A Biblically Based Response to Neurophysiological Reductionism." *Andrews University Seminary Studies* 51, no. 1 (Spring 2013): 69-82.

——. "The Challenge of Spiritual Individualism (And How to Meet It)." *Andrews University Seminary Studies* 43, no. 1 (Spring, 2005): 113-31.

——. "Creation, Evolution, and Evil." In *Understanding Genesis: Contemporary Adventist Perspectives,* edited by Brian Bull, Fritz Guy, and Ervin Taylor. Riverside, CA: Adventist Today, 2006.

——. "Divine Foreknowledge and Free-Will Theism." In *The Grace of God, The Will of Man: A Case for Arminianism,* edited by Clark H. Pinnock. Grand Rapids: Zondervan Academic, 1989.

——. *The Openness of God.* Washington, DC: Review and Herald Publishing Association, 1980. Republished as *God's Foreknowledge and Man's Free Will.* Minneapolis: Bethany House Publishers, 1985.

——. "Process Theism and the Open View of God." In *Searching for an Adequate God: A Dialogue Between Process and Free Will Theists,* edited by John B. Cobb Jr. and Clark H. Pinnock. Grand Rapids: Eerdmans, 2000.

——. "Wolfhart Pannenberg's Crowning Achievement: A Review of His *Systematic Theology.*" *Andrews University Seminary Studies* 37, no. 1 (Spring 1998): 55-72.

Ricoeur, Paul. *Freedom and Nature: The Voluntary and the Involuntary.* Translated by Erazim V. Kohak. Evanston, IL: Northwestern University Press, 2007.

———. *The Symbolism of Evil*. Translated by Emerson Buchanan. New York: Beacon Press, 1967.

Rissler, James. "Open Theism." In *The Internet Encyclopedia of Philosophy*. September 1, 2019. www.iep.utm.edu/o-theism/.

Robinson, John A. T. *The Body: A Study in Pauline Theology*. Philadelphia: Westminster, 1952.

Roy, Steven C. *How Much Does God Foreknow? A Comprehensive Biblical Study*. Downers Grove, IL: InterVarsity Press, 2006.

Sanders, John. *The God Who Risks: A Theology of Divine Providence*, 2nd ed. Downers Grove, IL: InterVarsity Academic, 2007.

———. "Why Oord's Essential Kenosis Model Fails to Solve the Problem of Evil While Retaining Miracles." *Wesleyan Theological Journal* 51, no 2. (Fall 2016): 174-87.

Sanders, John and Christopher A. Hall. *Does God Have a Future? A Debate on Divine Providence*. Baker Academic, 2003.

Schmid, Manuel. "Der offene Theismus als bibeltheologische Reformbewegung." ["Open Theism as a Biblical Theological Reform Movement."] PhD diss., University of Basel, Switzerland, 2008.

Schrag, Calvin O. *The Self After Postmodernity*. New Haven, CT: Yale University Press, 1997.

Seligman, Adam B. *Modernity's Wager: Authority, the Self, and Transcendence*. Princeton, NJ: Princeton University Press, 2000.

Smith, James K. A. "What God Knows: The Debate on 'Open Theism.'" *Christian Century* (July 12, 2005).

Sowers, Sidney G. *Salvation in History*. New York: Harper & Row Publishers, 1967.

Spiegel, James S. "Does God Take Risks?" In *God Under Fire: Modern Scholarship Reinvents God*, edited by Douglas S. Huffman and Eric L. Johnson. Grand Rapids: Zondervan, 2002.

Stendahl, Krister. "The Apostle Paul and the Introspective Conscience of the West." *Harvard Theological Review* 56 (1963).

Stump, Eleonore. *Wandering in Darkness: Narrative and the Problem of Suffering*. New York: Oxford University Press, 2010.

Swafford, Jan. *Beethoven: Anguish and Triumph. A Biography*. New York: Houghton Mifflin Harcourt, 2014.

Swinburne, Richard. *The Evolution of the Soul*. New York: Oxford University Press, 1986.

Taliaferro, Charles. *Contemporary Philosophy of Religion: An Introduction*. Malden, MA: Blackwell, 1998.

Taylor, Charles. *Sources of the Self: The Making of the Modern Identity*. Cambridge, MA: Harvard University Press, 1989.

Tiessen, David Alstad. *The Openness Model of God: An Examination of Its Current and Early Expression in Light of Hartshorne's Process Theism*. Colorado Springs: Providence Theological Seminary, 1998.

———. "The Openness Model of God: An Evangelical Paradigm in Light of Its Nineteenth-Century Wesleyan Precedent." *Didaskalia* 11 (Spring 2000): 77-101.

Tracy, David. *The Achievement of Bernard Lonergan*. New York: Herder and Herder, 1970.

Tuggy, Dale. "Divine Deception, Identity and Social Trinitariansim." *Religious Studies* 40 (2004), 269-87.

———. "Three Roads to Open Theism." *Faith and Philosophy: Journal of the Society of Christian Philosophers* 24, no. 1 (January 2007): 28-51.

Vaage, Leif, ed. *Religious Rivalries in the Early Roman Empire and the Rise of Christianity.* Waterloo, ON: Wilfrid Laurier University Press, 2006.

Viney, Donald Wayne. "Jules Lequyer and the Openness of God." *Faith and Philosophy: Journal of the Society of Christian Philosophers* 14, no. 2 (April 1997).

Walton, John H. *The Lost World of Genesis 1: Ancient Cosmology and the Origins Debate.* Downers Grove, IL: IVP Academic, 2009.

Ward, Keith. *Religion and Creation.* New York: Oxford University Press, 1996.

Ware, Bruce A. *God's Lesser Glory: The Diminished God of Open Theism.* Wheaton, IL: Crossway Books, 2001.

Watson, Gary. "Free Agency." In *Free Will*, edited by Gary Watson. Oxford: Oxford University Press, 1982.

White, Ellen G. *The Ministry of Healing.* Mountain View, CA: Pacific Press, 1905.

Whitehead, Alfred North. *Process and Reality: An Essay in Cosmology.* New York: Macmillan, 1929.

Wierenga, Edward R. "Review of *The Openness of God*, by Clark Pinnock, et al." *Faith and Philosophy* 14, no. 2 (April 1997): 248.

Wilson, Douglas, ed. *Bound Only Once: The Failure of Open Theism.* Moscow, ID: Canon Press, 2001.

Winter, Bruce W. *Seek the Welfare of the City: Christians as Benefactors and Citizens.* Grand Rapids: Eerdmans, 1994.

Witham, Larry. *The God Biographers: Our Changing Image of God from Job to the Present.* Lanham, MD: Lexington Books, 2010.

Wright, R. K. McGregor. *No Place for Sovereignty: What's Wrong with Freewill Theism.* Downers Grove, IL: InterVarsity Press, 1996.

Zagzebski, Linda T. *The Dilemma of Freedom and Foreknowledge.* New York: Oxford University Press, 1991.

Zbaraschuk, Michael. "Process Theology Resources for an Open and Relational Christology." *Wesleyan Theological Journal* 44 (Fall 2009): 155.

▶▶▶▶▶▶▶▶▶▶▶ **CREDITS** ▶▶▶▶▶▶▶▶▶▶▶

I WOULD LIKE TO THANK SPRINGER NATURE, publishers of the journal *Philosophia*, for permission to include (in chapter seven) my article, "Trinity, Temporality and Open Theism" (*Philosophia: Philosophical Quarterly of Israel* 35, nos. 3-4 [Special Issue: 'Models of God'] 2007). The essay was also included in *Models of God and Alternative Ultimate Realities*, eds. Jeanine Diller and Asa Kasher (Dordrecht: Springer, 2013), 299-307.

I also appreciate *Andrews University Seminary Studies* granting permission for me to incorporate material from three essays. The discussion of human freedom in chapter eight includes material from the article, "Are We Really Free? A Biblically Based Response to Neurophysiological Reductionism" (*AUSS* 51, no. 1 [Spring 2013], 69-82). (A version of this essay will also appear in the forthcoming volume from Wipf and Stock, *What's with Free Will? Ethics and Religion After Neuroscience*, edited by Philip Clayton and James Walters.) The discussion of the church in chapter ten draws from "The Challenge of Spiritual Individualism (And How to Meet It)" (*AUSS* 43, no. 1 [Spring 2005], 113-31). And chapter eleven on last things, incorporates portions of "Wolfhart Pannenberg's Crowning Achievement: A Review of His *Systematic Theology*" (*AUSS* 37, no. 1 [Spring 1998], 55-72).

Chapter six incorporates my answer to the question, "Does Open Theism Limit God?," which originally appeared in *Wesleyan Theological Journal* (48, no. 2 [Fall 2013], 30-43). My discussion of the church (chapter ten) includes portions of an article originally published in *Spectrum Magazine*, "From Adventist Anthropology to Adventist Ecclesiology" (43, no. 2 [Spring 2015], 60-64, 80). I appreciate receiving permission from both *WTJ* and *Spectrum* to include portions of these articles here.

Chapter five includes a few paragraphs from *Suffering and the Search for Meaning: Contemporary Responses to the Problem of Pain* (IVP Academic, 2014). And I have received permission from the Association of Adventist Forums to include material in chapter ten from *Believing, Behaving, Belonging: Finding New Love for the Church* (Roseville, CA: AAF, 2003).

I am grateful to these journals and publishers for their permission to reproduce and/or adapt these discussions of some of the central aspects of Christian doctrine.

▶▶▶▶▶▶▶▶▶ AUTHOR INDEX ▶▶▶▶▶▶▶▶▶▶

⟩⟩⟩⟩⟩⟩⟩⟩ SUBJECT INDEX ⟨⟨⟨⟨⟨⟨⟨⟨⟨

:::::::: SCRIPTURE INDEX ::::::::